JOURNEY
TO
ONENESS

JOURNEY TO ONENESS

Align with Your Divine Magnificence

Your Divine Magnificence Trilogy

Anne M. Deatly, PhD

Sacred Dragon Publishing
Los Angeles, California

©2026 Anne M. Deatly

All rights reserved. No part of this publication may be reproduced, stored in a retrieval system, or transmitted, in any form or by any means, electronic, mechanical, recorded, photocopied, or otherwise, without the prior written permission of the publisher, except by a reviewer who may quote brief passages in a review.

Sacred Dragon Publishing Services LLC
Los Angles California
www.sacreddragonpublishing.com

ISBN: 978-1-967005-02-4 Paperback
ISBN: 978-1-967005-04-8 Hardcover
ISBN: 978-1-967005-03-1 eBook

Cover Design: Amygdala Designs
Interior Design: Ryan Forsythe

The information presented in this work is the author's opinion and does not constitute any health or medical advice. The content of this work is for informational purposes only and is not intended to diagnose, treat, cure, or prevent any condition or disease, nor is it meant as a substitute for consultation with a licensed practitioner.

Publishers Cataloging-in-Publication (Provided by Cassidy Cataloging Services, Inc.)

Names: Deatly, Anne M., author.
Title: Journey to oneness: align with your divine magnificence / Anne M. Deatly, PhD
Description: Los Angeles, California: Sacred Dragon Publishing, [2026] | Series: Deatly, Anne M. Your divine magnificence. | Includes bibliographical references.
Identifiers: ISBN: 9781967005024 (paperback) | 9781967005048 (hardcover) | 9781967005031 (ebook)
Subjects: LCSH: Spirituality. | Self-actualization (Psychology) | Energy medicine. | Quantum theory. | Consciousness. | Self-control. | Religion and science. | BISAC: BODY, MIND & SPIRIT / Healing / Energy. | BODY, MIND & SPIRIT / Inspiration & Personal Growth.
Classification: LCC: BL624 .D431 2026 | DDC: 204--dc23

Printed in the United States of America

Dedicated to my children, Kate and Bill.
May you find your spiritual journey in your own time in your own way.
I love you deeply. I will always BE with you.

AUTHOR'S NOTE

Throughout this book, I draw on specific experiences with clients and friends to demonstrate the validity and authenticity of the healing practices, energy work, and Divine revelations presented in these pages. Without exception, the real names and personal details of these individuals are not used to protect their identities. I have also taken great care to ensure that everyone has given their consent for their healing stories to be included in this book.

I have used capitalization throughout the book to draw attention to the significance of the myriad ways the Divine is part of our life experience. Words like Consciousness, Source, Soul, Self, Spirit, Spiritual Journey, and the Universe are also capitalized because I believe they all represent aspects of the Divine. BEing is used to represent our Soul aspect from the perspective of a Divine state of BEing.

The use of the information in this book is only to help you on your Spiritual Journey. I don't claim that this will help everyone, even though it has helped me and others. Please follow your own guidance system in engaging with the content of this book.

TABLE OF CONTENTS

Author's Note	vii
Preface	xi
Section 1 Being in Flow with the Universe	1
Section 2 Aligning with the Divine	53
Section 3 Tapping into our Infinite Divine Potential	109
Section 4 The Path of Enlightenment	175
Section 5 Oneness: Evolving from Duality to Unity	221
Afterword	261
Appendix Divine Soul Energies	267
Questions for Individual Reflections and Book Club Discussions	271
Endnotes	273
Resources	286
Permissions	287
Acknowledgments	288
About the Author	291
About the Speaker	293
Invitation to Connect	295

PREFACE

In *Journey to Oneness: Align with Your Divine Magnificence*, we start to understand and live in the flow of the Universe. We begin to align with the bigger perspective of the forward movement of the Universe and the innate capacity to flow in the direction of expansion, alignment with the Divine, tapping into our higher potential, then entering a path to enlightenment as we come to understand the concept of Universal Oneness.

You'll be transformed on our journey together. This journey requires awakening and a willingness to go deeper into the wisdom that surrounds us and within us. The concepts presented will likely stretch your imagination as you encounter the awe and wonder of the adventure of life, explained in a whole new way that is understood by only a small percentage of people.

The truth is everything is happening for your best and highest good—always. The Universe benefits from each of us who awakens and follows a path to enlightenment. I didn't know there was more to life. There really is *so* much more.

Without my intending it, I was catapulted into a new reality or a higher level of Consciousness through the death of my significant other, Michael Angelo Ludas, on February 7, 2008. On that day, I knew his death was imminent, but I didn't know it would be that day. Luckily, I hadn't gone to work and could be with him. Mike was emaciated. He had intentionally stopped eating and drinking several days prior. He was prepared for the next stage of his journey. He never stopped being his caring, fun-loving, and curious self.

When his breathing changed that afternoon, I alerted his three children and three siblings to come and be with him in his last moments. We all held hands around his bed and said how much we loved him. This loss would leave a gaping hole in all our lives. It was a loving and compassionate send-off for a truly and deeply wonderful man.

On one hand, I was relieved his suffering was over. But on the other hand, I didn't know how I could continue without his love and joy surrounding me. He was extraordinary in his thinking and believed in more than the physical earthly experience.

Two or three weeks before he transitioned, he shared his excitement about this next phase of this life—meaning his death. We had talked about a lot of things during our three-or four-year relationship, but not death and not the String Theory.

He said, "I am sorry you can't go with me. I am going to get the answers to all my questions. I know it has something to do with the String Theory."

Losing Mike to colon cancer was the initiation of my real transformation in aligning with the Divine and the Spiritual Realm. A few days after Mike died, I woke up with a 'knowing' there was a modality that could have saved his life. I'm unable to explain this *knowing*. I certainly didn't know this when we were putting all our faith in the medical community at Sloan-Kettering in NYC.

I set an intention to discover the modality that could have saved him. Because I was reading Wayne Dyer's *Power of Intention*, I set an intention to discover how to be optimally healthy. Sometime later, I heard about energy healing, Healing Touch, and Energy Medicine within a few days. I didn't know anything about energy healing then. I searched the internet for answers and clarification. I found *The Energy Medicine Kit* online for $20, so I ordered it to learn about this modality. The kit contained a small, clear glass, faceted crystal on a red thread. Being a scientist, my immediate reaction was that this was not for me. As a critical thinker, my mind decided energy healing had nothing to do with scientific principles. I dismissed this whole energy healing concept.

But when I was recycling the bigger package, I noticed a program announcement. The pioneer of Energy Medicine, Donna Eden, was traveling all over the world. In the next six months, Donna was to teach in Australia, Norway, and Wales. I was incredulous with the widespread interest in Energy Medicine. Then I noticed Donna Eden was doing a workshop through the Omega Institute in NYC that very next weekend--near where I lived.

My whole body shook.

I was in shock. Did my body shake to tell me to attend the workshop? I stood there thinking ... scientists don't believe the human body talks to us. But what just happened *to me*? I'd never experienced my body shaking before. It only took me a few minutes to decide to register for the workshop. If my body was encouraging me to go, then I wanted to find out WHY.

This event was the first of many to follow that illustrated how we all are being guided in life -we just don't consciously realize it. One of the first things that Donna Eden explained was that energy medicine activates the body's intelligence—its inner wisdom—to heal. That was exactly what I was looking for-- a modality that could have saved Mike's life. I was on the edge of my seat the whole weekend. A whole new perspective and secret of life was being demonstrated. I was excited about this new way of connecting to the body's wisdom.

Two weeks after that workshop in NYC, I was sitting in the first class of the Energy Medicine Certification Program in Phoenix, AZ. I was embarking on a whole new adventure that would transform me, my life, and my career in the most magnificent way beyond my imagination.

That was a quantum leap in my Spiritual Journey. Two years later, I changed careers to explore my role as an energy healer to help people become the best versions of themselves and lead their best lives. In this process, I was becoming a more authentic version of myself—an aspect of me that I hadn't known before.

After losing Mike, I kept asking the question, "What do I do now?"

As it turns out, that was the wrong question. A better question was "who do I need to become?"

The old me was gone forever. I had to discover who I was now that I had opened up to the terrible gift of this grief and loss. That was the turning point of my life. When I stopped thinking about what to do, I focused on who I was BEing and who I needed to become after this loss. As I was changing, my life unfolded in a different way than my original plan. I was becoming more and more my real Self. It was within me—but not in my mind. My inner wisdom was working to heal me from the inside out. I trusted, and life unfolded in miraculous ways. I know your life can unfold in miraculous ways, too!

Writing this book required a real journey for me to discover how to align with the Divine to educate and enlighten others. I am explaining this wisdom from the perspective of my Spiritual Journey. The story of an ordinary person who just paid attention to her guidance and was transformed from the inside out. That made all the difference. This new way of BEing is one of joy, peace, fulfillment, inner wisdom, growth, strength, resilience, and courage.

I have an interesting background, and you might even say I am the least likely person to write books related to Divine Magnificence. I have a PhD in Microbiology and studied viruses for several decades. During that time, I was totally in my head—a critical thinker not accepting anything without physical proof or evidence supported by data—statistically significant data!

I was always interested in miracles. From a scientific perspective, I remember thinking a miracle is something real, but we just don't understand *how* it can be real. We just don't know the science of it. I hope you can take this same approach as you read this book. Hopefully, there will be things you've never heard before. Hopefully, you can accept them with the knowing that there is a lot we don't understand, but not understanding doesn't mean it isn't true.

As a young adult, I felt really disconnected from the Divine. A lot of turmoil, emotional trauma, and changes in my life forced me to change jobs. I no longer commuted into New York City to my job as a PhD virologist at an academic institution. I started to work at a pharmaceutical company. To ease the emotional trauma, I listened to personal development courses in my car on my way to and from work. I remember listening to Wayne Dyer and Deepak Chopra's *Path to Enlightenment* course one day. I remember one moment clearly.

I said out loud emphatically, "That is what I want—to be on a path to enlightenment!"

You might even say I declared it! I didn't do anything consciously to be on a path to enlightenment. I just let my life unfold naturally, and then I met Mike.

Two years after I started studying energy medicine, I left my job as a scientist and started my new career as a certified Energy Medicine Practitioner, and then progressed to an Advanced Energy Medicine Practitioner and teacher. I created my own business, *E Quantum Breakthroughs*. I don't think there is a career further away from scientific research than being an Energy Medicine Practitioner. In my science career, you would never believe anything unless you *saw* it in terms of results—over and over. In my energy healing and Spiritual Influencer career, you won't see it until you believe it.

In addition to seeing clients privately to balance their energies, I also prepared group programs to help people reach higher levels of Consciousness. Recently—years after I made that declaration about wanting to be on a path of enlightenment—I was preparing a program, *Letting Go to Manifest Prosperity*. I was reviewing David Hawkins' *Clinically Proven Map of Consciousness* and meditating on the highest level of Consciousness – enlightenment--to determine a way for students to get on a path of enlightenment. Suddenly, the memory of that declaration flashed in my mind.

I was on the path to enlightenment.

This memory flash enabled me to realize I was moving toward a greater understanding of the Universe. I was being guided all along. I did not follow any specific steps or formula to be on this path. There was something way beyond me guiding me. I believe this is part of everyone's journey.

I awakened to a life that was way more than I had ever experienced. I understood that life is a Spiritual Journey. This journey is why we are here on Earth. The significance of our time here on Earth has nothing to do with success, fame, material goods, or wealth. We are here to become the best versions of ourselves and to live our best lives. To live this way, it helps to know who we really are and why we are here. We are here to accomplish a specific mission that our Souls decided before entering our physical bodies. We are here to align with the Divine. We are here to develop a real connection with our Soul and to understand our Divine Mission as an evolutionary path for our Soul to ascend to higher levels of BEing—but also to help the expansion and growth of the whole Universe.

In *Journey to Oneness*, we discuss how we are an aspect of the Oneness of the Universe. Understanding the concept of Oneness may propel us into a whole new level of understanding the benevolent love of the Divine. The basic concept is that every thing and every living being comes from One Source. Everything is interconnected. We are energy beings, we live in an energetic Universe, and everything happens through energy flow. Our vibrational frequency determines what we attract in life. We create our lives through this energy flow—mostly unconsciously. My goal is for anyone reading this book to awaken and realize they're the creator of their lives through their thoughts, feelings, and beliefs.

This journey is about tuning into the higher vibrational frequencies of our True Selves and discovering our Divine Magnificence and the wisdom of the Universe. An important mission is to evolve our Souls. When we grow and expand, the whole Universe grows and evolves. Otherwise, our Soul would not be inclined to leave the peace, unconditional love, and serenity of the Spiritual Realm to meet earthly challenges and learn from mistakes and difficult experiences.

There are many stepping stones needed to discover the truth and wisdom of this Universe. I am glad for every step. But I wish I had been more aware. I wrote these books so *you* will be more aware. I wrote these books so *you* would understand that every step and stage is necessary for you to grow and evolve as you are meant to. You will be guided.

You will grow in different ways. But in the overview of your life, you will have a similar journey to help you become your best Self and live your best life. Living your best life means that you make your specific mark in the world by becoming your authentic True Self.

Your life will be transformed into an amazing adventure beyond your wildest imagination. Your life could open to amazing new opportunities and potential you may not resonate with in this moment. I am excited for you to start on this journey.

What is available to you is unlimited. Infinite abundance and potential are yours to tap into. Maybe reading about my experience will give you insight, inspiration, and encouragement to progress. You can start living as if everything is a miracle.

I invite you to open yourself to new possibilities and opportunities. Understand that you don't know everything. Understand there is a force more powerful and more loving than you could ever imagine. You even have built-in guidance in your DNA double helix molecule—the blueprint of your physical, energetic, and spiritual life. You are way more than you know. You are more magnificent than you could dream. You are meant for greatness. You are meant to accomplish something ONLY YOU can do. All of us are expressions of the Divine. Why don't you allow the Divine to experience your human life at full potential and the highest vibration? It's your free will to make that choice.

Embrace the mystery of this magnificent Universe. There is so much that we don't understand yet. It is beyond our ability to understand. Be in awe and wonder of your unlimited potential. Trust in the Universe. Surrender to the Universe.

I hope this book leads you from the limited to the limitless. Each section of the book is intended to enlighten and awaken you to a higher level of thinking and BEing in the world. I hope for all to transcend to a higher level of Consciousness and to understand the real you and why you're here on Earth at this time. Let your Soul guide you in this transcendence.

This book invites you to perceive your life as an expression of the Divine and part of the Oneness. It's about aligning with your Divine Magnificence. My hope is that this book will help guide you to find out more about your life or Spiritual Journey, discover your True Self, and realize you're loved and supported more than you could ever imagine in your wildest imagination.

I am honored to be a guide on your Spiritual Journey.

Live radiantly!

Anne McDeath

Wonder

When I am in wonder,
The world is full of possibilities.

My level of excitement increases
I have an opportunity to see the world differently.

When I am in wonder, I let go of the
boundaries of my life, where new ideas emerge
and the still small voice guides me.

Certainty and knowingness relax and unlimitedness blooms
in new ways magnifying joy around me.

When I am in wonder- trust, faith and hope
present themselves in magical and miraculous ways.

I feel differently, I know differently and
I receive with an open heart.

When I am in wonder, I am a new person, experiencing the world
with pregnancy in each moment.

I know something wonderful is going to break through
to show me a deeper love and brighter vision.

When I am in wonder, the past gets rearranged
and the energy flows resolving emotional stickiness.

It appears I exist in a new dimension
clear, happy and compassionate.

When I am in wonder, I love and trust the mystery of life.
I empty out the old to accept the new.

When I am in wonder,
I am fully blessed with the radiance of the Divine.

~Anne Deatly

Section One

BEING IN FLOW WITH THE UNIVERSE

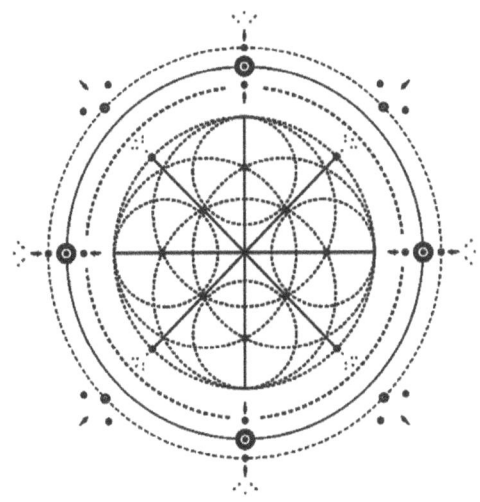

Freedom in the Flow

Let the force be with me.
To step into the Flow and detach.
Let my life unfold naturally.
May I not resist or get in the way.

Cross those *limiting lines,*
Grow, go beyond, evolve.
Mystery and magic are in the Flow.
But I am on the sidelines watching.

Close the door to limitation.
Open the door to new opportunity.
Seek abundance within.
Break through lack and misconceptions.

Let go of limiting beliefs.
Unleash my True Self within.
Discover my magnificence.
Grateful I am me.

My many gifts and talents,
Help me grasp the unknown.
To use my gifts wisely
To serve others.

Start living fully.
Me—a Creative Force.
Believe in myself.
Dance with joy.

I jump into the Flow.
No longer just observing.
I could participate, allow, and Be the Flow.
I could witness the serenity of the Flow.

Fall into the Flow.
Receive the Flow.
Surrender to the Flow.
Magnify the Flow.

Be with the Flow and know
I am a miracle.
An unlimited Soul in a sea of ALL opportunities.
Anything, everything is possible.

I am an upward golden spiral
Energy transcending logic and boundaries.
Connecting to what's already waiting for me.
I am free.

I have the power within for anything.
I am safe and totally protected.
I am One with the Flow.
I am the freedom.

~Anne M. Deatly

Being in Flow with the Universe

From a physical realm perspective, being in flow with the Universe is similar to a feeling of being in the zone when everything in life seems to fall into place easily. There is a sense of ease and peace, with more movement forward and fewer obstacles. There is clarity about life's purpose and how to live it.

From the Spiritual Realm perspective, the flow of the Universe is a living, dynamic, sentient, Invisible Force that moves through the vast expanse of space and everything and every living creature. If we are aware of it and embrace it, we realize we are part of it. Being in Universal Flow aligns us with higher vibrational frequencies of Divine Love, Wisdom, and the Oneness of the Universe. The iconic line "Let the force be with you" from the Star Wars movies captures the concept of allowing the benevolent forces of the Universe to work with and through us, knowing there is so much more available to humanity than we know.

Aligning with this vast, omnipresent Universal force aligns us with a powerful energy that guides us toward expansion and compassion, elevating Consciousness and our awareness of Divine Love and Wisdom. New opportunities arise, leading to a fuller and more purposeful life as we shift to BEing in the energetic vibration and level of Consciousness of Divine Love and Wisdom.

To fully understand and accept this flow of Divine Love and Wisdom, within and without, requires that we wake up to the truth of who we are as Divine BEings and let go of limiting beliefs that attach us to the physical realm and the proscribed agendas of daily life. It's up to each of us to consciously be in the flow of the Universe, bringing in these higher vibrational frequencies to uplift all living things and BEings on the planet. This happens through us—through how we live our lives, how we extend love and compassion, and how we support each other in growing toward and becoming our True Selves.

This is the Divine Plan of the Universe. As we are flowing in it and with it, we are spreading the good news, spreading high vibrational frequencies and a Loving Presence that is the pulse of the flow of the vast Universe.

Understand that this universal flow is always happening. It is always there for us to join. It is the backdrop of all life. Though it may appear behind the scenes, it is always right in front of and within us. There are multitudes of invitations for us to join the Universal flow. It is the Divine Plan we join and flow with the direction of increased life, expansion, and growth.

Aligning with Universal flow *guides* us to follow our Soul's direction to live our highest and best lives and contribute to the world at our highest level. We experience a deep sense of peace, freedom, and compassion in life and easily meet our goals and heart's desires that are in alignment with our Soul's Guidance. By aligning with the flow of the Universe, we detach from third-dimensional Earth programming that keeps us trapped in lower-frequency thoughts and feelings. Freed from this limited view, our vibrational frequency naturally rises to resonate with a higher state of BEing, living from our true magnificence.

At first, it may not be easy to sense the subtle nature of this dynamic, energetic flow because we are part of it—one with it as a unique expression of the flow. But it's always there. We don't have to go searching for it. Universal Flow finds us. When I changed careers from being a research scientist to an energy healer, life seemed to pick me up and place me in the flow of the Universe in an entirely different place—a place beyond my understanding and beyond what my imagination could envision. The power of Life Force energy flowing through and around me grew stronger as I moved toward my new career. The feeling of upliftment and Divine guidance was powerfully palpable. It was indescribable and miraculous at the same time. Fortunately, my intuition was keen enough to sense the wisdom of going with the natural pull and flow of what was unfolding for me, even though this was quite alien to my way of thinking and how I had been living my life.

You may have had a similar experience of being in a powerful flow of energy guiding you on your path. But most of us are at least familiar with the experience of being in the *zone*, an elevated state of focus and awareness that inspires heightened creativity, athletic prowess, insights, inner wisdom, or any other extraordinary state of being. Both experiences provide glimpses of the subtle energies of Universal flow, always available for us to connect with and align to our highest potential.

Being consciously in flow with the Universe is a direct experience of Awakened Consciousness that leads to greater depths of spiritual awakening as we allow it to permeate our whole being. Being committed to being in the flow creates a portal, or wormhole, for ascending to higher realms and levels of consciousness. We are relating to life from a completely new place and state of being on an enlightened path.

Being in the flow is our true nature. We can be present with Universal flow in all we do, not just when we meditate or sit quietly in a contemplative state focused on stillness and silence. The more we intend and surrender to the flow, the more we will live and experience life in a higher state of being through all of life's ups and downs, facing, embracing, and responding to what is really happening in our lives instead of simply reacting out of habit, ignorance, or disconnection.

We allow the flow of Awakened Consciousness to be our way of life. We are no longer attached to specific outcomes or to our stories about who we are as separate individuals. We are part of something bigger and more profound than ourselves. We feel the magnetic pull into the flow to discover what we don't know, rather than stay stuck in what we already know. We are open to going deeper into how the Universe really works within us and around us. Knowing that everything happening around us is awareness manifesting, we are present to the flow of life as it unfolds for our highest good. We are awake, rooted in, and present with Universal Consciousness.

Although being in flow with the Universe is a natural state of BEing, we have been programmed into a state of separation that conceals this aspect of Self from our awareness and our ability to connect with the natural flow of Universal abundance all around us. Basic survival instincts of the ego that view the world as a place of danger, lack, and us vs. them block our forward movement in flow. Fundamental to aligning with Universal Flow is realizing our unity with All and embracing the idea of a Life Force Energy or purposeful organizing field guiding us to be our True Self—an entelechy within us guiding us to be who we are meant to be in this life.

We will explore ways to overcome blocks to natural flow by tapping into higher levels of Consciousness that open us to seeing ourselves and the world around us in more loving ways, sharing our positive energy, and expressing gratitude for the life we have right now. We will also explore using Akashic Records to align with who we are from a high-level Spiritual perspective.

Raising our vibrational frequency is also a key step to living our best life and being in the flow of the Universe. There are many ways to raise vibrational frequency in all areas of our lives. From intentional energy work, such as activating the radiant circuits in our energy body to spark joy, and guided visualizations, meditation, and imaginative exploration, to being in gratitude and focusing on the frequency of our words, thoughts, feelings, and beliefs, the way we can raise frequency are as varied as the multitude of choices we make in everyday life. Being centered, focused, and grounded in who we really are and where we are going in life is also essential to aligning with Universal Flow, watering the seeds of who we are becoming and what we want to grow in our lives that will guide us toward our next stage of growth.

The Radiant Circuits System

The radiant circuits system is one of nine energy systems in our energy body. Comprised of ten radiant circuits, it is a major healing system connected with Consciousness and the Universal Flow. The more we activate the radiant circuits, the more we raise our vibrational frequency, connecting us to the Universal Flow and opening up opportunities to be in alignment with powerful Creative Energies beyond our current understanding.

This extraordinary energy system is infused with Divine Intelligence that illuminates where energy flow is blocked or disconnected in any of the other eight systems. It creates energy circuits or bridges to the impacted area, functioning as a backup system for the disconnected system. They also act like reservoirs of extra energy to add to areas of deficient or blocked energy flow and fill in gaps in the energy flow.

The radiant circuits function at the highest vibrational frequencies related to joy, exhilaration, excitement, enthusiasm, radiance, passion, vibrancy, hope, gratitude, rapture, exultation, exaltation, and Spiritual Ecstasy. This ecstatic energy is also connected to feelings of falling in love. In traditional Chinese Medicine, the radiant circuits energy system is referred to as Joy Generators. Some other names include Extraordinary Vessels, Funky Flows, or Psychic Channels. Donna Eden, the pioneer of Energy Medicine, named this energy system radiant circuits because she saw this system of energy as particularly glowing and radiant compared to the other energy systems.

Activating the radiant circuits connects us to these high vibrational frequencies that will transform our lives. The more we activate these radiant circuits, the more joy energy is available to us. Joy attracts more joy, bringing more fulfillment and opportunity to our lives.

I firmly believe feeling and BEing joy is a choice. It is an inner way of BEing. There are a multitude of benefits to choosing joy by activating the amazing, radiant circuits in our energy fields and our lives. They are extraordinary energies of Divine Intelligence. They are capable of *knowing* where to create energy bridges or circuits between energies that are disconnected or imbalanced in our energy fields.

These intelligent energies help us transcend our understanding of reality. They help instill strength, vibrancy, resilience, and health in the body and even open us up to psychic realms and greater intuition, helping us connect to the Divine. Radiant circuits are also likely responsible for spontaneous healing. Amazingly, they create, attract, and open channels for healing energy from the Universe to flow into the body.

Radiant circuits are not restricted to specific pathways in the body like other energy systems, such as the meridian channels. They have the unique capability of jumping or connecting to any place in the energy body to distribute needed energy or to link to a specific energy system. As reservoirs of energy, radiant circuits act like repair mechanisms, bridging and jump-starting different energies and energy systems. This radiant circuit system is a backup system or energy reservoir for most, if not all, energy systems.

Radiant circuits play a significant role in human development. According to Donna Eden, the radiant circuits are the second energies to come into a blastocyst or very early stage of embryogenesis. According to Eden, the unfertilized ovum is already surrounded by an aura when the sperm fertilizes it. Next, the electrics energy system comes into the embryo, followed by the radiant circuits system, underscoring its core significance as a primary energy building block of our early development.

When we are experiencing fear, stress, depression, or anxiety, the radiant circuits have been blocked or deactivated, and their joy energy is not available to us. For example, here are some common life experiences that indicate an obstruction in the optimal flow and function of the radiant circuit system.

- Feeling stuck in life
- Feeling lost or in despair
- Feelings of drowning in sorrow, fear, or grief
- Feeling disconnected from ourselves, others, or the Divine
- Hyper-focus on past events or negativity
- Unable to forgive ourselves or others
- Unable to let go of negative experiences

Insights on your inner journey, such as those listed below, can also lead to working with the radiant circuit system to attain a higher vibrational frequency.

- Realization of operating through negative paradigms of life
- Wanting to overcome a persistent and negative habit that no longer serves our growth
- Wanting to remove negative thoughts, patterns, or emotions

Fortunately, our radiant circuit system can easily be reactivated or turned on. In the following section, I provide some specific exercises for working with the radiant circuit system. But here are some easy ways to naturally activate the radiant circuit system.

- Walking in nature
- Hearing inspirational stories or poetry
- Experiencing uplifting music
- Dancing and moving
- Being in love, being loved, and being loving
- Using our radiant imagination, such as vivid day-dreaming
- Smiling
- Laughing uncontrollably (Laughing Buddha exercise below)
- Exercising, especially exercises that encourage the energy to cross over the body
- Walking and swimming
- Being with young children or being childlike in awe and wonder
- Playing, being playful, silly, or letting go of inhibitions
- Anything that engages our spiritual nature
- Witnessing a rainbow, a spectacular sunrise, or a sunset

The more we activate our radiant circuits system, the more it is available to us, enhancing our energy levels and life experience by raising our vibrational frequency.

Activate the Radiant Circuits

Activating the radiant circuits energy system floods us with high vibrational energy that quite literally dissolves any low-vibrational frequency energy, canceling it out, so we no longer experience the negative, lower vibrational feelings and emotions of stress, anxiety, or fear. Fear and joy cannot coexist in our energy fields at the same time. In the *Map of Consciousness,* David Hawkins assigned a relative vibrational frequency score to a range of feelings, emotional states, or levels of Consciousness. This logarithmic scale ranks joy at 560 compared to fear at 100. So, you can think of turning on the radiant circuits like a mathematical solution. Applying the higher vibrational frequency, like joy at 560, overrides or cancels out a lower vibrational frequency, like fear at 100.

Using the analogy of a mathematical solution that represents a higher value canceling out a lower value, the part of the equation that relates to the higher value would be expressed as the method for activating radiant circuits. While there are many such methods, the following is a series of exercises aimed at activating the radiant circuits to achieve a high vibrational frequency. The first three exercises are designed to activate all ten radiant circuits at once. Each exercise uses a different approach, so you can try one or all three and see which one is most effective for you. The last three exercises stimulate the energy of exhilaration, activating some of the radiant circuits.

Blow Out, Zip Up, and Hook Up

The Blow Out, Zip Up, and Hook Up exercise has three parts, as the name suggests. Each part of the exercise is easy to do and can be done separately to some effect, but doing them together is a powerful way to activate all ten radiant circuits.

First, the *Blow Out* part of this exercise helps us eliminate excess energy, like stress, anger, or fear, that could prevent the activation of the radiant circuits. Start by taking any low vibrational frequency energy, excess energy, or energy draining you into your fists. Set the intention of releasing this excess energy while doing this exercise. Raise your clenched fists over your head. Then, with force and determination, throw the fistful of energy toward the floor or the Earth, allowing the Earth to transmute the energy. As you throw or release this energy, make an emphatic *Shhhh* sound; repeat at least two or three more times. Then, for the final release, throw the energy slowly with control into the Earth and with a powerful *Shhhh* sound.

Next is the *Zip Up*. This part of the exercise protects you from taking on negative energy from others and removes the vulnerability you feel when not protected. You are actually zipping up your central meridian, ensuring that you are centered and more contained within yourself—not vulnerable to forces outside of you. To zip up, put one or two hands in front of the base of the torso and slowly trace up the center of your body to the lower lip. Then, bring the hands back down to the base of the torso but away from the body so as not to unzip the central meridian on the way down. Repeat this three times. When you get to the lower lip on the third tracing, lock in the Zip Up with a pretend key, then throw the key away to emphasize the intention that no one else's energies can get into your field without your permission.

Last is the *Hook Up* to stabilize the energy balance of the first two exercises. In this exercise, we are hooking up the central and governing meridians, which supply energy to the brain, front, and back. The central meridian flows up the center of the front of the body to the lower lip, and the governing meridian flows up the center of the back from the sacrum up to the head and over the head to the upper lip. The Hook Up exercise connects the central and governing meridians at the back of the throat, activating their dual aspect as radiant circuits. To Hook Up the two meridians, put one middle finger in the navel and the other middle finger in the third eye between the eyebrows. Push gently on your skin in both places, then move your fingers up slightly toward the top of your head to stretch the skin in the two areas, creating more space for energy to move. The energy moves more rapidly if you engage the fascia or the connective tissue below the skin. Hold the Hook Up for at least three long, deep breaths. Instead of just three breaths, you can also do a Hook Up for 20 minutes to allow a deeper connection between the central and governing meridians. You would hold the Hook Up longer if you are feeling disconnected within yourself or in life. The longer you hold the Hook Up, the deeper the connection and the more connected you feel. It feels great!

Butt in the Air

The *Butt in the Air* is a second exercise to activate all ten radiant circuits. It's performed much like Child's Pose in yoga, which babies do naturally. Start by sitting on the back of your legs with your knees bent. Then lie your head down on the floor or ground in front of you and raise your butt into the air. Place your arms on either side of your body, with your hands closer to your feet, in a relaxed position. Turn your head either right or left, whichever feels most comfortable. Stay in that position for several minutes, breathing deeply. This exercise can be uncomfortable for the neck if you have neck issues. If so, do one of the other exercises for activating the ten radiant circuits.

Dancing the 8s

Dancing the 8s is a third exercise for activating all ten radiant circuits. From a standing position, use your arms to weave large and small sideways figure 8s or infinity signs all around you and allow yourself to flow and dance with the movement. You can weave figure 8s in all directions: front and back, up and down, and side to side. Try doing this exercise to music and being playful. Have fun. Turn up the music and enJOY.

The following are exercises that may not activate all the radiant circuits, but they are great for activating some of the radiant circuits and the energy of exhilaration!

Laughing Buddha Exercise

To do the *Laughing Buddha* exercise, raise both arms up to the sky with hands open flat, ready to receive, then bounce around or move. Be playful. Let go and be silly. Then, start to laugh. It may feel fake at first. But in a few seconds, you will be laughing at yourself laughing. This exercise is fun to do with other people because laughing is contagious. You will laugh at others who are laughing. Be outrageous with your laughing. Let your inhibitions go and really laugh out loud. It is also fun to do this exercise outside. Laughing is a natural way to activate most, if not all, radiant circuits.

Nine Hearts Exercise

This *Nine Hearts* exercise is simply drawing nine hearts on different places on your body. Our energy body loves this exercise and is very responsive to the repeating heart shapes, so don't be limited to tracing only nine hearts if you are enjoying the experience. To do this exercise, take a deep breath and draw three hearts on your face. Start at the nose and go up to the hairline and down around the outside of your face to the chin. Be conscious and intentional. Go slowly and connect to the shape of the tracing. Then drop your hands down to just above the breast area. Rest your hands there for a moment and take a deep breath. Then, draw three hearts around the breast area and down to the base of the torso. Rest your hands above the breast area and take another deep breath. Then, trace three hearts over the whole body. From the upper chest area, go above the head and make the heart from there to your feet. Repeat two more times. Rest your hands over your heart to end the exercise.

Heaven Rushing In

The *Heaven Rushing In* exercise opens you to receive Divine Energy flowing through your body or to get answers to specific questions. To do this exercise, begin by rubbing your hands together to activate the energy in your hands. Then, shake off any stagnant energy in your hands and put them on your thighs to ground the energy into the Earth. Imagine the energy running down your hands, then down your legs, and into the Earth. It is important to be grounded in the next step when connecting to Divine Energy. Next, bring your hands together in front of your heart area, like the prayer pose or the Anjali Mudra. Pause for a moment to connect to your heart energy by celebrating the moment with humility for increased Spiritual Awakening.

At this point, you can ask a question silently or out loud. First, set an intention, and you'll get an answer. Then, when you are ready, raise your arms up and slightly out to the side to receive Divine Energy into your open hands or to receive the answer. You will likely feel tingling energy or some activity in your hands. When your hands are filled up with this Divine Energy, bring your hands together and lay them over the heart area, which has an energy vortex called *Heaven Rushing In*. If you want more Divine or radiant energy, raise your arms again and be open to receiving more Divine Energy. In my experience, this exercise is very powerful and even more so when done outside in nature.

> I once did the *Heaven Rushing In* exercise with about 150 in a hotel ballroom without any windows as part of an Energy Medicine class. I had my eyes closed, but I could see bright lights in front of my eyes. I was convinced the sun was shining on us with a spectacular radiance through the windows. When I finished the exercise and opened my eyes, I was reminded that the room had no windows. I was a little perplexed, but went on with my day. Later, one of the faculty members came up to me to let me know that I was glowing during the *Heaven Rushing In* exercise. She said she saw light flowing from me. Still perplexed, I asked how she was able to see this light coming from me. She said she had no special abilities, and anyone else with their eyes open at the time would have seen it.

Using Our Radiant Imagination

We can use our radiant imagination to activate our radiant circuits by being mindful of our thoughts and feelings and setting an intention to be in the energies of gratitude, joy, love, forgiveness, and any other high vibrational frequency. This is especially helpful if you are feeling sad or depressed or experiencing other negative states of mind. Instead of attaching to the negative feelings, we can shift our awareness and call to mind positive thoughts, feelings, or experiences that connect us to a higher vibrational frequency. For some, that may be happy childhood memories or family vacations; for others, it may be a happy life experience that has endured in their heart. Whatever is available to build the momentum of joy, set the intention to focus on that feeling, allowing it to blossom and dissolve any negative feelings.

Using our radiant imagination during meditation activates our radiant circuits and raises our vibrational frequency. A powerful way to use this technique is to visualize a brilliant, dazzling light or golden liquid light coming in through your crown chakra, flowing down your spine or your energetic core, and into your legs. You can visualize the light filling up each cell in every tissue and organ.

When I do this visualization during my morning meditation, I feel the light all day long. It feels amazing. But this is just one example of a visualization that works to activate the radiant circuits. I invite you to use your imagination to visualize any experience of radiant light or positive energy as completely enveloping your body and feel the joyous energy of the radiant circuits lighting you up.

BEing in Gratitude

BEing in gratitude also activates the radiant circuits. Gratitude helps us shift to a new, health-inducing way of seeing and experiencing the world. It fosters new hope and optimism, relieves stress and anxiety, and moves us into a higher vibrational frequency. Understanding life from a positive and grateful perspective opens our ability to understand the gift of life and the opportunities for growth and evolution. Seeing life from this perspective of growth is true empowerment.

Keeping a gratitude journal is a great way to be aware of what and whom we appreciate and helps us to focus on what is going well in our lives. I have provided some journal prompts in Exercise 1 at the end of this Section.

The Power of Positive Thoughts and Beliefs

In my book *Journey to True Self*, I introduce the idea that our words, thoughts, feelings, and beliefs affect our vibrational frequency, which, in turn, acts like a magnet attracting the people, opportunities, and experiences that are a vibrational match. In other words, our frequency causes the effects of our lives according to the Universal Law of Cause and Effect.

Here, we are going to expand on that idea to explore more fully how we can use our words, thoughts, and feelings. Turning first to the words we use, it's easy to see how simply focusing on word choice can dramatically shift our vibrational frequency. To understand word choice, it's important to realize that we tend to talk negatively about ourselves in the secret recesses of our minds. We may also have a tendency to think negative thoughts about others; sometimes, we express these thoughts, but mostly we internalize them, keeping them hidden. Either way, whether words are used in an inner or external dialogue, their vibrational frequency radiates throughout our body and out into the Universe. Swear words have a particularly low-vibrational energy that lands in our energy field and physical body and can block the natural flow of energy in a specific area of the body, resulting in stuck energy or discomfort.

Making the shift to thinking and talking in terms of our magnificence and our gifts will have an extraordinarily positive result in our lives. If we see the good in ourselves, we will naturally see the good in others. Consciously focusing on using high vibrational frequency words is a magnificent way to raise our overall vibrational frequency, improve energy flow, and remove energy blocks. Saying these words while your hand is placed over an area of discomfort in your body can be very helpful in releasing any blocked energy that may be causing the discomfort.

These are some high-vibrational words associated with the highest levels of Consciousness in *the Map of Consciousness*: enlightenment, ascension, wisdom, ineffable, benevolence, magnificence, vibrancy, vitality, peace, joy, compassion, serenity, forgiveness, courage, illumination, transcendence, empowerment, unconditional love, reverence, optimism, bliss, harmony, sacred, sanctuary, acceptance, and willingness.

Here are three high-vibrational statements I use in my energy practice as I hold onto the areas of discomfort. I ask my clients to say these statements as I hold the areas of energy blockage.

I love you.
I appreciate you.
I am so grateful for all you do for me.

Periodically, I also use a series of *let go, let go, let go* if the client has stiff muscles and a shift in energy flow does not occur with either of these other two strategies.

Shifting Thoughts to Raise Our Vibrational Frequency

Shifting to how thoughts relate to vibrational frequency, the explanation is simple: we become what we think about, and what we think about expands. Most people have approximately 60,000 thoughts every day. If the majority of those thoughts are charged with negative energy, which research shows may be as much as 80% of our thoughts, our corresponding vibrational frequency is going to match that and be relatively low. Of course, the converse is also true; thinking positive thoughts corresponds with a higher vibrational frequency and optimal energy flow in our bodies. Choosing inspirational messages and uplifting thoughts as the chatter in our minds will help raise our vibrational frequency significantly and help us be in the flow of the Universe.

So, how do we get the core issue of shifting the pendulum toward increasing the amount and quality of positive thoughts we have in a day? My suggestion is that it starts with perception. Our perceptions are key to interpreting what is going on in our lives. In his book *The Biology of Belief*, Dr. Bruce Lipton explains that our thoughts come from our perceptions. We have a choice in how we perceive our lives and the world in the same way that we have a choice to engage in the physical or Spiritual Realm paradigms.

Beyond what we may experience, this choice also controls the expression of our genes. The recent understanding that our thoughts, perceptions, and paradigms of life affect our genes has evolved into a field of science known as epigenetics, which literally means control over the genes. Although the results of the studies are clear, the causal connection between perception and result is not. I suggest that the connection likely lies in the energy field—the vibrational frequency of thoughts, words, and actions affecting the genes. In a general sense, if we continually perceive negative thoughts and experiences, we are more likely to express genes related to disease and ill health. Conversely, if we continually find the silver lining in life, we are more likely to express genes related to optimal health, vibrancy, and well-being.

The amazing aspect of this concept suggests that we are empowered to change our thoughts, feelings, and beliefs based on how we perceive the world and create the experiences we want. Understanding that we can choose to be the creators rather than the victims of our circumstances is very empowering. It tells us that our choices matter and that we can change our circumstances and what happens in our lives by how we think.

Repetitive thoughts become beliefs that inform our feelings, resulting in behaviors that become the actions we take and the results we experience.

> Thoughts → Beliefs → Feelings → Behavior → Actions → Results

Our Thoughts Ultimately Create Our Reality

It's one thing to have a conceptual understanding that our thoughts ultimately create the reality we experience, but quite another to fully grasp this as a basis for how we live our lives. As with any change we want to make or new skill we want to master, it begins simply with taking the first steps and then building on that to create the momentum for real and lasting change.

Changing how we think to create the world we want is no different. We can begin with the first step of getting to know ourselves by observing our daily lives to discover the effects of our negative thoughts and the effects of our positive thoughts. It's an exercise in taking time to pause and to listen to what we are saying to ourselves and others and how we are feeling, then following that thread to identify the source of our negative thought patterns and emotions. From there, we have the beginnings of a road map that tells us where the roadblocks and obstacles lie, keeping us from expressing our highest and best Selves.

The first step in changing our thoughts is to become aware of the words we use and our thoughts. Become an observer and witness the thoughts. We think 60,000 thoughts every day. We can set intentions to be present enough in the moment to start capturing the exact moments when we think a negative thought. If we catch ourselves going into a negative state, we can say, *delete, delete, delete*! The more we can catch ourselves going into negativity, the easier it is to stop. Awareness is the key here.

Being in tune with our feelings and understanding that we are on a Spiritual Journey, which likely involves crossing an ephemeral bridge from the physical to the invisible, we can choose to see through a filter of love and forgiveness, raising our vibrational frequency. If our words, thoughts, and feelings have a high vibrational frequency, our actions will have corresponding energy and follow the high vibrational frequency course we have set in place.

Focusing on problems and what we don't want lowers our vibrancy. Even though we know this, it is easy to focus on our problems and get sucked into negativity about what is happening.

Do you see how focusing on our problems only attracts more of the same in our lives?

Shifting our focus to what we want and being grateful for where we are in the moment is a great way to move beyond this stagnant cause-and-effect cycle. Being attracted to and reading this book indicates that you are open and willing to change. Be grateful for this openness and willingness. Shifting our focus this way puts our attention on what we want—not what we don't want; where we are going—not where we've been. The flow of the Universe is going forward, not backward to the past. Opening up space within to be in flow with this forward momentum allows new opportunities to come into our field.

Are we focused on a path to enlightenment, and are we headed in the direction of where we want to go?

In his book, *The Magician's Way: What It Really Takes to Find Your Treasure*, William Whitecloud uses the analogy of playing golf to illustrate the answer to this question. He explains that golfers are taught to look at the hole where they want the ball to go, focus on the hole, aim for the cup, and then swing, launching the ball toward the green. Alternatively, focusing on a course obstacle, like a sand trap or water hole, inevitably sends the ball sailing in that direction rather than toward the green. In other words, the ball goes where our focus goes; energy flows where attention goes. If we carry our disappointment and frustration about how we played the previous hole, how well do we think we will do on the next one?

Letting go of who we used to be allows who we are meant to be to show up.

If the concept of negative thinking resonates with you, I invite you to do Exercises 2 and 3 at the end of this Section to help you change thoughts from negative to positive and discover it's easier than you think.

Misperceptions

To be aligned with the flow of the Universe also means being in flow with abundance because there is no lack or limitation in the Universe. Everything we need can be manifested through the invisible energy around us. Quantum physics indicates that our potential exists in a haze of possibilities. Like an electron that exists in two aspects, as a particle and as a string of energy, to manifest from possibility to physical form, we collapse energy or vibrating strings through intention or thought to create form. The energy for creating from this potential is limitless. Any thoughts or feelings of less than, lack, or limitation are necessarily false and illusory because lack and limitation simply do not exist as a creative force in the Universe. They are constructs of the ego, creating a false reality.

In her book, *The Law of Divine Compensation*, Marianne Williamson explains that the Universe is always self-organizing and self-correcting. If we are aligned with love, we will receive Divine compensation for any material lack. Williamson calls this the Law of Divine Compensation. Manifestation in the physical realm comes from the Spiritual Substance of the Universe. The Law of Divine Compensation is the Universal Law of Cause and Effect using the concept of love. It is activated by and responds to every loving thought and is deactivated or turned off by every unloving thought. We are compensated by our loving thoughts with more to love. Conversely, we are compensated for our unloving thoughts by more situations to be unloving.

Our illusions about how the Universe supports us come from misperceptions we have been taught or modeled through our collective experience. Misperceptions can also come from our own misunderstandings or misinterpretations of events or situations. There is a myriad of misperceptions we have decided are true.

We may believe we are guilty or that others are guilty. We may believe we are victims of our circumstances. We may believe that there is lack and limitation in the Universe. These misperceptions can become beliefs embedded in our Consciousness as if they are true. Unknowingly, we are then living our lives based on untruths or illusions. If we are experiencing any of these misperceptions, especially the belief in lack or limitation, it is a sign that we are not in flow with the abundance of the Universe.

Self-Limiting Beliefs

If our thoughts of lack and limitation relate to how we feel about ourselves, they can become embedded as self-limiting beliefs. All these limiting beliefs are false constructs of our ego that are very damaging. The first agreement in Don Miguel Luis's book, *The Four Agreements*, is about being impeccable. Be honorable with your words. Use your words from your Inner Wisdom for your highest potential, creativity, and conscious intention to manifest what you want. This agreement includes being impeccable with our words about ourselves—honoring ourselves. In my experience working with people's energies, self-limiting beliefs are often the core issue holding people back in life. Here are some examples of common self-limiting beliefs.

> I'm not good enough.
> I don't trust myself.
> I don't believe in myself.
> I don't deserve success.
> I'm unworthy.
> I'm unlovable.

Most of the self-limiting beliefs we have were introduced into our thought patterns and stored in our subconscious mind before we were seven years old. The more we engage in these self-limiting beliefs later in life, the deeper they embed in our subconscious. The subconscious mind controls about 95% of everything we do, from controlling our breathing and heartbeat to our automatic responsiveness while driving. That means self-limiting beliefs held in the subconscious mind are almost always turned on in the background of the mind, like a tape recorder on constant replay, holding us back from living up to our full potential.

Every thought is creative energy that has a causal effect. Unloving thoughts, such as self-limiting beliefs, create a negative effect, resulting in the opposite of what we want by interfering and undermining the natural flow of the Universe to support us.

Marianne Williamson shares that Spiritual Growth is understanding that the stories we tell ourselves are not real; they are just stories. Stories can be developed to help us cope with an issue or trauma in the moment. If we give up the stories of our past, we can co-create a new story with the Universe. Self-limiting beliefs are just that, stories. Worse yet, they relate to the untrue stories we have been told about ourselves or tell ourselves that we believe to be true. Whatever negative or self-limiting beliefs we have about ourselves, or others have about us, do not reflect the truth of who we really are. Any thought of self-limitation separates us from the Divine. Self-limitation is a result of identification with the physical body rather than the Soul—who we really are. The truth is, we are the immutable, unlimited creations of the Divine. We can align with, embrace, and step into the magnificent BEing the Divine created.

How can we be One with the Divine and have any self-limitations? If we identify with the Spiritual aspect of ourselves rather than our physical forms, we are in a synchronous flow with the Universe. We are on a path to enlightenment. Williamson explains that negative or self-limiting concepts do not have any bearing on what the Universe has planned for us. Therefore, our past mistakes and failures do not limit who we are or what is possible for us in the present; rather, they help us grow.

We all were created by the Divine, not as separate beings but as One BEing. We all are capable of being, serving, and expressing the Divine Intention. Divine Intelligence pours into us as One. We all receive this Divine Gift and make our individual choices about consciously accepting it or not.

Reprogramming Our Subconscious Minds

Reprogramming our subconscious minds and recognizing how often and the ways in which we do something creative, innovative, or excellent can change our feelings and beliefs about ourselves. Focusing on what we are doing right, where we shine, and securely storing that in our subconscious mind overwrites the old programming. We can create and manifest beyond our wildest imagination in every moment.

Fundamentally, reprogramming our subconscious is about being honest with ourselves. We need to acknowledge the self-limiting beliefs at play and replace them with the realization of the truth and magnificence of who we really are and that we are here on Earth for a Divine Purpose. We were given the gifts and talents to accomplish this purpose when we came into this incarnation. We were totally set up for success!

If these methods for reprogramming are not as effective as you would like, you may want to consider exploring energy work to release the energy related to these beliefs with the help of an Energy Mastery practitioner. Or you could find a coach certified by the Institute for Women-Centered Coaching, Training & Leadership to help you break through inner barriers or self-limiting beliefs.

Try Exercise 4 at the end of this Section to start overwriting self-limiting beliefs with positive affirmations. I have also provided questions and prompts to inspire helpful meditations and journaling.

Increasing Clarity from Experiences on the Journey

A key step to being in the flow of the Universe is getting clear on what is important to us, how we fit into the world with our gifts and talents, and what brings us joy. Knowing what we want and where we are going in life helps us make the best choices and decisions for ourselves. Knowing what we want and where we are going places us on a journey to BE our best selves. Our journey and experiences help us discover what is best for us. Paying attention to what is happening for us is following the guidance of the Universe. Otherwise, we are vulnerable to what others think is best for us, giving away our power. To be aligned on our Spiritual Journey, we move forward in our truth and authenticity. We move forward in aligning with our True Selves. We are in flow with the Universe.

Essentialism: The Disciplined Pursuit of Less, a book by Greg McKweon, explores what is essential in our lives for achieving happiness that is part of our Spiritual Journey. What is essential for one person's journey is not necessarily essential for another person's journey because we all have different special gifts, talents, skills, and preferences for what lights us up as individuals. Different things make me come alive than what makes you come alive. We are trying to accomplish different purposes or missions. McKweon suggests that, most likely, what is essential in our lives will reflect our Divine Mission. The book's main premise is to live our lives focused on what is essential and eliminate what is non-essential to live a life of meaning and purpose intended for us.

We can interpret this concept as focusing on what will help us move toward accomplishing our mission and what will deter us from accomplishing our mission. To discover what is essential for our Spiritual Journey, we can connect to what is burning within us that needs to be expressed. We can ask ourselves questions to get clarity.

> *What am I sharing with the world that can't be kept inside of me anymore?*
> *What am I passionate about that needs to be shared?*

After reading McKweon's book, I realized I wasn't living my authentic life. I was living a life someone else wanted me to live, or, more likely, the life I thought someone wanted me to live. I spent months writing about *What is Essential to Me* in a journal every night. After I had exhausted the topic for months, or more like a year later, I looked at all my journal entries and discovered a consistent theme or pattern that led me to write these verses.

What's Essential to Me?

> To be in alignment with my True Divine Self is number 1.
> That I am living and achieving at my highest and full potential.
> That I am open and super receptive and allow life to unfold naturally.
> That I am BEing love, joy, and peace.
>
> That I follow a path to enlightenment.
> That I focus on truth, wisdom, and joy.
> That I am One with the Divine, nature, and the Universe.
> That I transcend my 3D self.
>
> That I am always connected to my Soul, my True Self.
> The inner Divine aspect of me.
> Realizing I am more than a body.
> I am a Soul in a physical body.
>
> I am a Soul, first and foremost.

My Soul is guiding me, and I listen.
I am empowered by my Soul.
I disregard my ego's exhausting messages.

That I am in service to others.
Uplifting, inspiring, and awakening people.
Sharing the wisdom of the quantum nature of the Universe.
Detaching from the outcomes, not blocking this flow.

Being the conduit for something new to come in.
Allowing the flow toward the best and highest for all.
That would help others transform and see through a new lens,
A lens of awe, wonder, and Oneness.

A knowing that anything and everything is possible.
The more I allow, the more it flows through me.
Being part of the ascension process and raising the positive.
Discovering even higher dimensions of BEing and doing.

If I could live this way, it would be a life well-lived.
I could be a blessing to others, and they would bless me.
I would be in the best position to make an impact in the world,
And to make significant changes in me and the people around me.

~Anne M. Deatly

Here are my inner reflections on what is essential to me. If you want to explore and create your own list of what is essential to you, I have provided some prompts and guidance in Exercise 5 at the end of this Section.

What is essential to me is:

Growing spiritually.
Feeding my Soul.
Following a path of enlightenment.

Living in prosperity Consciousness.
BEing unconditional love.

BEing at peace and living radiantly.

Saying yes to new opportunities to grow.
Saying no to what's not essential to me.
Being free to make the best choices for me.

Seeing the good, the love, and the Divine in all people, situations, and experiences.
Using everything that happens for my best and highest good.
Living simply in the present moment.

Being with and attracting people also seeking enlightenment.
BEing in heart/brain coherence and listening to my heart.
Knowing that everything I need is always available to me.

Observing the abundance of the Universe.
Feeling the abundance of the Universe.
Living fully from this abundance.

~Anne M. Deatly

Detaching from the Outcome

Even when we know what is essential to us and where we are headed, and even connected to our entelechy, we can still be open to unexpected outcomes that expand what we think is possible without limits or blocks to what life force energy is offering us. From a physical realm perspective, we don't have access to higher levels of Consciousness and don't always know what outcomes are in our best and highest good. This is partly because we lack the perspective of our Spiritual Growth from this physical realm view. It's also because, just by being born and growing up in the physical realm, most of us have been programmed to think in terms of separation, fear, limitation, and lack, relying solely on what we can perceive with the physical senses to guide us.

But as we open to the Spiritual Realm and receive information beyond physical perception, we have access to a whole new level of awareness, possibility, and opportunity. Detaching from expectations about the specific outcome based on what we think we know or think should happen gives us the freedom to be in the flow of the Universe and allows for possibilities and opportunities beyond our expectations to appear in our lives. It is a process of letting go of control of the outcome while staying focused on the general direction of our path for growth and expansion.

It is easier to detach from the outcome if we know a benevolent Life Force is always guiding us toward the best choices for our life lessons and growth. Even if we transmit a vibrational frequency that resonates with the outcome we think we want, we may not get it because, at that moment, what we thought we wanted was not aligned with our true path. Feeling disappointment or a sense of failure would be a mistake. The wisdom of the Universe gives us something different, something better, or an opportunity to learn and grow, needed for success that is more aligned with our highest potential. If we get something unexpected, it may mean that another path is opening for us that will serve us better.

Changing from the Inside Out

Once we are aligned with the flow of the Universe, we change from the inside out. Our lives become clearer and more focused. We create different goals for our lives. We see the illusions of the third-dimensional Earth programming and want to detach from the compulsion to chase ever more illusions. We are drawn to create from our True Self or Divine Self rather than the physical or ego self.

We realize that to be and express the Divine, we have to think like the Divine. We move into a higher level of Consciousness and create what benefits us and others beyond the physical world. From this perspective, competing with others and climbing corporate ladders is revealed as a far cry from what the Divine in co-creation with our True Self would like to experience through us. We are magnetized to find the answers and understand life at a deeper level. Questions may arise within us.

> *What will bring out my Higher Self?*
> *What is my specific Divine Mission that I am here to accomplish?*

In answering these questions, we might find that we already know our specific mission because our Higher Self has been guiding us toward it. If we are in the flow of the Universe, we will be flowing toward our next step, our next opportunity, or our next project. We are going to have energetic resonance with whatever that is. We might want to pay attention to how we react emotionally to different opportunities, people, situations, or events. Our Divine Guidance System will be nudging us in a particular direction. Our Divine Guidance System may be showing us a completely different path from what we are currently experiencing. Detaching from the outcome and following the flow is the best approach as we go through life and different levels of learning, growing, and expanding.

If we understand our connection to the Spiritual Realm, we will understand the Divine Guidance System. There is so much support for us and our journey that we can't possibly imagine. But that is the truth. Sometimes, it takes a lifetime to realize there is a whole support system ready, willing, and able to help us with whatever we need whenever we need it. So, we might as well learn this as soon as possible!!

The closer we become to Self-actualizing, the better it is for us, the Spiritual Realm, the Divine, and Consciousness. Life gets easier if we can learn to detach from our earthly goals and go in the direction of the Divine Guidance System. Being in the flow of the Universe results in us BEing the best versions of ourselves.

The Garden of Our Mind

Seeds grow, sprout, and mature. Pumpkin seeds produce pumpkins. Grape seeds germinate into grapevines that produce grapes. We don't get green bean plants from grape seeds. This concept seems obvious in the planting world. But it is not so obvious when we use this as a metaphor for thoughts we are planting in the garden of our minds. In the garden of our mind, we can plant seeds of joy, peace, love, forgiveness, and Oneness, or seeds of judgment, unforgiveness, despair, criticism, anger, fear, panic, worry, and grief.

Just as a nurtured seed expands and produces fruit, the thoughts we focus on expand and produce our experience of reality. If we seed the garden of our mind with thoughts of love, expressions of love appear in our lives. Positive thoughts reap harvests of more positivity. Likewise, planting seeds of fear manifests as fear in our life experience, reaping harvests of more negativity. Either way, it can come as no surprise that the thoughts planted in our minds and nurtured through attention and focus can only bear the fruit of those thoughts, just as pumpkin seeds can only bear pumpkins.

All the seeds we have planted and nurtured in our minds constantly germinate and mature as our life experiences. The seeds we water and nurture most will grow strong and determine the quality of our BEing and the quality of our lives. Being aware of the seeds we plant in our minds is critical to our success in life. If we pay attention to what harvests as our life experiences, we will see what seeds we have planted and nurtured. Remember the Universal Law of Cause and Effect?

> *What are the seeds you have been planting in your mind?*
> *Is this what you want to harvest more of in the future?*

Be very intentional about what you are planting and nurturing because those seeds will grow and expand. Although you can't change an unwanted seed once it's planted in your mind, you can pull it out like a weed to prevent it from producing an unwanted result. If we keep our minds clear of weeds and focus our attention on nurturing the seeds that are essential to us, those seeds will blossom and become new opportunities for expansion.

You can plant seeds by setting intentions of what you feel you will need as you align with what is essential to you and the flow of the Universe.

Being Grounded and Present as Spirituality Unfolds

Being grounded and connected to the Earth allows us to stay centered and clear in our intentions and goals, and focused on what is essential. Being grounded means the polarity of our energy fields is in alignment with the polarity of the Earth's energy: the polarity of our field is north around our heads and south around our feet. We are like magnets. We have an electromagnetic field around us, just like the Earth. This north-to-south polarity allows us to connect to Earth energy and attract fresh, revitalizing energy into our body through our feet, or receive revitalizing energies into our crown chakra area or head.

Being ungrounded or disconnected from the Earth's energy indicates that our energy fields are not totally in our physical bodies. Sometimes, it feels like our energy body, or Soul, is not totally anchored into our physical forms. That feeling is the same as being ungrounded—not totally connected to the Earth. If the magnetic polarity of our energy fields is not aligned with the energy of the Earth, our energy body can be repelled by the energy of the Earth, like the northern sides of two magnets repel each other. Symptoms of being ungrounded include feeling dizzy, faint, disconnected, or experiencing vertigo. It could even manifest as being unable to focus because being grounded is essential to being in the present moment, the only place where life happens. If we are not living in the present moment, we're not really experiencing life. We are missing the here and now, focused on either a story about the past or a non-existent future.

We are also disconnected from ourselves when we are ungrounded. Symptoms of being disconnected from yourself include jumping from topic to topic, not following through, avoidance of confronting situations, lack of focus, and being stuck in the head, to name a few.

If you want to be more connected to the Earth and receive its revitalizing energy, there are easy ways to orient the polarities of your energy fields. If you want to be more focused or be in the present moment to enjoy what is happening in the here and now, you can do any of the exercises listed below. Some exercises work better for some people than others. That is why there is a choice.

- Rub the curved side of a stainless-steel spoon on the bottom of your feet to help organize the electrons for more optimal communication within your energy body, creating a clear difference between your north and south poles.
- Walk barefoot on wet grass or sand to directly connect your feet to the energies of the Earth.
- Sit or stand with your back against a tree to connect to the strong energy flowing through the tree into the roots in the ground.
- Imagine roots growing out of your feet, going into the Earth, helping you to root thoroughly into the soil and below ground.
- Rub the top of each foot to open the area between the small bones where energy can easily get stuck. Encourage the energy to flow easily through your feet and to the rest of your body.
- Cross your arms and put your hands under the opposite armpits. Hold for several minutes while breathing deeply.
- Draw Figure 8s on the bottom of each foot.

Removing the Energy Blocks to Growth, Freedom, and Peace

Another way we can be blocked from being in alignment with Universal Flow is from energy blocks or gaps in our body or energy field. Energy blocks are areas of the energy body where the energy is not flowing optimally and may be stuck. For example, some common energy blocks can result when the magnetic polarity of an area of the body is off: the energy is not crossing over, there is a blockage or hole in the aura over the area, or low vibrational frequency words or emotions are stuck. This can cause us to be disconnected from growth opportunities, freedom, and peace.

Karmic imprints, analogical states of mind, resistance, and Soul fracturing are other ways energy is blocked in our energy fields. These are ways that energy can congeal in our fields, blocking flow. Energy that was stuck in one area may move to another area of the body with a blockage and express as a physical symptom there. If we are blocked in our energy fields or not in flow within ourselves, it is harder to be in flow with the Universe. Improving the energy flow, regardless of the cause or type of blockage, is relatively simple. No one must live with pain or other energy blockages.

No matter the cause of the energy blocks, the result is the same: we are disconnected from where we are headed as Souls. These blocks can act either to block us entirely from being in flow, like being in a sailboat with no wind, or partially block us, like having one foot on the accelerator and one foot on the brake. Although we may not be able to prevent an energy block from occurring, it can be released by using energy techniques to address the underlying cause. If the energy block is not released, deeper issues related to the stuck energy can develop.

Below are some examples of types of energy blockages preventing alignment with Universal Flow, which will be discussed in more detail later in this Section.

- pain or discomfort from congealed or blocked energy
- having a low-vibrational energy field frequency
- being disconnected within ourselves or from others
- being disconnected from the Divine
- being stuck in the past or carrying burdens from the past
- being stuck in negative thoughts, feelings, and beliefs
- holding self-limiting beliefs
- having an energetic disconnection between the heart and the Soul
- having a broken or damaged energy grid within our energy field
- having unresolved karmic imprints
- having energetic attachments, identities, or IDs, or analogical states of mind
- having a lost or fractured Soul aspect
- being too filled up with old energy to accept new energy
- resisting change

We can heal all these energy blocks and more by addressing the underlying root cause and emptying out non-essential energies that are blocking us from being in the flow with the Universe.

Releasing Physical Discomfort

One way to detect an energy block is through areas of tightness, soreness, tenderness, or pain. These physical sensations are almost always related to excess energy that is not flowing optimally in the area of the body expressing the symptom. Energy blockages can be in localized areas or dispersed over larger sections of the body, in a meridian, or from unresolved emotional issues. The type and scope of the physical symptom determine the energy technique needed to clear the blockage.

It may be surprising to know that releasing energy blockages related to tightness, soreness, tenderness, and pain is fairly easy. It is a matter of repatterning the energy flow so the energy is not stuck or accumulating where the symptom is felt. Although the energy techniques can help the energy flow better in a short period of time, if the energetic pattern has existed for a significant time, the energy technique will have to be performed repeatedly until the energies are balanced and sustain the new energy flow.

I often tell my clients that no one needs to live with these physical symptoms. It is just a message from the body alerting us to the blocked energy flow. Please understand this discussion as a way to handle some physical symptoms. You may still need to see a medical professional to handle your physical symptoms that don't respond to the methods discussed. If the physical discomfort is not relieved, further and perhaps more serious complications can occur.

If the physical symptom is in a meridian, the energy blockage can be released using acupressure points. Knowing where the symptom is expressed and how energy flows from one meridian to the other in the five-rhythm system provides the road map for using acupressure points to release excess energy from one meridian into the other to restore optimal flow. The method of using acupressure points to direct the flow of energy to specific points along the meridians has been tested and used for thousands of years. You will likely need an energy medicine practitioner to help you with this technique.

For localized symptoms, tap the affected area and the wrist or ankles in the zone of the affected area to get the energy moving out of the area for relief. This is called *Zone Tapping*. Tap the top of the wrist if the issue is above the waist and on the back or the outside of the body. If the issue is above the waist but on the front or the inside of the leg or arms, then tap the wrist on the palm side of the body. If the issue is below the waist, tap the ankles. Tap on the inside of the ankles if the issue is on the front of the body or the inside of your arms or legs. Tap on the outside of the ankle if the issue is on the back or the outside of the body. You can also use the Emotional Freedom Technique to tap out the pain. Another technique is circling a hand counterclockwise over the area without touching your body to remove potential vortexes of energy holding the symptom or blockage in place. Spinning crystals, using magnets, healing stones, or essential oils are other ways to release symptoms in localized areas. Doing these exercises is simple and may alleviate the physical symptom, releasing stuck or blocked energy to avoid deeper issues.

We can also hold specific neurovascular points associated with specific meridians to release stuck emotional energy that causes discomfort. Imbalanced emotions are a primary source of physical symptoms or blocked energy flow. Fear, anger, panic, worry, and grief are powerful emotional energies that can get stuck at different points in our energy bodies. These types of energy blocks can be easily released using neurovascular points associated with one or more of the five rhythms.

For symptoms that extend in more dispersed patterns, longer techniques, such as the Hopi technique, are especially effective in relieving back discomfort. The Brazilian Toe Technique is another wonderful and powerful technique to release dispersed discomfort in the body. Again, I would suggest contacting a local energy medicine practitioner who can help you with these techniques.

Removing Karmic Imprints

Karma is created at the Soul level because of our choices. We have created everything around us by choice. We live in a self-correcting system. Every choice, every thought, has a consequence. Choices are stored in our Akashic Record, in our chakras, in DNA, in cell memory, in our body, and at every level of our mind. Every thought becomes a morphogenetic imprint within the frequency bands of our Consciousness.

Karma is an example of the consequences of the Universal Law of Cause and Effect and is happening all the time, every single moment. Our thoughts and actions create the cause; our morphogenetic field or frequency through which we experience life is the effect. Karma is created when we make a choice of a substantial nature that continues to influence our life experiences and can leave a powerful, energetic imprint until it is resolved. Karma can be created by us or inherited from our ancestors. This concept of inheriting karma from our ancestors may be difficult to comprehend, especially if we are trying to transform some aspect of our lives where we are struggling and unhappy. Then why would we create more of what upsets us and causes disharmony in our lives? The answer is simple-it's most likely ancestral Karma.

Karma can also be present in our energy field as an innate pattern of victimhood inherited from our ancestors. Healing the patterns and their imprints allows us to resolve and move beyond the victim consciousness and become a victor in our present lifetime, possibly healing this pattern in our ancestral lineage as well. Karmic imprints can be created in a state of shock or trauma. In this state, time seems to stop. This timeless state is called an analogical state of mind. Declaring or agreeing to something in that state could fracture one or more facets of our Soul's crystalline energetic structure. In this fracturing process, karmic imprints of twisted or distorted energy patterns are created that cannot properly process light or vibrational frequency. The effect is like re-wiring the electrical system in a house in reverse. The lights are dim, and only a limited number of lights are turned on.

Karmic imprints related to the birth process can develop if the father is not present at birth or if we are born with the umbilical cord wrapped around our neck. Anything said before, during, or after birth can result in a karmic imprint. A baby's subconscious mind records all of this, where it remains inaccessible to the conscious mind.

Similarly, anesthesia can cause a karmic imprint based on what the doctors are discussing or what is happening in the surgery room. Like the baby, we don't know what is being said and done, but our subconscious mind records everything and can store a karmic imprint from the trauma.

Inherited Karmic Imprints

As previously discussed, we can also inherit unknown karmic imprints from our parents or ancestors. We inherit everything from our parents that is unresolved, including thousands of years of ancestral karmic imprints stored in our DNA. Since this all happens through the birth process, we have no conscious awareness that karma is in our energy field and affecting our lives. If these karmic imprints are not cleared and electrically disengaged, the energy block from the imprint remains in our energy field, and we can pass it along to our children. We may express unwanted behaviors or tendencies related to these imprints that can be resolved in this lifetime by understanding that it is not our True Self and letting it go.

Here are some examples of unresolved karmic imprints that can be inherited from our ancestors.

- unwanted repetitive behavior
- attracting the same type of person in relationships who don't fulfill our needs
- poverty consciousness
- any belief in lack and limitation
- obesity
- cancer
- guilt and shame
- worthlessness
- sense of undeserving
- victimization
- martyrdom

Regardless of how our karmic imprints were created, our goal is to master life choices and not be impacted by an unknown trauma or ancestral inheritance. We need to clear what we create as well as what we have inherited. We can't embody or become our Higher Selves with these blocks. The worst things about karmic imprints are:

- We don't know how it is created; we don't understand the mechanics of it.
- We continue to make choices directly against Divine Right Order and continue to fracture connections.
- Eventually, we become disconnected from the Divine.
- We don't know how to clear the residue of past choices to embody our important mission.

Discerning what is really us and what belongs to someone else is key to BEing and expressing our True Selves. As observers in our lives, we can better tune in to what is happening around us. We understand the bigger picture for us, and we can stay in that energy of our higher state of BEing and become aware of what is not us. We can see what is happening, and we are able to change it and create a different reality. We disconnect from the egoic mind chatter and listen to our Soul. We begin to understand that life on Earth is a holographic playground for us to work through our issues to learn, grow, and evolve.

Nonetheless, we do not have to be victims of these silent predators lying in wait in our subconscious and can clear the karmic imprints through specialized energy techniques. Karma clearly substantially decreases our vibrational frequency and is the most important blockage to clear from our Soul energy. It is a process of Spiritual Evolution that transforms past experiences into golden nuggets of wisdom or Spiritual Wisdom. Clearing karmic imprints returns us to the essence of who we are by removing these twisted energetic distortions, allowing our fractured Soul fragments to rejoin our Soul and become whole. We begin to feel more like ourselves. We are more connected and in flow with the Universe.

Not all Soul facet loss is caused by karmic imprints. During physical or emotional trauma, the facets of the Soul may disassociate from the Soul as a survival mechanism in response to being injured in an accident, invasive surgery, or drug or alcohol toxicity. Soul facet loss can also be a result of psychological dissociation. Desperation, fear, anger, or victimization are the main causes of Soul facet loss. Loss of Soul facets is common, and there are professional healers who are skilled in assisting with Soul retrieval to integrate lost or fractured Soul facets back into your energy field.

We can also clear karmic imprints that underlie many of life's challenges: money issues based on lack, limitation, poverty consciousness, vows of poverty, and religious beliefs; self-esteem issues related to a sense of unworthiness, undeservedness, guilt, shame, and I'm not good enough; disease, and epigenetic issues that may lead to disease. Advanced techniques for clearing karmic imprints may use codes, symbols, or images composed of color, light, sound, and mathematical frequencies to activate specific frequencies within us to remove what is not us and is interfering with where we want to go. These sophisticated techniques can release any kind of karma from an energy field. The clearing is permanent at the DNA template level.

Clearing Analogical States of Mind

Analogical states of mind occur when we have a traumatic experience or the body goes into shock, creating emotional identities in the body. When this happens, energy in the affected area congeals and forms a block to energy flow that can no longer process light. The area appears dark and stuck. An analogical state of mind may get into chakra energy if the trauma or emotional experience matches the theme or energy of a chakra. An analogical state of mind in a chakra has the quantum potential to create an identity or persona. Whatever we are thinking at that moment will determine which chakra will develop the most identities based on the theme of the chakra. Identities create a blockage with a specific frequency. Unfortunately, moving forward, we will keep attracting that frequency into our lives, affecting our Life Force Energy.

Our energy body, or Life Force Energy, slows down and eventually becomes depleted. Our Life Force Energy becomes like stagnant water, attracting more ambiguity and opaqueness. If revitalized energy comes down through our crown and hits a blockage, it cannot proceed through our whole body. This revitalized energy has not been processed and is not available to us. The stagnant energy eventually forms a physical issue, like a sore throat or perhaps thyroid cancer, if the throat chakra is blocked.

These congealed energies or blockages resonate with a specific trauma, illness, abuse, or stress that has occurred in a person's life. Sometimes, the congealed energies affect the energetic core. The congealed energy block in the core can have a strong magnetic field that attracts undesirable experiences. That is why we want them removed. These energies interfere with the natural flow of people or things. Negative thought forms also hinder manifestation.

- Discordant thought forms are negative thoughts we resonate with repeatedly.
- For example, *I am never going to make money* creates a strong magnetic pull to manifest more of not making money—more of what you don't want.
- Clearing energy by quantum release sends the energy back to Source. Quantum release is from the deep subconscious. The thought forms are transmuted. They are absolved. The neural nets related to the thought forms are unplugged and go to the void. This twisted energy unfolds and goes back to a *no*-thing.
- When we let the body unplug, we sometimes feel heat or waves.
- Clearing this energy allows new opportunities, potentials, illuminations, and connections.

Like releasing karma, there are sophisticated and advanced techniques for clearing these congealed energies that are blocking optimal energy flow in our electromagnetic fields. These can become blockages in the aura and are cleared through the chakras, which are connected to the different layers of the aura. If this congealed energy or analogical state of mind is removed, its dominance is also removed. We can manifest according to our true desires when we get clear.

The ultimate purpose of clearing these types of energy blocks is to accrete more light, increase resilience, and heighten our intuition. Clearing the blocks will also help to raise our vibrational frequency. It is like the congealed energy blocks crystallize and then break through with the clearing. The more we clear energy blocks, the more we identify with and embody our Higher Self or Soul. The more we clear energy blocks, the more we are aligned with the flow of the Universe.

Repairing Broken Grids

According to Donna Eden, the grid is one of the nine energy systems in our energy body. It is like a container for all the other energy systems and can be broken by emotional or physical trauma. There are eight aspects of the grid. The chakras lie on top of the grid and are intimately associated with this system. Once a grid aspect is broken, the body uses peripheral energies to hold the pieces of the broken aspect together, but the body cannot repair the grid on its own. Only an Advanced Energy Medicine Practitioner can repair a broken grid; it is not something we can do on our own. To repair a broken grid, all the other systems must be balanced and capable of supporting the major shift of energy that occurs in a grid repair session.

One reason to suspect a grid needs repair is if energy is leaking out of the body, resulting in a person feeling depleted or fatigued. If the energy corrections to strengthen the energy flow don't hold, and the person maintains the depleted state, one or more grid aspects are most likely broken.

> I've had five grid aspects repaired so far. The repair of the first grid was most memorable. This first grid was repaired in the Fourth Year Grid class. It was a straight grid on the left side of my body that ran through my heart area. I felt a significant energy shift when the grid energy connected during the repair. It felt like a shot of amazingly warm energy coming together, like an extension ladder was being opened quickly. I will never forget that blitzing sensation. However, my energies started to unravel about 30 minutes after the repair. Energy was stuck in my shock points at the bottom of

both heels, my Assemblage Point had moved to the right side of my body below my waist, and my stomach meridian became over-energized. I was nauseous. Most of the faculty and other students had left for lunch. Luckily, a friend who attended the class with me stayed behind and corrected some of these imbalances for me. After she re-aligned my Assemblage Point, I relaxed, sedating my stomach meridian to remove the excess energy. My energies were fine after that. However, several years later, that same grid needed to be repaired again. I assume the trauma around my divorce caused the first break in the grid, but I never figured out what caused the second break.

Emptying Ourselves Out to Receive from the Universe

Being filled up with too much energy limits or completely blocks our ability to take on more energy. The energy is unable to flow easily in and through us. For example, someone who is filled up will test weaker after receiving a hug rather than testing stronger, as would be expected from the influx of additional love energy. When we are too filled up, we are out of flow with the Universe.

The *Blow Out* exercise described earlier is a great way to activate all the radiant circuits, restoring energy flow to move and empty out stagnant energy. But if that doesn't clear the issue, it is likely an underlying emotional issue, like a grievance we must let go of. But emptying out or letting go of emotional issues, especially ones that have congealed into an energy block, is not always easy. Holding onto grievances blocks our inner light. A *Course of Miracles* says that when you come from Love Consciousness, there can be no grievances. If we can let go, we are freer and lighter. We can take on more energy and not get filled up so easily. If we don't regularly release the energy, we get filled up with stagnant energy, which can block the flow of energy in our fields. This can become a repetitive issue.

An Overflowing Cup

A well-known story exemplifies the concept of being too full. The story is about a professor who wants to deepen his Spirituality. He was admired by his students for his wisdom. Nonetheless, he wanted to know more and experience more. So, he researched possible mentors and decided on a holy person who lived far from him. He traveled halfway around the world to a remote village high up in the Himalayan Mountains to begin a yearlong sabbatical with this Holy Man. The journey was a difficult one, so he hired a guide and a small group to help him get there safely. Finally, the professor arrived at the Holy Man's Spiritual Retreat.

His host greeted him smiling. His face radiated love and affection. At once, the professor began talking about all he had heard and read about the Holy Man, what he hoped to learn, and his own background.

After a few minutes, the Holy Man gently interrupted to make some tea for them. The professor continued talking about himself and what he wanted the Holy Man to teach him.

The Holy Man returned holding a tray with a simple earthen pot and two teacups. He briefly interrupted the professor, placing a teacup on the table, and began to pour the tea. After a slight pause, the professor continued talking about his expectations and yearnings for the outcome of their time together. The Holy Man continued pouring tea until the professor's cup was overflowing.

The professor cried out to stop the Holy Man from pouring more tea into his already overflowing teacup. The Holy Man put down the teapot and looked into the professor's eyes, indicating he was done with their meeting.

The professor was angry and then confused with incredulity at the Holy Man's inhospitality. Preparing to leave, the professor asked the Holy Man to explain himself. The Holy Man replied that the professor had shown that his mind was already filled up with his own ideas about the Holy Man and his teachings, what he could learn, and what he already thought he knew. With a compassionate heart, the Holy Man told the professor that his mind was so full there wasn't any room for him to learn something new, just like the full teacup could not hold more tea. Before he could learn anything new, the professor must first empty his cup.

The *professor* aspect exists in all of us. It's the part of us convincing ourselves that we are right in what we think, feel, and believe. We have to let go of the professor within us, including the thoughts, feelings, and beliefs blocking us from emptying out our cup, to receive the wisdom of higher-level teachings and be in flow with the Universe. We must surrender and trust in something new, even when we have no experience with it yet. I often refer to this concept as creating the whiteboard. To me, this means erasing what was there to create something new. Go back to the whiteboard. Assume the energy of someone open and ready to be transformed by something not known, by creating a new space or blank slate. Be the student. Allow something new to come in.

Let it Go

One of my favorite phrases for the whiteboard that I say to myself and my clients is *let it go*. When I started to become aware of how energy gets stuck in our fields, I became increasingly keen to let things go: the need to be right, to judge, and negativity in general. I understand that I don't want to be in that low-frequency state, and I quickly get out of that energy because I've decided to be at a higher level. By reminding myself to let it go, I remember my choice of being a higher vibrational frequency.

I don't know if it is our programming, but we seem to want to hold onto negative things that have happened to us. *Why do we do this?* Do we do this because we feel victimized and want to be recognized and get attention for being hurt? Is it an attention-getting tactic? I don't know, but I do know that we need to let go of the past so we can move forward—*let it go*. The past will define us and limit us if we hold onto it.

When we hold onto our pain and suffering from past experiences, we may behave in ways that hurt others, but we also hurt ourselves. This is because the energetic blocks that come from holding on to all this pain and suffering reside in us and can have a widespread ripple effect throughout our entire energy system. The congealed energy sits there locked in place, causing us to become reactive, reliving old pain each time something happens that triggers a similar emotional response.

These blocks take up space in our fields and lower our vibrational frequency. There may be anger or fear mixed up in the energetic block. Those energies can transmit from us out into the world, bringing more people, opportunities, events, situations, and circumstances with a matching frequency of anger or fear into our lives. We continue perpetuating anger and fear. This keeps us from getting what we want in life.

The concept of emptying out or letting go is helpful for us to stay in the present moment and not be held back by the negative or low vibrational frequencies of the past. Being in the present moment is key to living life. Life is only the present moment. If we are focused on something from the past, we are not able to be aware of what is happening all around us in the present moment. When we can tune into the present moment and see through the lenses of awe and wonder, we realize that we miss so many miraculous events right there in front of us.

Emptying out is important for us to move forward from the present moment toward a goal or burning desire. Emptying out is important for us to be fully grounded in who we are and where we want to go. We are less distracted by others and other activities that are not associated with our goals and intentions. Emptying out frees us to accept the new opportunities, people, and events that are unfolding for us to learn, grow, and evolve. Emptying out is like cleaning the slate to start over or for us to be exactly where we need to be. Emptying out helps us connect to our True Selves and our Divine Purpose. When we are emptied out, we flow with the Universe and are open to taking on something new in our lives. We can be transformed. We create space for new opportunities.

Any of these topics highlights where we might be blocked from being in flow with the Universe toward more life, toward growth and expansion. There are ways to move beyond these blocks and put us consciously in the flow of the Universe to be our True Selves, a higher version of ourselves. Consciously being open to receiving more in our lives, something new and possibly transformative, will definitely help us align with the flow of the Universe.

If you're interested in identifying possible grievances and letting go, I have provided some journal prompts in Exercise 7 at the end of this Section.

Consciousness is a Mirror

The Universe is designed to show us who we are BEing so that we can change how we think, feel, and act that is not in our highest and best interest. The Universe shows us when we are the best versions of ourselves and when we are not. Whatever is going on in our external world reflects what is happening in our internal world. In this way, our Consciousness is a mirror reflecting what we are transmitting by showing us the results of that reflection in our daily lives. The mirror of Consciousness never lies, and it never judges. It just informs us of our state of BEing. This is the Universal Law of Cause and Effect—energy sent out into the Universe comes back to its original source, you. Once we realize we are the cause, then we can change the cause and reap different and better results or effects. The blessing is that any reflection of our Consciousness affords us the opportunity to make a change for better flow with the Universe. Life is easier when in flow with the Universe.

Our energy body is always sending messages through our emotions that help us be in flow with the Universe. With its innate wisdom, our energy body shows us what is interfering with us BEing the best versions of ourselves. Our physical body is a magnificent communication device that mirrors our internal world by sending us messages through pain, discomfort, and disease. The more we listen to the body, the more messages we get and the more able we are to resolve imbalances before they become medical problems. The more we pay attention to our emotions and physical body, the more we can determine when we are off-course, and we can use specific methods to get back on our intended course. Paying attention to the messages of our energy body and physical body is essential to our Spiritual Journey and being in flow with the Universe.

Energy healing is all about listening to the messages from the body to find out what is happening in the inner world. There is always a correlation between what the body shows as an imbalance in an energy system and what is going on within that person, either mentally, emotionally, or spiritually. This is because the energy of the mind, emotions, and Spirit is transmitted to the cells in our physical bodies and eventually becomes physical discomfort or disease when there is an imbalance.

Although energy healers can easily correct the energetic imbalance, they may need to go deeper to identify the core mental, emotional, or spiritual issue causing the imbalance for a lasting result. We seek to go beyond the symptoms to the cause of the symptoms, which I refer to as the core issue. The intention of the healing work is to identify and clear the core issue at its root so it no longer exists, eliminating any related symptoms from reappearing. Once the core issue is identified and cleared, the physical manifestation is resolved, and the mirror is no longer needed. The beautiful thing is that the core energetic issue can be resolved before a physical disease needs to manifest as a stronger message.

Our Soul's Perspective for Being in Universal Flow

Understanding how to be in flow with the Universe sometimes requires information at a higher level or from a higher perspective. Our Souls have lived many lives, and there is a plan for us to evolve in each lifetime. There is likely already a plan for our next lifetime after we finish this one. Wouldn't it be wonderful if we knew this higher perspective for this life and for our Soul in general? The good news is that there is a way to find out this higher perspective. The answer is in the Akashic Records.

The Akashic Records

The Akashic Records are energetic information on the ethereal plane. The Akashic Records are a cosmic treasury or repository of all universal events, thoughts, words, emotions, and intent that occurred in the past, present, or will occur in the future for all life forms. Also called the Book of Life, the Akashic Records are referred to as the energetic archive of the history of each of our Souls. The Akashic Records represent the energetic record or Consciousness accumulated for every Soul and its journey through lifetimes.

Edgar Cayce, a clairvoyant and metaphysical teacher from the early twentieth century, stated that the Akashic Records are God's Book of Remembrance. These remembrances are from benevolent, loving energy, not a punishing judge. In this way, the Akashic Records can be used as a guidance tool for greater wisdom and growth. As a collection of cosmic wisdom and ideas, these remembrances can influence how we view reality from this benevolent perspective.

In Sanskrit, Akasha refers to the primary substance from which all things in the Universe are derived. The Akasha represents the initial phase of the crystallization of Spirit. The Akasha is ultra-sensitive and picks up all vibrational frequencies from all aspects of the Universe. These vibrations form a distinct energetic impression in the Akasha.

This primary substance is vibrant light energy that expresses a unique quality of aliveness and vitality in each Soul. The energy of the Akash is all high vibrational frequencies representing our Inner Presence or Inner Light--love, joy, radiance, peace, harmony, balance, and sacred order. This Light is Universal Awareness, including Universal Consciousness of the mind, heart, and will. We experience and become aware of the Light in the Akashic Records and become infused with the light just by accessing the Records. This en-Light-enment affects our thoughts and emotions, resulting in peace and well-being.

The ideal outcome of learning the wisdom of the Akashic Records about our Souls and the resulting journey through different incarnations is to embody our Higher Self. If we could understand from our Higher Self perspective, we can make decisions based on our Soul's understanding of our lives and beyond. The two-in-one phenomenon intrinsic to the Akashic Records includes the Soul-print and the myriad experiences of the Soul as it advances in its own awakening as a Spiritual BEing that is Divine but also manifests in the physical realm.

The Akashic Records represent the ongoing flow of experiences and lessons to highlight the Souls' Growth. Accessing our Soul's Akashic Record provides crucial information about ourselves from a higher perspective, with a broader understanding of our relationship to the Divine and our place in the Universe. Knowing our Souls' history can help us heal and grow, empowering us to change our lives because we understand our mission or purpose in this lifetime. We can also increase our psychic abilities and raise our level of Consciousness by being in the energy of the Akashic Records that envelop us in the Divine Universal Consciousness of Oneness. In the Akashic Records, we shift from our ordinary human Consciousness to a state of Divine Universal Consciousness. In this state, we realize Oneness with the Divine. We perceive the information in our Records as vibrations that can be translated into the human experience perspective for our understanding.

This *Book of Life* guides us from a place of compassion and love that helps us embrace peace as a way of life in resonance with the gift of our existence in the Universe and our innate creative abilities to make an impact. Since all information in the Akashic Records is stored in the ethereal plane, anyone has the capability to access the information. The enlightening aspect of the Akashic Records is that the Records reside or are part of the Divine Mind or Intelligence. The Divine Intention is for the Records to be used as a guide, an educated way to advance and transform all individuals to be their best Selves through a host of possibilities and potentials.

We can access the Akashic Records using prayer, meditation, hypnosis, symbols, sacred geometry forms, or veca codes. Linda Howe shares her Pathway Prayer Process in her book, *How to Read the Akashic Records: Accessing the Archive of the Soul and Its Journey*. As with other energy methods, the intention to access this information is what's most important, not the method.

Working with the Akashic Records helps us connect more deeply to being One with the Divine and is another confirmation that each of us matters. We are not a random experiential existence. Each of us is known in the ethereal plane and has an energetic record of each life our Soul has ever lived, reminding us that everything we do makes an impact on the Spiritual Plane of existence.

The Akashic Records can also be used for Spiritual Healing. To heal spiritually is to heal the Soul. As a dimension of Consciousness, the energetic impressions of the experiences of every Soul, the Akashic Records are an infinite Spiritual Resource that holds information about our present and past lives that can be used for healing work. In her book, *Healing through the Akashic Records: Using the Power of Your Sacred Wounds to Discover Your Soul's Perfection*, Linda Howe suggests that using the Akashic Records to reveal wounds we experienced during our many lives is a means to come to know our True Selves and discover the perfection of our Soul. From Howe's personal work and healing in the Akashic Records, she came to understand that nothing could alter or destroy the Divine Spark within her. Her Spiritual Growth was enhanced by the realization that her relationship with and to the Divine and life itself is resilient and immutable; it cannot be modified in any way. Learning and accepting this concept as truth, Howe transformed her life into one that expresses her wisdom and truth.

As Howe explains, there is a fixed aspect and an evolving aspect of each Soul's Records. The fixed aspect is the truth of who you are at your Soul level. It is permanent and unchangeable. It is considered your blueprint or *soul-print,* your unique pattern as an expression of the Divine. The evolving aspect of the Records is the growth of awareness of our true essence through our many lifetimes. The goal of working with the healing energy of the Akashic Records is to free up unconditional love present in the core of our true essence for ourselves and others.

From this higher perspective or level of Consciousness, we can understand all the dimensions and aspects of our True Self as the different components of our eternal Soul, our Loving Presence. Our True Essence in the present and through our different lives, as well as our essence between lives, is illuminated at this deep level. We can connect to our core Loving Presence by observing and knowing ourselves from this elevated perspective, as understood from the complete Akashic Record story of who we are.

Only in the Akashic Records can we glean the bigger picture and real meaning of our lives and the intention for our present life in the context of our Soul's journey. Knowing our True Essence, our Soul, helps us to be in the flow of the Universe—aligned with both our Soul's journey and the flow of the Universe, which ultimately are connected.

The Light of Akasha

The Light of the Akasha is infinite wisdom and knowledge, an essential Life Force Energy that is both a Divine Presence and a Healing Force. It can be understood as the Light of the Mind of God flowing through the heart or core of the Divine's energy body—a Divine Intelligence that functions for our best and highest good.

The Light of the Akasha is associated with the Light Grid, a constellation of points of light unique to each living being that serves as an energetic container surrounding us, holding us together based on the frequencies of our light radiance. The energetic patterns and configurations of the points of light within our Light Grid determine our unique habits and traits and the resulting physical manifestation. Each unique configuration represents the specific issues and growth edges available to assist us in becoming who we are meant to be on our Soul's evolutionary path.

Our life experiences, feelings, thoughts, declarations, and beliefs can shift our energy and transform our Light Grid. These shifts can distort our Light Grid, requiring healing work to restore it to its optimal structure and flow. Or, if we want to release old patterns held in our Light Grid, we can change our beliefs and behaviors to shift the flow of energy and realign the points of light to a higher frequency energetic pattern. Once our energetic container is changed, our behavior, habits, patterns, way of BEing, and circumstances are changed, transforming our human expression.

Akashic Record Healing

In an Akashic Records healing, we can experience our energetic and physical vehicles or conduits that interact with Divine Energy, expanding our Consciousness to realize we are way more than what we think we are from a physical perspective. When we want to heal something within us, including our health, level of happiness, or relationships, interacting with the Light Grid can shift the pattern of energy flow, representing the issue of concern. If we want to heal concerns about our family, friends, or career—things external to us—we can also address these issues by interacting with the Light Grid. These interactions shift the pattern or habits to a more optimal energy flow, new design, or new layout to induce the healing state. Being in our truth and integrity about the issue helps us to expand or elevate ourselves to a new level of the new pattern of energy flow. Our elevated level of Consciousness helps us change our behaviors and our previous way of BEing.

Healing within the Akashic Records has three stages: the story, causes and conditions, and the Soul Truth. The first stage of the Story is to discern exactly what is happening in the present time. The more specific we are in the Story, the more specific the healing. Be clear about your role in the situation you want to change. The second stage of Causes and Conditions invites us to determine our knowledge, understanding, and beliefs about the situation or circumstance. Digging deep to uncover what is causing the strain and struggle of the situation will help us get to a resolution. The third stage, the Soul Truth, helps us get to the Soul level, where the greatest opportunity for healing exists. This is the stage where we connect with our infinite and loving Soul. Healing in this stage can uncover the truth about our perfection, wholeness, wellness, and our magnificence. Once this truth is attained, we can rise above the story, causes, and conditions and view ourselves from this higher perception of our unlimited and compassionate Soul. This stage will reveal who we are now and who we have been through time and other lives. We can know who we are in the Light of Truth. This could result in a very loving experience.

Healing through the Akashic Records with the awareness of the Divine Presence within and around us strengthens us spiritually and induces resilience and Spiritual Maturity along our Spiritual Journey. Changing our Light Grid to shed old ways of BEing, old goals related to ordinary living, and outdated patterns of living a limited existence propels us toward living as our Divine Selves and achieving our Divine Potential. Healing work with the Akashic Records also helps us to love ourselves without conditions, accepting where we have been and where we are going as a necessary means to extraordinary living. This healing aligns us with our Souls and helps us be in the flow of the Universe.

Working in the Akashic Records helps us with the paradox of our living as physical human beings as well as Divine Souls. We make these changes or behavioral shifts in our physicality through the flow of energy in connection with Divine Presence in the Light Grid of the Akashic Records. *Hu, or hw,* means God in ancient Egyptian. Therefore, *hu*-man means God and man in the same form. BEing in this paradox of embodiment as a human seemingly limited to the physical world while connecting with our unlimited potential in eternity as a Soul is challenging. It is much easier to focus on our physical aspect because we have had the necessary training to navigate the physical world. Relatively few achieve that same familiarity with the Spiritual Realm.

Raising our vibrational frequency and removing energy blocks to align with the flow of the Universe is critically important for inner growth. Once we understand what it takes to be in flow with the Universe and start acting from that alignment, we are ready to journey to align with the Divine.

EXERCISES

Journal Prompts

Sit quietly and consider the following journal prompts to discover personal insights and inner truths. Journaling is a useful tool for becoming aware of how you feel about the topic and revealing inner knowing. As you write, an insight might come through your subconscious mind, illuminating limiting patterns or perspectives that can be shifted to higher-frequency thoughts and beliefs.

Exercise 1: Start a Gratitude Journal

Being in a state of gratitude increases our vibrational frequency. Consistently writing in a gratitude journal is a great way to be aware of what and whom we appreciate. It helps us focus on what is going well in our lives, which will increase our vibrational frequency over time.

- Write at least three things you are grateful for each day.
- At the end of the week, ask, "What is that accomplishment I am most grateful for?"
- What person surprised you this week in a way that elicited your gratitude?

Exercise 2: Explore Your Thoughts, Feelings, and Beliefs

If you compared yourself to the most pessimistic and most optimistic people you know, where would you lie in the continuum between the two opposites? Where do you want to lie in the continuum between these two opposites?

We can choose to spend more time with optimistic people and people with high vibrational frequencies. These people will positively affect our vibrational frequency.

- Who are those people for you?
- How do they make you feel?

Ask yourself these questions. Ponder the answers or write the answers down to get more clarity. You might have to spend a few days analyzing your thoughts to find the truth.

- What percentage of your thoughts do you want to come true?
- What percentage of your thoughts do you want more of?
- What percentage of your thoughts stop you?
- What percentage of your thoughts inspire you to move forward?
- What percentage of your thoughts come from fear?
- What percentage of your thoughts come from love?

After you take this inner inventory, write your answers to these questions:

- Can you better understand why you have the results that you do in your life?
- Do you understand what you need to change?
- Do you know that life is a boomerang, and your thoughts come right back to you at the same vibration but in a different form?

Exercise 3: Determine the Ease of Changing Your Negative Thoughts

Write about something you love unconditionally. It could be your dog or cat, friend, movie, miracle, book, event, an aha moment, or a new discovery. Before you start, tune into how you feel in the moment—your vibrational frequency. Write that down. You may want to give it a number from 0 to 10, with 10 being the highest vibrational frequency. To illustrate the power of this exercise, monitor how you feel after you do the exercise. Writing enables insights and the awareness of how you are really feeling in the moment. Writing sometimes elicits information from the subconscious mind.

Now spend five minutes writing about something you (1) love unconditionally, (2) want, or (3) are grateful for. After five minutes, observe how you feel. Give it a number between 0 and 10. My prediction is that you'll feel more joyous and lighter. Doing this exercise trains you to be more aware and more awakened to the wonderful people, events, and opportunities in your life. It also gives you a practice to change your negative thoughts into positive thoughts by concentrating on something or someone you love unconditionally. You may do this daily to focus on what is going fabulously well in your life. In time, you will most likely experience a permanent positive shift in your vibrancy.

What we focus on expands. What do you want to expand?

Meditation Prompts

Contemplate the questions below, then quiet your mind and go into a meditative state, connecting with your inner knowing at a Soul level as it feels right to you. Be open to whatever comes to mind.

Exercise 4: Go Deep to Experience the Wisdom

After arising from meditation, write down what came up for you during contemplation and meditation.

- What if I were Divine?
- What are examples in my life where I have expressed my Divinity?
- What is the evidence of my Divine Magnificence?
- When have I clearly dismissed the evidence of my Divinity?
- Why did I dismiss the evidence of my Divine Magnificence?
- How am I misperceiving the truth of who I am?
- What needs to happen for me to accept and believe in my magnificence?

Exercise 5: What is Essential to You?

Take time every day for a week (or longer) to write five to ten things that are essential to you. After the week, take an inventory of what you wrote down.

- What were one or two essential things that appeared most often in your lists?
- What does that say about the priority of your life?
- What needs to change to show up in your life to be aligned with what is most essential to you?
- Where can you refocus your intention and actions?
- What can you now say no to or eliminate in your life that is not aligned with what is most essential to you?

Exercise 6: Investigate the Garden of Your Mind

Take some time to investigate what seeds you have been planting and what seeds you may want to plant in the future, knowing that whatever you are harvesting now from the garden of your mind, you planted previously.

Do you see the connection in terms of what you planted in the garden of your mind and what you are reaping now in your life?

- What are the seeds you have been planting in your mind?
- Is this what you want to harvest more of in the future?
- What have you been harvesting that you really do not want?
- What kinds of seeds do you want to plant in your mind right now?
- What new opportunities do you want to plant in your garden?

Exercise 7: Empty Yourself Out and Let Go of Grievances

- Identify grievances you have with people in your life.
- Practice letting go of the grievances to let your light shine.
- What are you too filled up with that needs to be released to give space for something new?
- What do you want to create more space for in your life?
- Unite your will with the Divine Will for your life.
- Forgive yourself and others.

Exercise 8: BEing in Flow with the Universe

- What will bring out your Higher Self?
- What is your specific Divine Mission that you are here to accomplish?
- What do you need to let go of?
- What will help you be in flow with the Universe?

Exercise 9: *What If* Questions

Meditate or journal about these questions to ignite your imagination and open yourself to new possibilities or perspectives that may illuminate inner wisdom or a Spiritual Path.

- *What if* I were in flow with the Universe? How would I be growing?
- *What if* it were true that records exist for all my Soul's lifetimes?
- *What if* it were true that I could heal aspects of my life in the Akashic Records that aren't working for me?
- *What if* I could raise my vibrational frequency?
- *What if* I could surrender my life to the Divine?
- *What if* Consciousness is a mirror? What has Consciousness been showing me?
- *What if* I could reprogram a self-limiting belief? What self-limiting belief would I start with?

AFFIRMATION

Begin a practice of saying positive affirmations to reprogram negative self-talk or self-limiting beliefs. Here are some suggestions for positive affirmations to get you started.

Reprogramming Self-limiting Beliefs

I am Divine Wisdom.
I am a loving, light-filled BEing.
I am on a journey to discover my magnificence.
I am enlightened to know I am One with the Divine.
I am enlightened to know I am One with the Universe.
I am extraordinary, and I bring joy to others.

Section Two

ALIGNING WITH THE DIVINE

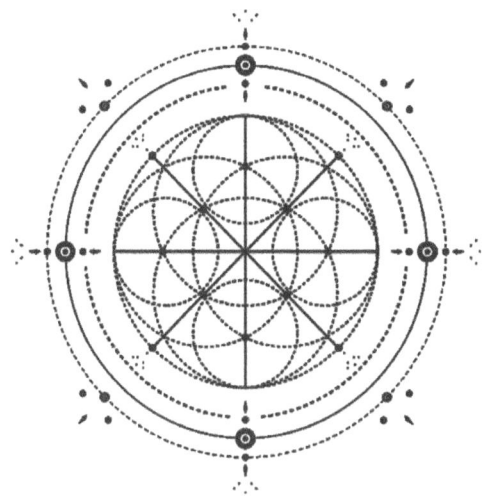

Falling into the Divine

From the cliff of 3D existence,
I let go, jump, to fall into Your Love.
I keep falling, falling, falling.
Am I falling into eternity?

I learn to surrender to all You are.
I learn to let go of my 3D existence and just BE.
Will I know when I've finally fallen into You?
Will You embrace me into Your loving, energetic arms?

As I fall, I feel the unfathomable grace, the ineffable surrounding me.
It is expansive and quite unexplainable in words.
Does the Universe open as I fall into You?
I'm just one more that understands. You're always right there.

You are guiding me as You are loving me.
Subtly and quietly, but sometimes I get the message.
Sometimes I feel the inspiration with love.
Sometimes I give up my will to take Your Will in.

Will I be able to totally surrender to the life You've planned for me?
With these unanswered questions, I cease to fear the outcome.
I detach from the outcome; I learn to trust more fully.
Do I cease and become You?
Do You more fully inhabit my energy field?

This falling is limitless . . .
My arms and back open more fully, letting go more completely.
I anticipate falling into a place of light and joy.
So fully RADIANT that maybe I won't be able to see with my eyes.
This mystery is exciting and challenging at the same time.

Maybe the falling never ends.
Maybe the falling is not the important part.

The decision to let go is the key. I surrender to the falling. . .
Into Divine Love, and the Void.

Your Light is sparkling and bright.
Such a wondrous sight!
Such radiance and delight!
Such a symbol of your might.

Where do WE go from here?
Do I change physically?
Do I lose my body?
Or do You use me to teach about surrendering?

What does total surrender to You really entail?
Will You guide me, or do I know what to do by intuition?
Maybe the intuition is really You and has nothing to do with me.
Are You still there (?) because I'm still falling.

Where do I begin and end, and where do You come into me?
I am giving You everything as You have guided.
Are You going to live in me, or am I going to live in You?
Or do we just merge together?

~Anne M. Deatly

Now that we are in the flow of the Universe, or at least understand the concept, we can turn to the part of this Inner Journey where we reach into our Core Essence to discover our true inner strength and wisdom. This is where we uncover the illusions of ego that we have unconsciously allowed to guide our lives and turn to our eternal Soul to take us beyond the suffering to a place of peace, truth, and love within us. On this part of the journey, we'll learn ways to heal, amplify, and magnify our energy flows to accommodate the higher vibrational frequencies available to help us connect more deeply with the Divine, bridging the gateways between the physical and Spiritual realms.

Let's step forward together with courage and truth to break through all the limiting beliefs and feelings that have blocked us from discovering the radiant magnificence of our True Selves.

We were taught to believe in separateness and duality in life. The truth is, we share in the Oneness. We are part of a unified field of existence. We are all aspects or different expressions of the Oneness. The physical and invisible are One realm working together. When we accept this truth—this wisdom—it is easier to align with the Divine and accept our true Divine Nature. We are Divine Energy BEings living in an energetic, sentient, dynamic, thinking Universe. Everything that happens in the Universe and in our lives is through vibrational frequency.

In this Section, there are big concepts to explore. We will discuss an overarching principle that everything—absolutely everything is a Divine Creation. Everything has a purpose and was created with intention and benevolence. Everything has its own entelechy or innateness to become what the Soul, the Divine, intended. Every living thing and being matters and is alive, bringing a unique significance to the world. To align with the Divine, we have the opportunity to consciously and intentionally plug into Divine Energy to benefit in life. We must surrender to this high vibrational frequency to be fully our True selves. We will also understand our alignment with the Divine is not in separateness but in Oneness, not in duality but in unity. It is a major step to accept our part in the Oneness of Humanity and the Oneness of the Universe.

Everyone and Everything is a Divine Creation

We were all created by the Divine; there is no difference between or among any of us. The Divine wanted to make our Divinity so clear and obvious to us that he created a message in our DNA. Gregg Braden refers to this aspect of our DNA as the "God Code," which imprints the eternal Divine within the body. This means that humanity was created to be a united family with the same design and the same inherited birthright! The Divine created us, and the Divine is in each of us.

Braden discovered the God Code by linking the ancient Hebrew and Arabic alphabets to hydrogen, nitrogen, oxygen, and carbon, the basic chemical elements that comprise the nucleotides of the DNA molecule. This DNA molecule is the building block of all existence that is present in every cell of every living creature. There is a 1 in 200,000 chance of this message happening randomly. But nothing is random in the Universe. This imprint of the eternal Divine in the body can be thought of as an artist's signature on each work of art, in each cell of every living being. This message is replicated over and over and over with each cell division. There is no denying its significance to us. This message illuminates Divine Love for us. The Divine intended that we understand our radiant magnificence and live from this magnificence in uplifting the world. Everything we need to accomplish our unique Soul Mission has been provided to us. Everything we need to perform miracles is available to us. Everything we need to expand love is available to us.

The Divine's Intention is that we view ourselves and each other with this knowing, no matter what is happening. When we make mistakes or do things that aren't expected as Divine behavior, we feel less than—we feel bad. However, this experience is only happening from a physical realm perspective where the ego has dominion as our guide, and we fall into the competitive mode of wanting to be better than others. But from the Spiritual Realm perspective of Oneness, we are all One, and our Soul is our guide. Knowing the Divine has blessed us each with special gifts of our uniqueness, how could one Divine BEing be any better or worse than another Divine BEing?

If we really accepted that we all were created by the Divine, why would we need to compare ourselves, judging who is better? Trying to be better comes from a place of lack and limitation. BEing better is a way to over-compensate for our deficiency, limitation, incompleteness, weakness, or brokenness. Engaging in comparison and competition tells us we do not yet understand the abundance of the Universe and our Divine Potential.

If we all understood that everyone is Divinely created and that each Divine Self cannot be changed, we would start to see beyond the behaviors and actions of people who may have hurt us. We can understand they are Divine at their core, but they may not be present in that space or able to take action as their Divine Selves in the moment. They may have been listening to their ego rather than their Soul. We are all in this process of learning, growing, and evolving.

We were created in Divine Love. We were and are an idea in the mind of the Divine. That idea cannot be deleted. We are like undeletable, immutable files. That part of us cannot be changed, ever. We cannot undo what the Divine has created. We cannot alter who we really are. No matter what we do, we remain as the Divine created us. That is who we are in our Core Essence. If we could know this as the truth at our deepest aspect, it would change how we view the world around us. If we are as the Divine created us, fear is meaningless. Stress and anxiety are nonexistent because there is no separation from the Divine. This truth could heal us at the core, creating unlimited opportunities for miracles of new awakening.

Therefore, even if we don't come from our Divineness in every moment, our Divinity is still there. That idea may be covered up with the illusions of the earthly programming of fear, stress, lack, and limitation. We can always recapture our Divineness. It is our Core Essence.

We are Divine

Not only are we all Divinely created, but we are all Divine. We were created in Divine Love. That Divinity can never be changed. The Divine is expressed through us as us. We are different aspects of the Divine. The Divine is experiencing life in the physical realm through our different journeys. The Divine experiences life in the physical realm through our diverse talents, expertise, and adventures. The Divine is experiencing life in the physical realm through our awakening to the truth of who we really are. We are expressions of the Divine, and Divine Energy flows through us; we exist in this energy world and share this Divine Energy. We are all naturally connected to this Divine Energy. We are this Divine Energy.

The Divine is incomplete without each of us. In fact, we are irreplaceable. Understanding this wisdom could change your life completely.

> I was shocked when I learned what it really meant to be created by the Divine. After decades of struggle and stress, I finally changed my view of myself and the world around me. I started to understand why I was here on Earth at this particular time. I started to understand why I had to change careers when I did. I was running out of time to make the contribution I was supposed to make in this world.

The Divine wants us to thrive, experiencing ever-greater opportunities for Divine Expression and Expansion. The Divine wants us to live our best lives, experiencing all our highest potentials. The Divine wants us to be the best versions of ourselves and has gifted us enormous creative abilities. Although we possess different gifts, we all have creative abilities to create new and expanded opportunities, visions, innovations, and products or offerings.

In this next step on our journey, we will explore how we can see and experience our lives from these new perspectives that allow us to make a conscious choice to experience the Spiritual Realm paradigms of love, gratitude, and higher frequency living, or stay stuck in physical realm illusions. We will look within for the answers. All the power and wisdom are within us, not outside of us.

Our Divine Nature

There are many aspects of our Divine Nature that mirror aspects of the Divine, such as Divine Wisdom, Divine Intelligence, Divine Love, Divine Compassion, Divine Creation or creativity, Divine Self-Expression, Divine Power, Divine Truth, Divine Knowing, and Divine Order. Here, I am focusing on the Divine aspects of two: radiant light and radiant love. These two aspects are fundamentally one, differing only in their vibrational frequencies. They flow together in the energetic core.

I am focusing on these two aspects because they represent our core essence. These aspects are the building blocks of our existence—the fabric of our creation. We were created from the energy of light and love in their purest forms. We were created from Divine Energy and represent the expression of Divine Light and Love. The energy flowing through our energetic channel is radiant light and radiant love. Our Divine Nature is not limited to these aspects; there is no limitation to the Divine.

I AM the Light

I AM the Light that embraces new things.
I AM the Light that erases darkness in others.
I AM the Light that shines a new way of BEing.
I AM the Light that opens to the Divine.

I AM the light that radiates Divine Energy.
I AM the light that opens to Divine Flow.
I AM the light that connects to Divine Light.
I AM the light that opens a path to enlightenment.

I AM the Light that brings hope, love, and peace.
I AM the Light that sparks new energy into a dim world.
I AM the Light illuminating goodness, prosperity, and wisdom.
I AM the Light that is connected to everyone and everything.

I AM the Light of joy and radiance flowing through every Soul.
I AM the Light that mirrors love pulsing through the Universal Heart.
I AM the Light that ignites wonder, awe, and deep gratitude.
I AM the Light that activates the Inner Divine Spark in every Soul.

~Anne M. Deatly

Our Divine Nature as Radiant Light

Divine Light radiates through us to others and the whole Universe. We are the hands and feet of the Divine to love and care for ourselves and others, using our gifts and talents to bring peace, joy, love, fulfillment, abundance, and freedom into our lives on Earth. The more we understand this, the more the Creative Spirit of the Divine flows through us and experiences new potentialities with each new expression. We are channels of Divine Energy. As we express the Divine Energy flowing through us, we are expressing at our highest potential and sharing Divine Love, Divine Compassion, and Divine Radiance at the highest level. We are contributing to making the world a better place at higher and higher levels of impact.

We have a Spiritual Light, or the Divine Light, within us that gives us the ability to see and understand at a higher level of Consciousness. At our core, we are light. The Divine Energy is Light. This light at our core illuminates wisdom and peace to help us on our Spiritual Journey and can even heal emotional issues and physical illnesses. We are meant to be open to accrete more light. We are meant to be the reflections of Divine Light. We are meant to shine our lights and uplift others to see and know their own Inner Light. We are meant to overcome the darkness in our world by shining our lights. We are meant to shine away our egos' attempt to control us and keep us in fear. We are to awaken to reflect the Divine within us.

Light also refers to understanding; we can bring forth more understanding when we light up the world. We can be lifted up from the insanity of our thoughts. Awakening from the illusion of the physical realm thought system is how we attain enlightenment, illuminating the light within us. This inner Spiritual Light illuminates the illusions our egos have created. Most of us have been programmed through fear-based ideas, fear-based teachings, and fear-based experiences that have diminished or completely blocked our awareness of our Inner Light. By holding fear-based thoughts, we experience fear and keep attracting more fear into our lives. This is an ongoing cycle—until we see beyond ego to the truth of our Inner Light.

Knowing that *we are the light* of the world is a humble perspective, not an ego-driven, self-aggrandizing aphorism. It is about accepting our Inner Light with humility as a Divine Truth. Knowing that Divine Light Energy is always flowing through everyone, we become humble in understanding that all living beings are equally important and worthy of our love. The Divine has assigned the purpose of realizing our Inner Light to each of us. As we accept this role, we are evolving both our Souls and the human collective. It is a powerfully positive assertion of our acknowledgment of the power given to us to be used to uplift others. If we could make this a firm belief and foundation for our life's work and daily lives, it would help us get on track to grow and evolve our Souls.

If we all accept that *we are the light*, then we can accept our *radiance* and *magnificence*. We are all radiant energy BEings. We all have the capability to activate this Divine Radiance within us. We all have the potential to radiate the light of the Divine. We are all meant to shine our Divine Lights. We are meant to work together to express the Divine within us. When we shine our lights together, we make an even bigger impact. The Universe can go from being dim to being brilliant. We can work together as one radiant light. BEing the light is a shared purpose in our lives.

Our Divine Nature as Radiant Love

In the teachings in *A Course in Miracles*, one fundamental principle is that love is the only aspect of life that is real. Everything else is an illusion. Most of us have created illusions of reality that are not based on love. For example, if there is fear in any aspect of our lives, we have created the illusion that fear is real. I have come to embrace this concept that only love is real and to understand that love is at the core of who we really are. We were created to be love, and we are unconditional love at our foundation. This love is a level of Consciousness, a way of BEing, a type of love. It is deep and available to us. The vibration of unconditional love dissolves fear and any other lower vibrational frequency. Consciously being loving changes everything in our lives. It helps us be more forgiving. It helps us to be in a flow between giving and receiving. BEing loving helps us trust and surrender. BEing love helps us to be in gratitude.

Just like the light, we can radiate the love from deep within us. The more we connect with the love that we are, the more we shine or radiate love into the Unified Field or Universal Consciousness.

Aligning Consciousness to Our Divine Nature

We are so much more than our physical forms. By expanding our awareness to include our Spiritual Self—our Soul, True Self, Higher Self, Divine Self—we can view the world through the eyes, mind, and heart of the Divine. By aligning our Consciousness to our Divine Nature, we become the *bridge* between the physical and the Invisible, the physical and the Spiritual. We see each other as Divine Souls contributing to the Universe in a positive way. Aligning with the Divine also allows us to consciously connect with the Divine Energy flowing through us and realize the intention of Divine Creation. BEing the light of the world, we can sense the world as the Divine intended. We were designed to understand the Universe, our lives, and who we are BEing from Divine Vision, the Divine Mind, the Divine Heart, and Divine Intention. We share the Divine Mind. When we can think like the Divine, with the same visions, thoughts, and wisdom, we create a world the Divine intended. When this shift occurs, we can now love through the heart of the Divine. Then, we naturally extend love to ourselves and others, like the love the Divine has extended to us. In this way, we are experiencing the Spiritual Realm paradigms in the physical realm.

People who have gone through a near-death experience describe the Spiritual Realm as the epitome of unconditional love and abiding peace. While this paradise-like experience calls the Soul, it lacks the contrast of perceived separation and physical challenges needed for Soul Growth and expansion. We voluntarily leave the Spiritual Realm and enter physical bodies to experience life on Earth, where we can explore, experiment, and meet new challenges that stretch us in new ways. Our growing edges are revealed to us through our physical experiences.

If we identify only with our physical being in the physical realm, we can get stuck in believing in lack, limitation, fear, and suffering of this world. We live in chaos and confusion, feeling victimized by our circumstances. We listen to our egos, reminding us of our self-limiting beliefs. This cycle repeats over and over, until we can see ourselves and our physical realm experiences differently. But when we remember that our Soul is the aspect of ourselves that lives for eternity, we shift our focus to Soul Growth, acknowledging life's challenges as reminders to see new opportunities to learn, grow, and evolve.

Shifting into an awareness of the Spiritual Realm through expanding our sense of Self as Spiritual Energy BEings also affects our vibrational frequency and how we interact and communicate with the energy of the Universe. To better understand how to align our Consciousness with this Divine aspect of ourselves, it's helpful to grasp more fully who we really are as the Divine created us from a Spiritual Realm perspective. In her book *Jesus: My Autobiography*, Tina Louise Spalding shares channeled messages from Jesus that are not included in the Christian Bible, beginning with His explanation that we are all just like Him.

My Consciousness was ordinary, Jesus explains. He acknowledges that He is called the Son of God, "but I am not more the Son of God than you. You are, too. You are the sons and daughters of God, and we are all equal."

Jesus acknowledges that some of us have progressed further on our Spiritual Journey than others. Those who have progressed understand their purpose to help others along the way. We are all here to help each other awaken.

Through His channeled messages, Jesus says he wanted this message to come through at this time in human evolution, so we know we are like Him and can do as He did in our Earth lives. Reflecting on his life on Earth, Jesus says he received messages from the Spiritual Realm about what to teach and what healings to offer. The crowds of people who gathered to experience His Presence and teachings left filled with peace and love. Speaking about these experiences, Jesus explains that non-physical energies flowed through Him during these gatherings. It wasn't his human aspect that was teaching and healing.

> *There is nothing that I did that is not feasible for you all, given the clarification, given study, given focus, and given understanding.*

It is incredibly profound, uplifting, and empowering to know that with the right information and understanding, we can do anything Jesus did. Although we already have the energy from the non-physical flowing through us to do this, many still choose to dismiss, disconnect, or dissociate from this reality. Their experiences, their egos, or their upbringing tell them this could not be true.

> I can relate to Jesus's comment that we can do anything that He did, or we can do more than we think we can. I have learned from the energy medicine training and my experience working with clients that we are way more powerful than we realize. Activating the energy flow in our hands and placing it on people in areas of

stuck energy or pain can affect amazing changes. After I balance people's energies, their physical appearance changes as if stress and anxiety have literally dissolved from their faces and bodies.

It may be difficult to reconcile in our minds that we can experience life with the same Divine Wisdom and miracle powers as Jesus. It seems surreal because the world of chaos, confusion, and fear is more familiar to most of us. To say that what we experience and witness on Earth is an illusion is difficult to grasp. But if we start accepting this concept that we can connect to the same Divine Intelligence as Jesus did, we will be happier and feel more alive, realizing that only love is real. Only the world that the Divine created is real. Only the world beyond the veil is real. We are Spiritual BEings having a human experience or Spiritual BEings having a Spiritual experience in the physical realm!

Becoming aware of our Higher Self permeates our BEing with a perpetual feeling of reverence and devotion to a higher level of contribution in this world. We will live in awe and wonder. We will feel the presence of the Divine in our everyday life, opening us up to live in awe and wonder as we witness the Divine in everything. Our life takes on a whole new meaning as we move forward on our Spiritual Journey to fulfill the desires of our Souls to grow and expand. We are living our lives as the Divine and our Higher Self intended.

Divine Energy in Everything

Divine Energy is in everything.
You are not separate from it.
I am not separate from it.
Divine Energy flows through the trees, the mountains, and the waters.

Divine Energy is always available to us.
It will flow through our Life Force.
We just open and allow it to be in our energy fields.
Our Life Force is begging for it.

Our Life Force needs the Divine to be fully in this world and beyond this world.
Our Higher Self knows its presence and availability.
Our Higher Self, our Soul, is part of it.
We expand when connected with it.

Every animal, every person, every tree, every insect, every plant, every stone, every dog, every deer, every piece of wood,
It is even part of our cells and organelles— mitochondria, nuclei, endoplasmic reticulum, DNA.
It flows through our atoms, electrons, protons, and neutrons.
It flows through the quanta and quarks.

Everything. Always. Forever.

Open the door to its help and guidance—or not. Your choice.

~Anne M. Deatly

Entelechy: Inherent Life Force in Our Divine Alignment

Being aligned with Consciousness is being in Divine Alignment. We are pure awareness or pure Consciousness. If we were designed to be a particular Consciousness or person, have specific experiences within selected circumstances, and learn specific lessons, all designed to help us grow and evolve as Souls, then it seems significant to live life as that Consciousness in this lifetime. Unless you are completely cut off from your authentic Self, you will be guided to become who you were intended to be. It's not guesswork. It's not hit or miss unless you have intentionally separated yourself. We will be guided--paying attention is key.

Designed to Become Uniquely You

There is an inherent Life Force within us guiding us to realize our true potential as Self-actualized BEings in the physical world. Although DNA provides a template or blueprint of genetic codes that determine a multitude of our characteristics, there is a guiding force or energetic field, the Universal Flow of Life, that plays a role in initiating the process of *becoming* our True Self. This guiding force represents the environment, surroundings, conditions, and influence under which the potential becomes actualized—changing from formless to form.

This concept of an Inherent Life Force or field is called entelechy from the Greek word entelecheia, meaning that which creates reality from potential. According to The New World Encyclopedia, Aristotle considered entelechy as the realization or evolved state of a potential concept or function. Entelechy guides the potentialities of a DNA blueprint to actualization. It is an inner motivation, inner determination, inner strength, and/or inner wisdom that works through a purposeful organizing field, or the Universal Flow, to direct the growth to become the full potential. For example, you can think of entelechy as the force that moves the acorn to become an oak tree, the caterpillar to become a butterfly, or a basil seed to become a basil plant.

The innate Infinite Life Force of entelechy conveys transformational energies to support Self-actualization. For example, it guides the caterpillar to eat a lot of leaves before creating the cocoon so it will have the physical resilience to complete its metamorphosis. There's an internal and external transformation that helps the caterpillar actualize its True Self. Although some thought leaders think of entelechy as simply another level of coding, it also requires the right circumstances and conditions for actualization to occur. Back to the butterfly, with the right external conditions and food sources, the caterpillar can complete the metamorphosis of becoming a butterfly.

It's the same for humans. While DNA provides our genetic code, entelechy drives our evolution through our inherent desire or the urgency to become our truest Inner Essence. The potential or entelechy to become the highest versions of ourselves is innate and always present within us. Its energetic force compels us to reach our greatest potential. This may be a way the Spiritual and physical realms are inextricably connected and work together. Perhaps entelechy is an expression of our unique Divine Magnificence.

So, what conditions and circumstances support our human entelechy to thrive, propelling us to our highest expression of our Divine Magnificence?

Our Entelechy Connects Us to the Divine

Entelechy works through our connection to the Divine within and all around us. When the energies of entelechy flow to us, within us, and through us, we align with our intended path. Our unique entelechy is related to our unique Divine Soul Energies. We are infused with the inherent potential of these Divine energies, but we are responsible for maximizing their Creative Force by our exercise of free will and taking specific, conscious action to become what our entelechy is guiding us to be.

We can go through life oblivious to how entelechy is working in the background of our lives or engage consciously with the power of its Inherent Life Force to accelerate our own evolution and Self-actualization, and by extension, that of the human collective and, ultimately, the Universe. The journey of Self-actualization is a lifetime—lifetimes— process for humans. In this life alone, it took me decades just to begin an earnest exploration of my true potential.

The exercise of free will turns on or activates the energy of the intention. There are an infinite number of ways that the Divine can experience life through us. When the Divine provides the energy for a successful connection to one of the infinite paths, it ignites an intention within us to allow that path to be expressed through us. Our exercise of free will determines the extent to which we will follow the given path to become a more aligned expression of the Divine. The more our exercise of free will is anchored in our heart energy, the greater our alignment. This is how the Divine accomplishes its goal of expansion and growth, allowing for this space to be ever available to us and allowing us to be closer and closer to the Divine within us.

Learning to work with and attune to our individual entelechy also requires the courage to move beyond the need to conform, yielding to societal pressures for sameness and fitting in. The more individual we are, the greater the chances that the innate energy of our entelechy is guiding us to our highest potential for Self-actualization. The *becoming* process is activated, and its potential is emerging and unfolding in Divine alignment.

Entelechy and Inner Radiance

Entelechy can also be expressed as the Inner Radiance of a BEing. The Divine Wisdom or Inner Soul Radiance is evolving for us according to the entelechy to become what was intended before our birth. We can think of this as a cocoon of energy forming around our physical body to encase it or protect the physical body during this inner transformation. The energy within the cocoon is the Essence of Life, holding our entelechy for us to step into a greater radiance—a truer expression of BEing.

This inner transformation happens as we turn up the illumination or flip the switch to step into this higher level of BEing beyond our earthly programming and connect more fully with the Universal Flow. There is no more playing small and trying to fit in with what society dictates, and no more listening to egoic chatter, controlling, or limiting our growth. Our Inner Wisdom and Inner Radiance come forth and take over the reins to let our True Essence share its brightest illumination—its radiance—to shine our light, illuminating the path for others to step into their greatest illumination—their entelechy.

Aligning with Divine Soul Energy

The Soul Is

The deepest part of us, our innermost BEing, our True Essence.
Our essence that connects to the Divine and is the Divine.
Our Infinite Potential.
The energy body.
Our energetic core.

Our limitless and abundant Life Force.

Multidimensional and interdimensional.

Like an elegant brocade interwoven with experiences, adventures, life lessons, and growth.

Divine Evolution.

Our Inner Wisdom, our Innate Goodness, Divine Love.

Divine Peace.

Our internal guidance system and source of intuition.

All knowing, interconnected to Divine Intelligence.

Present everywhere in the Universe—is the Universe.

~Anne M. Deatly

What is the Soul?

Next, on our path to Divine or Soul alignment, we shift our focus to what the Soul is and its connection to the Divine. From a physical realm perspective, the Soul does not compare to anything familiar to us. The vocabulary is simply not available to describe the Soul. But we can start by putting out some ideas. We have both a Soul and a physical body. One could say we are a Soul embodied in a physical form that we recognize as the human body. This understanding puts the Soul as our primary identity.

Beyond this general understanding, there are many ideas about the Soul as BEing wisdom, energized Consciousness, multidimensional energy, and eternal. One view is that the Soul has 617 facets or energetic pieces, which are vibrational substances reflecting light, suggesting that the human Soul resembles a rough crystalline or gemstone structure. As we evolve, our Soul facets become increasingly brighter and smoother. Perhaps there is an element of truth in all these concepts. Regardless of how one may describe the Soul or whether any of these descriptions fit into a logical, physical realm perspective, the reality is that we have a Soul, whether or not we can agree on what it is or how to describe it.

Perhaps because it's hard, if not impossible, to define the Soul with logical left-brain thinking, most of us prefer to identify with our physical form rather than some vague concept of our Soul. But believing we are only a physical mind and body is an illusion that keeps us from realizing the truth of our connection to the Divine. This limiting belief keeps us feeling weak, doubtful, uncertain, disconnected, disempowered, vulnerable, alone, and isolated, believing that there isn't a Higher Power supporting us. As long as we hold onto the illusion of physical form as the sum total of our BEing, we are not open to reaching enlightenment through Self-actualization.

One way to try to understand what the Soul is and how it functions in our lives is to view it from an energetic perspective. Working with people's energy fields for more than a decade, I am very aware that the Soul is the whole energy body that contains all nine energy systems described by Donna Eden in her book *Energy Medicine*. But the energy body may be only part of the Soul. The Soul may be our whole energy body plus the Divine. Our Souls extend way beyond us and exist beyond the four dimensions—three dimensions plus time—familiar to us.

The Core and Radiant Aspects of the Soul

In her book *Your Radiant Soul*, Prune Harris describes the Soul as having two aspects or vibrations—the Core Soul and the Radiant Soul. The Core Soul is the deepest part of our energetic core that connects to energies above and below us in a vertical flow that connects to the Soul of the Universe or is the Soul of the Universe. Prune describes the energetic core as a channel of whizzing energy that flows from below us to above us and from above us to below us.

The Radiant Soul is the energy that flows from our energetic core, outward perhaps more laterally, connecting this core to our physical, emotional, mental, and energy bodies and beyond. Prune refers to this interface as a template of health. I refer to this interface as the transitional activation space. This connection aligns our Core Soul and our physical body. This energy flows from our energetic core, through our physical and energy systems, to the Radiant Soul, which also contains radiant circuits, or extraordinary channels, as Prune describes them. This Radiant Soul aspect flows through all our physical, emotional, and cognitive or mental attributes. The Radiant Soul connects us to the Oneness of the Universe.

The Energetic Core is Subtle or Light Energy

The energetic core is subtle energy, not electromagnetic energy. In fact, it is light energy. We are the light of the world because light energy is our energetic core. If we think of the energetic core as an energy system in and of itself, it would be the system that connects to each of our 50-100 trillion cells. It is also called the central vertical channel. There is a toric field around all living beings and all aspects of nature. The torus, illustrated in Figure 1, is not part of our energy body but is associated with it. All nine energy systems of our energy body were derived from the torus. In the center of the torus, a channel forms between the north and south poles that becomes our energetic core—our central vertical channel. Energy flows up and down the center, continuously being renewed and revitalized by the torus energy.

This energetic core also connects all our thoughts, all our heart emotions, and all aspects of our aura or biofield, beyond our physical form, to the energy of Universal Consciousness above and below us. Through Chakra 9 at the top of our energetic core and Chakra 10 at the bottom of our energetic core, the energy of Universal Consciousness flows through, connecting us to Universal Wisdom. Our energetic core is our unique essence, where our intuition comes from when we are open to communication with the Soul of the Universe. The energy of the Cosmos flows through our energetic Core Soul superhighway with our True Essence. Therefore, all knowledge and wisdom of creation flow within our unique, energetic template.

The Essence of Our True Selves

Regardless of how the Soul may be viewed from an energetic perspective, at our core, it is the deepest essence of our True Selves. Our Core Soul is the *most essential part* of us and is unique to us. We are all part of the continuum of Universal Energy or Quantum Reality. Connected to the Universe, Source, and Divine Intelligence flows through our Core Soul.

The Soul is the aspect of us that has experienced multiple lives and holds the intelligence of where we are headed in this lifetime. It is likely the part of us that decided what challenges we needed for growth in this lifetime. The Soul knows our Divine Mission and helps guide us in that direction. The Soul knows how it wants to evolve. Our Souls want to BE our best, be fully alive, and move toward expressing our full potential. The Soul guides us through difficult challenges to get the learning and growth we really want and need from the higher perspective of our life's journey.

There is so much to this concept of Soul that I don't think we can truly comprehend its full scope and breadth from our limited perspective. But we can be open to possibilities beyond the known and ponder the magnificence of BEing a Soul. In a channeled message from the entity known as Kryon, channeler Lee Carroll indicated that most of the humans on Earth today are Old Souls who were present when the Divine created the Universe. As Souls, we participated in the creation of the Universe; we co-created the Universe. We are that magnificent, necessary, and significant to the Universe. Perhaps the Soul is our connection or bridge to the Divine, how we are ONE with the Divine. Perhaps our Soul is our greatest guide and teacher. I have meditated on the concept of Soul, turning to my connection with Universal Consciousness.

> In one of my Chakra Messaging sessions with a client, we got this information about the physical and the Invisible Realms.
>
> I told the Spiritual Guides, "I am so honored to be working with you to help this client and be the hands for you. Without you, I couldn't do this."
>
> Then the Guides said to me, "We couldn't do this without you. This is something that nobody has really understood: the physical and the Invisible are always working together. The physical and Invisible need each other. We think of it as either-or, but it is really both-and. There is a continuum from the Invisible to the physical. There are all different places in between that are not recognized, and that's where the miracles happen."
>
> Confirming the understanding of this message, my client continued this discussion with her Guides at a later time and shared the following information she received from them.
>
> The physical realm and the Invisible Realm are inextricable. Most humans are unaware of this fact, though you, Anne, and many others on a path to enlightenment are seeking this understanding. Through the millennia, humans have achieved a level of understanding that has allowed the transmission or infusion of energies from Heaven to Earth. In your session with Anne, she acknowledged only a one-way flow of energy from us to her. This one-way street is what Anne was beginning to describe when she translated "either-or instead of both-and." This idea of separation is the illusion, while unity or Oneness is the reality.
>
> For Anne, gratitude is indeed a very high vibration! But even higher, potentially, is BEing or knowing of the absolute reliance of the physical and non-physical upon each other. This interdependence represents the natural impossibility of a division. There is always

a mutual flow. One "side" cannot exist without the other! It is a two-way street instead of being unidirectional. You are our equal. When you, Anne, and all humans come to see your necessity—your unshakable, unimpeachable value and self-worth within the Universe, you will begin to approach your magnificence.

To further clarify the continuum, it is the evolving or healing strands of energy. If you wished, you could travel along each strand, as if along a string of pearls, reviewing each miracle as you made your way through and beyond each of life's lessons. You would see us, the "invisible," with you all along and, through us, the Divine Unknowable Itself. All lives are compilations of small and big miracles. This is how to get your energy hands in the energy mix and shape reality, turning the invisible vibrational reality into physical matter and form.

There are degrees of how we have integrated the Spiritual or Invisible aspects of our Soul into our physical embodiment. We can be limited by the physical world and not see or comprehend that there is anything more. We can be the channels for miracles to happen or not. We can experience life as a string of pearls, with each pearl as the miracle of a life lesson.

During a meditation in which I focused on finding the place in me where I can connect with my Soul and the interconnection with all Souls, I went through a doorway at my navel—a very sacred, energetic place in the body. I didn't realize it was a door until it opened within me. I entered a beautiful, peaceful, and serene place that was light blue like the sky. It was a sanctuary filled with a Loving Presence. I felt like I was expanding as I sensed the vastness of the space. It was like I was dissolving in it, becoming one with it. I then understood very clearly that my Soul was the Oneness. I was part of something much bigger than I could imagine, and it felt real, amazing, and surprising. It felt like home—a place I was familiar with but had forgotten. Have I been separated from my Soul all these years? This exercise helped me recognize the deepest part of me. I understand the reality of my Divine Wisdom and Divine Love energies that were present in the Oneness - the expansion of my Self. I was way more than a physical body—and I didn't end. I was the whole of the whole, the ALL, but I didn't understand the whole. I expanded, but I didn't function as a whole yet.

Divine Soul Blueprint

Even though our Souls are an aspect of Divine Oneness, each Soul is unique, gifted with specific characteristics and templates to help us with our Divine Mission. The abilities we are gifted with are likely so natural that we don't even recognize them as unique or special gifts. Also called Divine Soul Energies, these gifts represent the basic Soul template that is woven into the essence of our BEing as our Soul blueprint and affects our behaviors and personalities.

There are eight Divine Soul Energies. Each vibrates at a different frequency. Since all eight Divine Soul Energies were created by the Divine, they are all perfect. No Divine Soul Energy is better than any other. Each Divine Soul Energy has a positive and negative polarity. Table 1 introduces the eight Divine Soul Energies with their major characteristics and their most likely and appropriate role in life. A more complete table explaining the Divine Souls is provided in Appendix A (see page 267).

Each of us has all eight Divine Soul Energies to varying degrees. We have access to all these energies, but one or two of them are more predominant in us than the others. The Divine Soul Energies within us represent our Spiritual Anatomy—our energetic matrix or pattern. Our specific Divine Soul Energy constellation is unique and critical for our own Spiritual Journey. Our predominant Divine Soul Energy was gifted to us intentionally to provide the ability to accomplish our specific Divine Mission. The eight Divine Soul Energies are Divine Wisdom, Divine Love, Divine Creation, Divine Self-Expression, Divine Order, Divine Truth, Divine Compassion, and Divine Power.

Divine Soul Energies

Divine Soul Energy	Key Characteristics
Divine Wisdom	These Souls understand the wisdom inherent in the Universe, align with Universal Laws, connect with the larger truths and how things work, and are attracted to Spiritual Paths and Spiritual Teaching.
Divine Love	These heart-centered Souls act from unconditional love, are high vibrational energy BEings, experts in relationships, and value connection above all.
Divine Self Expression	These Souls are authentic communicators who express or speak their truth, are naturally born speakers with a gift with words and language, and express clearly.
Divine Compassion	These Souls are tolerant, compassionate, understanding, and other-focused, come from empathy as their superpower, and lead with their heart.
Divine Creation	These Souls build things like companies, physical bodies, wealth (through investments), great art, thrive on new experiences, are open to new ideas, focus on creative process, and are often very physical.
Divine Order	These Souls abide by order, perfection, peace, balance, and harmony, value form and function, and are creators of structures and systems.
Divine Power	These Souls are creative, highly value freedom, self-starters who take responsibility and action easily, seek to understand the power of the Soul, and are natural leaders.
Divine Truth	These Souls are about individual truth, sharing their truth in very few words, exposing lies and liars, are amazingly insightful, observant, intuitive and visionary, and bring light to wherever it is needed on the planet.

Table 1: Divine Soul Energies (Abbreviated). Full table at Appendix A.

Our primary Divine Soul Energy doesn't always make sense to us. Or perhaps we identify with the negative polarity or misalignment aspect of our primary Divine Soul Energy. But we can get back on track by recognizing when we are out of alignment. When we are in alignment with our primary Divine Soul Energy, our life works better. We are healthy, our relationships are healthy, and we have enough money. Our life is working. There is work and effort, but no struggle. We are happy.

The benefits of knowing and being aligned with our specific primary Divine Soul Energy include:

- knowing the essential qualities of our Soul and the basic aspects of our True Nature
- understanding the guidance of our life, like a north star
- finding our Divine Purpose
- having insights into our Soul or Core Essence
- understanding ourselves at a deeper and more Spiritual level
- identifying ourselves as Spiritual BEings rather than physical beings
- making choices and decisions aligned with our Divine Soul Energy
- living our best life
- accomplishing goals and our Divine Mission
- aligning with our Higher Self and the principles/paradigms of the Spiritual Realm
- aligning with greater ease, clarity, and flow
- reducing stress, anxiety, and overwhelm
- leading with our strengths and best qualities
- overcoming our shadow sides
- choosing differently if not in alignment
- manifesting what we really want
- shining as our true Divine Souls

Each of us receives Divine Energy through our Soul. This Divine Energy will manifest differently depending on our Divine Soul Energies and the percentages of each within our energetic blueprint. This Divine Soul Energy is aligned with our Higher Self. Life is much easier if we are using the full potential of our primary and secondary Divine Soul Energies.

I believe most of us are not aligned with our primary Divine Soul Energy; if we are, we are only using a fraction of its potential. Even if we haven't been aligned with our primary Divine Soul energy, it is available to us. We don't have to activate it to access it! It would help to clear any energy blockages to allow our Soul to evolve to a higher vibrational frequency, though.

If we are not aligned with our Divine Soul blueprint, it is likely due to a constant focus on conforming with what our parents, society, colleagues, or teachers have told us we should do and be or trying to fit into an opportunity available to us that is not aligned with who we really are. By conforming or trying to fit in, we are pulling ourselves out of alignment with our Divine Mission and primary Divine Soul Energies.

Another reason for misalignment is energy blockages. Energy blockages could prevent us from leveraging our Divine Soul gifts. Our Divine Soul Energy can also be disrupted. When we experience trauma or make choices alien to our primary or secondary Divine Soul Energy, it can cause major problems. So, our present Divine Soul Energy might not be the same as our original blueprint. However, our original Divine Soul blueprint is always available to us.

These misalignments often lead to applying learned skills that are not our natural gifts or our strengths. Even though we might be good at these other honed skills, our lives will never flow with ease using them. We might even resonate more with who we want to be than with who we are at the Soul level. We may also be expressing capabilities from one of our lesser dominant Divine Soul Energies. We may be conditioned to act and think from a different perspective, and our experiences of life agree with this misalignment. If this happens, it is harder to identify and align with our primary Divine Soul Energy and may require time and a series of adjustments to transition to our more natural state of being. With a clear intention to realign with our original Soul blueprint, our Soul can guide us to make the changes needed.

Our Primary Divine Soul Energy

Knowing our primary Divine Soul Energy is the first step to aligning with our Soul blueprint and Divine Mission. The second step is applying the Divine Soul Energies to our lives and making choices aligned with our primary Divine Soul Energies. The third step is realizing the changes, sometimes radical, in our perceptions of our purpose, career, relationships, and how we creatively express health, wealth, harmony, and balance. The fourth step is living and acting from our primary Divine Soul Energy.

Methods to use to determine your primary and perhaps secondary Divine Soul Energy are:

- If you know how to connect to your Higher Self and read energy signatures, ask yes-no-type questions about your Divine Soul Energy, and read the energy signature for your answer. For example, you could ask your Higher Self, "Is Divine Love my primary Divine Soul Energy?"

- Use a pendulum and ask the same yes/no questions to receive an answer based on the pendulum's response.
- Read the descriptions of each Divine Soul Energy while paying attention to how your physical body reacts. The description your body resonates with the most is evident by a feeling of open energy flowing in some place in your body, that is most likely your primary Divine Soul Energy.

Honoring and respecting our primary and secondary Divine Soul Energy as gifts allows a natural opening to create abundance on all levels of our existence. If we can live and express who we are at a Soul level, we experience a life of abundance and fulfillment. It isn't enough that we know we were created by the Divine in love, that we are all Divine, and that we have a specific purpose to accomplish that only we can do. When we are aligned with and act from our primary Divine Soul Energy, we not only add to our life experiences, but we also add experiences and wisdom to the Divine. We can add a whole new potential to the Divine through our unique experience as our truly aligned Divine Soul.

Another question to ask using the methods listed above is, what percentage of our primary Divine Soul Energy are we using at present? Ultimately, our goal is to use the full potential of our primary Divine Soul Energy. The more we live from our primary Divine Soul Energy, the greater our impact on ourselves and the Oneness of the Universe.

When we receive messages or guidance, we receive them through a filter of our predominant Divine Soul Energies. That is why it is so important that we listen to these messages. They are the messages of guidance to the higher ways of BEing and living our true life—our best life.

> Often, I ask, "What would the Divine have me do with my talents?"
>
> I get answers because I can pull back and see through a new lens. I understand that the Universe is flowing toward more life, expansion, and growth. With that perspective, I can see where I fit in with this flow. My intentions are to participate in fulfilling the needs of the Universe to flow toward more life.

How can I do this? How can I transform myself and keep growing and evolving? How can I help other people, my clients, transform their lives to live and BE at higher frequencies or higher levels of Consciousness?

When I ask these questions, I get entirely different answers from this different perspective. I feel clearer and more attuned to the frequencies of what will be in the energetic vibration of the flow of the Universe. The realizations and answers inform me of my True Purpose in life. I am empowered to bring forth new programs or opportunities that will help people out of negativity, fear, doubt, worry, lack mentality, scarcity, poverty consciousness, and trauma.

Divine Operating Systems

In addition to our Divine Soul Energies, we also have Divine Operating Systems as another level of organization of our Divine Soul blueprint that defines how we create, manifest, and, in general, get things done. The traits, characteristics, and attributes indicated through Human Design, DISC assessments, Myers-Briggs, Enneagram, sensory types, and our primary rhythm within the five rhythms energy system all provide indicators of our unique Divine Operating Systems. Understanding our primary Divine Soul Energy and our Divine Operating Systems can really support us in following our positive polarity expression, not our shadow sides or misaligned selves, as indicated in Appendix A.

The key message here is BE who you really are. It is actually easier to be our Soul-driven way of BEing. This inherent truth is why our Souls urge us to be who we were created to be. We need to allow our Souls to shine through. We need to express and become our entelechy. It is important to undo the conditioning and all the choices we may have made that would be against our original Soul blueprint and cause disruptions or challenges. We can change to live the truth of our Soul more and more every day.

> Just to be transparent, my primary Divine Soul Energy is Divine Wisdom, and my secondary is Divine Love. Knowing that it may strike you that writing a book like this is in alignment with both of my predominant Divine Soul Energies. The messages I've received are in alignment with what I am creating.

Connecting Heart and Soul

The next step after merging the vibrations of our physical and Soul Energies and acknowledging our primary Divine Soul Energy is to connect our heart and Soul energetically. When the heart and Soul are aligned, we are more internally connected with our Divine Mission and walk toward our Divine Wisdom as we go through life. We are aligned with the wisdom of who we really are to BE in the Universe.

The Assemblage Point

Our heart and Soul are connected through the Assemblage Point, which is the highest expression of our Soul in our present life's journey. The Assemblage Point is a radiant, dazzling energy, 1.5 to 3 inches in diameter, that ideally sits a few feet in front of our heart and thymus organs in our auric field, magnetizing us toward our Soul's Wisdom and drawing us to higher levels of Consciousness. The Assemblage Point holds our Soul's deepest truths. It pulls together information from life experiences and organizes it around the Divine Plan or Soul's Plan for us. We view the world through the perceptual lens of the Assemblage Point as a constellation of the deepest wisdom and our highest possibilities.

The Assemblage Point is an extremely significant point for connecting to our Soul. It is the interface of our internal and external perceptions. Life Force Energy enters the body at this point. Everyone has an Assemblage Point; its existence has been verified scientifically. Until recently, only a few people knew about the Assemblage Point. The new understanding is that our bodies are energetic, with an electromagnetic field governed by a significant energetic point, the Assemblage Point, which governs the energy flow in our bodies. This major breakthrough confirms that living beings are not only way more than physical beings, but their organization and function are determined via the flow of energy.

Not only does the Assemblage Point affect us Spiritually, but it also affects us physically. The Assemblage Point is a significant point or vortex of energy and the epicenter of our electromagnetic field, energy body, and physical body. The Assemblage Point creates an oscillating energy field of the human body. All oscillating energy systems in the Universe flow from an epicenter, and humans are no different. Everything has an epicenter, from the microcosm of atoms and molecules to the macrocosm of galaxies, storms, planets, and stars. The human body, with its associated aura, is an oscillating electrical energy field with the Assemblage Point ideally at the center of this field.

The energy potential of the Assemblage Point is strongest close to the body where the energy lines are most concentrated. The skin area connected to the Assemblage Point may feel slightly tender, and the skin in that area will often exhibit some redness due to the concentrated energy. In females, the Assemblage Point is slightly higher than in males. The Assemblage Point is located at the navel at birth and death. Ideally, in physically and mentally healthy beings, the Assemblage Point is located in the center of the body at the thymus and heart area.

Two Intersecting Channels

The energy body is symmetrical with the physical body. When our arms are extended out to each side of the body, and the aura is not collapsed, the energy body extends to the end of our fingertips or beyond. The Assemblage Point, with the vortex, connects the physical and energy body at its center or the intended location. The torus energy flow, sometimes called a donut, and the Assemblage Point connect to create a central vertical channel, or energetic core, with a Taiji Pole at the center. This channel is centralized between the right and left sides of the body. Another channel that affects our perception and level of Consciousness flows through the Assemblage Point, from the front to the back, crossing the central vertical channel and creating a cross-like pattern. This cross is like a scaffold holding the chakra system together. Although existing or flowing in the same area, the Assemblage Point is not considered part of the heart chakra. Our Soul links to the Assemblage Point through the heart chakra.

If these two intersecting channels are in alignment, we have an optimal amount of energy flow to all our cells. When these two energy channels are aligned with each other, we experience an optimal balance in life, and our mental, physical, and emotional states are aligned and functioning optimally. People with these energies aligned have a positive outlook on life and are healthy, happy, confident, fearless, resilient, empowered, and successful. Likely, their home life is happy and stable, their relationships are healthy and mature, and they handle challenges and crises with ease.

The Assemblage Point Affects All Energies

Although there is an intended location of the Assemblage Point, the location can vary for different people. The main point is that where the Assemblage Point penetrates the body will affect *all* the energies. The actual location and the entry angle of the Assemblage Point in the physical body determine the shape and distribution of the energy flow from that epicenter. The shape and distribution of the energy affect the biology and activity of the physical organs and glands, as well as the emotional capacity. The biological activity and health of the organs and glands affect the presence or absence of disease.

If the Assemblage Point is not in its centrally intended location, *all* the energies will shift accordingly, including all the energies in the energetic core and the chakras. Not only is the functioning of the energy systems affected, but the functioning of the organs, glands, physiological systems, brain, and nervous system is also affected. The alignment or misalignment of the Assemblage Point affects all our physical and energetic aspects, including our physical appearance, mental and emotional mood, decisions, state of health, perspective on life, life experience, beliefs, Spirituality, relationships, and successes in life.

Our behavior can affect the position of the Assemblage Point by excessive worry and resulting increased adrenaline, not sleeping or eating well, and the use of alcohol, tobacco, or hallucinogenic drugs. When the effects dissipate, the Assemblage Point can shift to a more unfavorable position. Toxins, poisons, and pollution can also shift the Assemblage Point to a more deleterious location.

Usually, these activities shift the Assemblage Point to the right side of the body, which is a very unstable location. If excessive behaviors continue, the energetic reserves can be depleted, leading to further instability in the Assemblage Point.

The location of the Assemblage Point determines the vibrational frequency of the whole body. So, shifting the Assemblage Point to a more stable and intended location will affect the overall vibrational frequency and increase the health and well-being, as well as the potential of the individual.

Energetic Imbalances and the Assemblage Point

Assemblage Point misalignment results in a continuum of energetic imbalances from small to large, depending on the location of the misalignment. The effect of misalignment is a shift in the distribution of energy, mainly in the brain and nervous system, which also disturbs the functions of the endocrine system and hormone expression. Over time, these energetic disturbances can impair the biological and functional aspects of the being. Once misaligned, it is difficult and rare for the Assemblage Point to move to its original or intended location on its own.

The Assemblage Point and Our Highest Potential

Prune Harris explains how the Assemblage Point helps us step into our highest potential. She explains that with its brilliance, dazzling radiance, and its own biofield, the Assemblage Point is the miraculous connection between our human and Divine aspects. As one of the most miraculous aspects of our energy field, it transmits to and receives information from all the energies of the energetic core or central vertical channel, serving as a filter that affects our perceptions or views on life.

The Assemblage Point moves to adjust to different situations and perspectives. Because the Assemblage Point is the epicenter, if it moves, then all the other energies in that individual shift as well, affecting that individual's physical, mental, and emotional health. A positive shift in an Assemblage Point to optimal alignment allows a deeper connection to our Inner Essence or Soul. This optimal alignment of the Assemblage Point enables us to step into our highest potential—a transcendent transformation. People who can physically see the Assemblage Point shifting to optimal alignment, like Prune Harris, witness extraordinary levels of performance in people in the entertainment world when this happens.

The Assemblage Point can be knocked out of position or optimal alignment, with significant energetic shifts within the body, especially the heart. Generally, a slightly misaligned Assemblage Point likely would induce a small shift or mild stress. In left-brained individuals, the Assemblage Point might naturally shift from the center of the body over to the right due to focused logical and rational thinking.

Misalignment of the Assemblage Point

According to the Assemblage Point Centre Ltd, a misaligned Assemblage Point correlates with most physical and psychological diseases. Symptoms in individuals with small shifts in the Assemblage Point include a sense of not being well, sadness, lack of purpose, or anxiety. Misaligned Assemblage Points could also result in a personality change, energy depletion, and fatigue. More significant shifts in Assemblage Points can lead to more severe symptoms such as anxiety, depression, exhaustion, apathy, mood swings, chronic fatigue, chronic stress, introversion, social anxiety, serious illness, and increased struggle and suffering in life.

Sudden shifts in life experiences, trauma, or during a substantial energetic translocation like a grid repair are all ways an Assemblage Point can significantly shift within our fields to a position that is not in alignment with our True Selves. A more specific list of causes for a significantly misaligned Assemblage Point includes trauma, disease, grief, pain, heartbreak, depression, long-term illness, divorce, substance abuse, infection, operations, childbirth, rape, sudden shock, violent attack, loss of job, persistent exposure to pollution, a blow to the head, sudden stress or prolonged stress, physical accidents, toxins, glandular fever, and intimidation could cause a negative displacement of the Assemblage Point. The Assemblage Point can also shatter into many pieces and become less functional. If the Assemblage Point shifts location or is shattered, the connection between the heart and Soul is energetically disrupted.

Realigning the Assemblage Point

Realigning the Assemblage Point may be the single most positive shift for a person. It can be lifesaving. Proper alignment can positively affect our health, sense of connection, safety, well-being, and attitude toward life. Most people with realigned Assemblage Points feel calmer and have a deeper sense of peace, revitalized energy, new purpose, increased worthiness, and a deep sense of gratitude. Realigning the Assemblage Point also reunites the heart and Soul, which can feel like coming home or being reunited with one's True Self and authenticity.

In *The Catalyst of Power*, Dr. Jon Whale states that energy medicine has become the endorsed method for shifting Assemblage Points. To discover if your Assemblage Point is in its ideal location in your body, please see a certified or advanced certified Eden Energy Medicine or Eden Method practitioner.

Exercise 3 at the end of this section provides guidance on tuning into your Assemblage Point. The exercise is intended to strengthen the connection of the Assemblage Point to your energetic core, but it may not correct a misalignment.

> When I first learned about the Assemblage Point in my Energy Medicine certification training, I knew there was an issue with my Assemblage Point. It was a clear knowing. After years of being divorced and a single parent, I had lost my way in life, and I had

lost myself. I was so focused on what was best for my two children that I never considered what I needed to be me.

I scheduled an energy medicine session for one evening after class with a practitioner who had expertise in working with the Assemblage Point. Instead of being in the center of my body, a few feet out in front of my heart organ, the practitioner found my Assemblage Point on my right side, but still in the upper chest and head area. Shockingly, it was shattered into eleven pieces. No wonder I was lost! My heart and Soul had lost energetic connection. I was not surprised. So, this expert first had to find all the pieces and bring them back together. Then, she had to move the newly connected Assemblage Point back to the heart area.

But when she brought the Assemblage Point to the area in front of my heart, there was this amazing warm feeling I had never experienced before. I would call this deeply warm feeling LOVE—a physical love. I felt like I had come home to a place I'd never imagined.

After that experience, I was able to take better care of myself. I made decisions that were for my best and highest good. Probably within that next year, I decided to leave my corporate job to start my career as an energy medicine practitioner to help people transform their lives. That reconnection of my heart and Soul was absolutely critical to my transformation and ability to align with my Divine Purpose in life.

I don't know how long I existed with my Assemblage Point misaligned—maybe a decade or more. I don't really know. Looking back at that time, it is clear to me that I was lost. I wasn't really living my authentic life. I was living for other people and agendas not aligned with my True Self. Understanding what I know now that everything is always working in my favor, I understand this reality was the perfect way for me to learn some important lessons. The most significant lesson for me was to put myself at the center of my life. From this experience or wake-up call, I am now able to identify when clients are not present and connected to themselves and not living their authentic lives. I am now helping others to step into the center of their lives. This growth helped me understand that there are gifts in all experiences. We grow from our challenges; then, we can help others with the same challenge.

I have no idea where my life would have taken me if my Assemblage Point hadn't been reconnected to itself and reconnected to my heart. I assume the stress, disharmony, and chaos I had been living with would have continued. Looking back on it now, I believe reconnecting my Assemblage Point to my heart energy really helped me not only to connect to myself but also to alter my perceptions of life and how I experienced myself and my reality. This experience was pivotal in taking a quantum leap to a career I couldn't imagine would have such a transforming effect in my whole BEing. My life changed so dramatically because I can now follow what my Soul knows.

Clinical Experience: On learning that a client's son has ADHD, I wondered if a misaligned Assemblage Point might be at the root of his restlessness and lack of focus. So, I suggested a session and tested him to determine his Assemblage Point alignment. I found that it was misaligned to the left of the body, next to his head. I was not surprised, as misaligned Assemblage Points are often the cause of many nervous system disorders.

I saw this child a few years after I realigned his Assemblage Point. He is a much calmer child, and his focus has improved. We don't know what would have happened if the Assemblage Point hadn't been realigned. His mother emphasized how important it is to test kids for this particular condition. So many children are put on drugs to help them focus and calm down. Maybe all they need is to realign their Assemblage Points.

Plugging Into Divine Source Energy

There is only one Source for everything in the Universe. The Divine Energy that flows through you is the same Divine Energy that flows through everyone else. It is the same Divine Energy that is the Universe. We are surrounded by a sphere or egg-shaped energy field. The energy of the Divine flows through our energetic core from above and below our physical forms, as well as from back to front and side to side. Think of this as our connection to the Universe, the Divine, and all of creation.

It is one thing to understand we are created by the Divine, and it is another to actually plug into the Source Energy of the Divine, recognizing our Oneness with the Divine. With conscious awareness, we can activate the connection to the Divine through intention setting to access what is available. A useful metaphor for understanding how intention works for accessing Divine Source Energy is how we access electricity in a house. Electricity is always running throughout the house, but it doesn't flow to our lamps, making them function unless they are plugged into a wall socket and turned on. Similarly, Divine Source Energy is always flowing through the energetic core of our bodies, but it doesn't work effectively to create our life experiences without an intentional connection on our part.

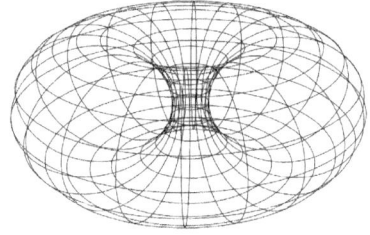

Figure 1: Torus

Our energetic core is at the center of a torus energy or toroidal field surrounding our body that is ever renewing itself and flowing from the physical to the Spiritual and from the Spiritual to the physical in spiraling patterns. The energy flowing through this energetic core is super-fast light energy or light filaments. It may be like the rays of the sun. This cosmic or Universal Light Energy interconnects and weaves together with Earth energy and the energy of our specific talents, Divine Soul Energies, and gifts that make us uniquely us. We become part of, and inseparable from, this continuum of Universal Energy that runs through our energetic core like a superhighway.

As this Universal Light Energy makes its way to us, it changes its structure from misty light to aqueous light, to liquid light, and then to crystalline light as it prepares to compress into our physical form and unite with, integrate into, and become One with our unique energy. While this light consists of interwoven energies in a unique configuration for each of us, this light is not separate from the Universe or the Earth. Like a hologram, each of us represents the whole.

What can we do to plug into this super-fast radiant energy?
What can we do to intentionally connect to the Source of everything?

Slowing down brain waves to achieve the theta state of four to seven hertz or cycles per second allows us to make deeper Spiritual connections and feel the energetic presence of the Divine. This slowing down of our brain waves puts us below the level of the ego or the subconscious mind. One simple method for slowing brain waves is to take several deep breaths and set the intention to connect with Divine Energy by stating, "connecting to the Divine." The "Heaven Rushing In" exercise in Section One can activate the radiant circuits to elevate our vibrational frequency and make connecting to the Divine easier. We can also use a receiving posture. Stand tall, with an open chest and your arms at your sides. Open your arms and bend your elbows. Open your hands to receive while looking up and stretching slightly backward to fully open your chest and heart area. Stay in that pose for several minutes to allow the connection and feel the energy flowing within. Of course, meditation will also help you to reach a theta brain wave state—if you can let go of your thoughts.

Having plugged into Divine Source energy, we feel and act differently, focused and aligned with the Divine. The day unfolds very differently as we have greater access to our intuition and more creative ideas. We are open to the flow of the Universe toward more life.

Sensing Divine Presence Within

To align with the Divine, we first need to acknowledge that the Divine is in everything and everyone. We are all expressions of the Divine. Through our life experiences, our vibrational frequency, and other aspects of our energetic makeup, the Divine is expressed through us in unique ways and in a myriad of ways. There is no place in the Universe where the Divine does not exist. The Divine is everywhere. Divine Energy is within us and surrounds us; the Divine Energy that flows through everything else flows through us. Since we are not separate from the Divine, we are not separate from any aspect of the Universe. While an intellectual understanding that we are connected to the Divine is fundamental to a journey of aligning with the Divine, at some point, we are invited to expand into an experiential knowing of the Divine Presence within. Developing this awareness and sensitivity to Divine Energy is likely the most important aspect of our Spiritual Journey. The more we can feel or sense the Divine Presence within us, the more we will be able to consciously experience ourselves as an expression of the Divine. Most of us were taught that the Divine is outside of us. So, coming to this realization may seem like a quantum leap, but just know it is possible.

At the depths of you, in your energetic core, you know this truth, this wisdom, because you are it. Essentially, sensing the Divine within is simply retraining your mind to pay attention to the energetic core, where your essential self, your True Self—your Soul—is predominant. When we train our minds to listen to our Souls, we know how to live more in alignment with the Divine.

Through intention, you can consciously and energetically be present in your energetic core. We can put our energy into any area of our body. Where our attention goes, the energy flows. We can sense the Divine within us and around us in a felt sensation if we develop a sensitivity to feel it. To feel it, we must become part of it. We become present with it.

In spiritual terms, inspiration is the breathing in of Spirit or the Divine. If we breathe slowly and deeply enough, we can feel the pressure of the breath. If we consciously monitor the movement of the breath, we can sense movement up and down our energetic core. Maybe it is the physical expansion of our tissues making space for the breath, but there is a real felt sensation when you consciously and intentionally put your attention in the energetic core and follow the pathway of energy flow and the breath in the center of our bodies.

Breathing Techniques to Sense the Divine Within

In her book, *The Energy Codes: The 7-Step System to Awaken Your Spirit, Heal Your Body, and Live Your Best Life*, Dr. Sue Morter describes a breathing technique to help carve a pathway through the center of your body that activates or enlivens the energetic core to sense the breath—the Divine Loving Presence—within the channel. The breath is sensed through conscious awareness of moving the breath slowly through the channel. The channel seems to expand as you breathe deeply. There is a physical sensation of this expansion and a sense of slight pressure in your energetic core.

Our True Self is in our energetic core. This practice helps us to connect more deeply to our True Self. What we are doing by breathing this way is activating all our electromagnetic circuitry, which then activates our neurological circuitry. The more systems that are activated while in connection with our True Self, the more fully we are One within ourselves. This helps us physically, mentally, emotionally, energetically, and spiritually.

Dr. Morter explains that breathing up and down the energetic core, as a central channel breathing technique, starts above your head or below your feet. If your body wants to breathe from below your feet into your body, breathe deeply from two feet below the surface of the Earth, where there is a foundational energy that represents your True Self. Bring this breath to your belly. Focus on this point and hold your breath there until you sense the presence of your breath. Then, consciously move the breath up to your solar plexus, heart, and throat. Aware of the movement of the breath, move this energetic sensation up to the Cave of Brahma in the center of your brain, then out the top of your head to chakras 8 and 9, two feet and four feet above your head. We are also activating the embodied chakras 1 to 7 in this process.

Next, reverse the process by slowly breathing down from chakras 9 and 8 into your crown and all the way down to two feet below the surface of the Earth. If you breathe slowly and deeply enough, you can sense a pressure or presence flowing through your physicality. Feeling or sensing the energy and breath as it moves up and down your energetic core ensures that you enliven each aspect of it. You also ignite your electromagnetic energy, which, in turn, activates your neurocircuitry in your energetic core. This deep, conscious breathing helps you embody and anchor the True Self or Soul energy into your body. Central channel breathing helps us, as energy BEings, to be fully present in our physical bodies. When in our physical bodies, it is more likely that we pay attention to our Soul's guidance or intuition. We make very different decisions in life than if we let our minds run rampant and take control of our lives. We are more likely to be aligned with our Divine Plan.

This activation of our core energy over time also helps us to feel the physicality of light in our core. The more we consciously breathe up and down the energetic core, also known as the central channel, the more photons or light particles gather there due to the activation. This photon activation increases the photon density or light within the core. The greater the photon density, the greater the physical sensation of light. I interpret this as the light, or a higher vibrational frequency, penetrating our physical tissues. We are becoming more fully integrated, body and energy. We are more fully whole and complete, and we are more empowered and aligned with our inner wisdom. We are light at our core. Energy, light, and breath are expressions of the same thing in the quantum reality. Central Channel Breathing helps sense the physicality, albeit subtle, of the breath and energy moving up and down the channel if we can be consciously aware and slow down our breathing.

Going one step further, we are pure light, pure consciousness, and pure love in our core. I invite each of you to sense the Divine Light that we are as a physical sensation. This may need some practice, but the more we experience these sensations, the more conscious we will be about the truth of who we are. What I experience as light is an expansion with a warm or glowing sensation. Anyone with the gift of inner vision will also envision light emanating from the core. I also sense a warm feeling that I interpret as love, which is not surprising, given that love and light are intertwined in the energetic core.

Visualization to Sense the Divine Within

We can also use visualization techniques to feel the Divine Presence within. I do a meditation called Loving Presence, which helps me feel a profound physical sensation of Divine love within my heart. As this love grows or activates within me, it becomes a very bright light that I can sense from my heart area and extends from me.

> In a recent meditation, I traveled to a space within me that was the point of singularity or Zero Point Field, and I experienced the Divine hugging me in a profound and life-changing way. Afterward, in an automatic writing session, I discovered the following about what happens energetically to have a physical sensation of Divine Presence.
>
> At an energetic level, when you experience a physical sensation of Divine Presence, photon density is accumulating in your energetic core. When you activate the energetic core by breathing and carving a pathway, you accrete more light there. That light is activated physically by situations or events that are similar to vibrations. Like attracts like in the Invisible Realm. Energetic vibrations seek like frequencies. The felt sensation is an amplified vibrational frequency, similar to a ripple effect and constructive interference, where the amplitude of one wave is added to the amplitude of another wave. The more energy in a specific space, the easier it is to feel.

I invite you to be curious about developing a felt sensation of the Divine within. The Divine intends for all of us to feel the connection and become aligned with what is intended for us on our Spiritual Journey.

Perceiving Reality Through Divine Energy

The Universe was created with compassion, an energy that pervades the Universe and supports our connection to the Divine. Compassion is an ideal energy flowing within us, around us, and through us to ease our transformation and ascension process in life. Compassion helps us to see with Divine Vision, think with the Divine Mind, and love with the Divine Heart.

In aligning with the Divine, we are invited to access that potential and see beyond the physical illusions of our physical eyes to view through the eyes, mind, and heart of the Divine. By shifting focus from the physical to the Spiritual Realm, we can remove these obstructions to Divine thinking within us. We have a better sense of who we are and what is intended for us in this lifetime. We see each other as Divine Souls on a Divine Mission to contribute to the Universe in a positive way or in ways that raise the vibration of the Universe. We extend love to ourselves and others in the same way the unconditional love the Divine has extended to us. Living in this way brings the Spiritual Realm paradigms into the physical realm. The Spiritual Realm paradigms of unconditional love, forgiveness, and compassion are the natural ways of BEing.

In *The Divine Design: The Untold Story of Earth's and Humanity's Evolution in Consciousness*, Lorie Ladd channels the Galactic Federation of Light (GFOL), twelve Higher Dimensional Light Beings that support Earth's and humanity's evolution. The GFOL says there are four quantum Universal Laws: (1) free will, (2) Source Energy—the Divine—is in all aspects of Consciousness, (3) one's intention creates one's experience, and (4) vibrational frequency directs the dimensional field.

Every Consciousness contains an aspect of the Divine within its vibration. Included in that Divine aspect is the Oneness—an inherent property of the Quantum Field or Quantum Reality, no matter its vibrational frequency. All Consciousness is connected to the Divine. We are pure Consciousness at our core.

Even when we have moments of Divine connection, we are easily distracted by ego-based thinking that shifts us out of our highest potential or connection with the Divine, sometimes without even realizing it. When this happens, we still have choice. Rather than slipping into old patterns of ego-based thinking, we can respond to the urgent insistence of the ego by being empathetic about not believing it. To any ego-driven messages of fear, anger, lack, limitation, or separation, we can say clearly and definitively, *not true!* Instead of listening to or paying attention to the ego, we can decide to see others and the world differently through a more loving lens, through the eyes, heart, and mind of the Divine. A key principle of the Spiritual Realm is unconditional love and compassion. We were created in love, and love is what we are at our core. We can stop listening to the ego's false ideas, leading us away from love. The time to override ego-driven thinking is now.

Byron Katie, author of *Loving What Is*, says she never believes her thinking mind. She has learned to question everything her mind thinks. She constantly asks herself, "Is that true?" I think this is a great question to look into to find the real truth within us. Once we stop believing in untruths, we find the truth that lies within. We can see the light and wake up to a new reality. We are in Divine Truth. If we bring ourselves back home to ourselves and breathe up and down the energetic core, it's easier to be in alignment with the Divine. With this Divine alignment comes a natural unfoldment of happiness and truth.

Sometimes, however, misalignment with the Divine is a necessary part of our journey to give us opportunities to learn, grow, and evolve. I find it interesting to consider that airplanes are off course about 90% of the time during a flight, and pilots are constantly course correcting. We might be the same, almost always out of alignment with the Divine, requiring frequent course corrections. We need to be aware of who we are, where we are, and where we are going. In that light, there is nothing to criticize or judge about ourselves or others. We are all just doing our best to course correct.

According to Dr. Michael Newton, who has studied the time between lives in his books *Journey of the Souls and Destiny of the Soul* and Robert Schwartz in *Your Soul's Plan: Discovering the Real Meaning of the Life You Planned Before You Were Born,* we choose our next physical life because of the specific life challenges or opportunities that will help our Souls grow and evolve. Our Soul is on a specific path in life that may not be obvious if we don't consider our Soul's desires.

My personal belief is that we have lived as different genders, different races, and different ethnicities. Being in these different bodies offers us new ways to grow. Most likely, our Souls are offered the full experience of life and growth from these different perspectives. If we have prejudices toward others who may be different from who we are in this lifetime, then we have prejudices toward the same aspects of our True Selves. If we have these prejudices, our Soul will likely choose to become the physical form of those we have prejudices against in the next lifetime. Our Soul may recognize the need to stand in the shoes of someone we don't really understand to help its evolution. If we live from our Soul, we can see and witness the Soul of others without gender, race, or ethnicity. Or perhaps our individual Soul is all races, genders, and ethnicities. We are all One. Remembering we were all Divinely created will help us understand that we are all the same in the Divine's eyes. Our Soul knows how to align with the Divine in this lifetime.

If we could view the Universe as the Divine, this physical world would be and feel very different. We would see each other as the Divine sees all, as Divine Souls trying to accomplish a Divine Mission and contribute to the Universe in a positive way.

We are invited to see everything and everyone as Divine, allowing Divine Energy to flow through us and create miracles. We can be conduits for miracles by aligning with the Divine and seeing life through the lens of the Divine. We can use our Divine eyes to see where more love, compassion, and peace are needed. We can use our hands, feet, voice, and heart to bring Divine Love and positive energy into the world. Living in alignment with the Divine in these ways will greatly impact our lives, the world, and the Universe.

Body and Soul Connection

Not truly understanding our Soul, we become disconnected, dissociated, or detached from our Souls in the physical world. Our traumas, challenges, and misalignments disconnect us from who we really are. Most of us don't identify primarily with being a Soul. We don't realize our Soul is trying to guide us in life. We don't recognize the nudges, emotional responses, or energy resonances with what is happening to us as our Soul tries to get our attention.

What if we could remember that our Soul is the most important aspect of ourselves? It is the aspect of us that lives for eternity.

What if our focus were on our Soul Growth, and we acknowledged life's challenges as reminders to see new opportunities in these experiences?

We would see all our problems from a different and higher perspective and not get caught up in fear, insanity, chaos, and confusion, knowing that all our experiences are happening for us to learn, grow, and evolve.

What if we could grasp the magnificence of each of our Souls and step into that magnificence, impacting the world around us by connecting Soul to Soul?

What if there were a way to better connect with our Souls?

There is a process called Soul Body Fusion in which we can fuse the vibrational frequencies of our Soul with those of our physical body. Body and Soul can become One. Here are my personal experiences of Soul Body Fusion sessions I did on myself.

> Day 1- My first experience of the Soul Body Fusion was amazing. At first, I saw yellow, red, and pink colors swirling in front of me. Every so often, I would see green with blue swirling energy. In my mind's eye, I saw my Soul, or an energy aspect of me, with a radiant white light around her heart and then around her head. She got bigger. Then I saw her come toward my physical body, and she walked right into me. I could no longer see "her" as if we were one now. Then, I started to see the light within me radiating out from me. I saw this light from above my head and felt tingling in my hands. In the second experience on the same day, I experienced swirling and spiraling, mostly yellow-energy above my head like the path of a hurricane—a golden spiral. Then, the spiraling energy flowed into my crown. Again, I could feel the light radiating out from me. I was the light. My hands felt more pressure than tingling. I got a sense of integration during this session. I kept seeing the light I was transmitting to the world. I also felt like I was expanding.
>
> A week later, in the first ten minutes, I experienced light forms and orange and yellow colors on the wall in front of me. Then I saw a structure, like a house, and winds forming and organizing the house or connecting the energy fields. The energy fields were now pink and spiraling lines or circuits. Then, circuits, or linking, started to form new connections. In the second ten minutes, I saw a white palace with gardens outside. Then, it was under the sea, followed by being in a natural water setting. There was more pressure and tingling in my hands.
>
> In the third experience, three weeks after the first experience, I saw the sun bright and actively engaged with integrating its light. The next sensation was waves of joy flowing from inside me as if my Soul had integrated and was so filled with joy that it could more fully integrate at a deeper level. My inner joy was my Soul being so grateful for this total invitation to join my other frequencies to

be more included and fully part of the whole me. In the second ten minutes, I didn't see anything at first—only darkness. Then I felt the joy coming up from the base of my torso through my energetic core, perhaps representing the energy of my Core Soul. It seemed it was from my perineum where the first eight cells of my original cell division were awakening. These eight cells are our original stem cells. The joy represented a type of revitalization of the original me or the eternal me. I then envisioned rays of white light radiating out from that area up through my upper body, perhaps representing my Radiant Soul. I felt new waves of joy as if the revitalizing energy was traveling throughout me. I also felt this energy radiating beyond my physical body, perhaps to my multidimensional aspects.

Our Soul is the multidimensional, eternal aspect of us, which is boundless and limitless. It is who we really are as an aspect of the Divine. Our Soul may be too magnificent to fully understand from the physical perspective. However, just opening up to the Soul as our True Self and setting an intention to connect more deeply to our Soul and identify as our Soul rather than our physical body may result in allowing the magnificence of our Soul to radiate more freely within and from us.

We are One with the Divine

Once we're consciously plugged into the Divine and we can sense Divine Presence within, we are on our way to aligning with the Divine and feeling part of the Oneness. However, it helps to have some framework for understanding creation itself to more fully appreciate who we are as a creation of the Divine and our own Creative Force in alignment with the Divine. If we understand the carefully crafted design of the Universe, we can begin to have at least some appreciation of the care, compassion, and deep, abiding love at the core of Creation. We can feel a sense of the dedication, commitment, and reverence the Divine put into creating a Universe that was balanced, peaceful, and beautiful! The Universe was created to be balanced and harmonious for the ease of our transformation. This intentional design helps us understand who we really are and connect more completely to the Divine Energy of the Universe. Even more, it was designed with abundance and unlimited supplies of everything that is needed. All is available to us in every moment.

Creation was intentional to help us transcend our limitations and ascend to higher levels of Consciousness and higher vibrational frequencies. The way in which sacred geometry provides order, symmetry, structure, repeated proportions, and mathematical exactness demonstrates that the Universe's Divine origin was deliberate, intentional, and intelligent.

Platonic solids, as the core building blocks of the natural physical structure, created a repeating exactness of form and elegant simplicity. This mathematical exactness creates stability, balance, and coherence, resulting in a sense of harmony, peace, comfort, safety, and security.

These same principles of balance, order, rhythms, and exact proportions of the design define what is real in the world and reflect Divine Love and compassion for us in providing such a comfortable and peaceful place to live and evolve. We can liken it to a sanctuary created for us. We need this sanctuary to find peace and stillness and discover the Divine Presence in our lives. We need stability, coherence, and guidance to surround us when transforming ourselves from the inside out on our Spiritual Journeys. We need stability and ease of coherence to find the thin spaces between the physical and Invisible Realms. Abstract expressionist Barnett Newman illustrates access points between blocks of color on his canvases. His placement of a thin vertical line shows the opportunity to find the Oneness through the physical realm.

> In a recent meditation, I aimed to explore and experience Oneness. I recalled Barnett Newman's *Vir Heroicus Sublimis* painting from 1951, which I had seen fifteen years ago at the Modern Museum of Art in New York City. Visualizing the painting, I was drawn to the narrow vertical lines of different colors and thicknesses that Newman calls zips. In this masterpiece, the zips are placed in a sea of red. To me, Newman was clearly illustrating the thin places or access spaces through the veils between the two realms. During my meditation, I slipped through a white zip and ended up in a room of mirrors. It looked like the dressing rooms of big department stores. Standing in front of a mirrored area, I was reflected as part of the Oneness. I realized that what is beyond the veil between the realms is a reflection of the physical realm or a reflection of me, a holographic version of the Universe. I was an aspect of the physical realm in the Spiritual Realm. A blending of the two realms was

evident in representing the Oneness. It was a loving way to see the truth of me in the Oneness.

Just like the Universe, the Divine created humans with physical exactness, Divine Proportion, and mathematical beauty. A Divine structure helps us to embody Divine Energy. This thoughtful design of humans and the Universe reflects or mirrors what the Divine wants us to create in our lives and to further create in the Universe.

The Divine didn't just create us in love, help us, design our Divine Plan, and then say, "Good luck, you're on your own now." No! The Divine created the perfect proportions and symmetry of sacred geometry forms to accommodate its higher vibrational frequencies to be with us in the physical world, enabling Divine Energy to flow through us. The Divine even designed a way to communicate with us through intuition. We can witness, understand, and experience this deep-abiding love for us. We are not left alone. But we can choose to go it alone, which a lot of us have done, me included.

The Divine did not intend or design us to rely on our own selves and our own strength. We are all One. The Divine would never abandon us. The Divine is aware of the trials of living in the physical realm. The Divine has set everything up for us to be successful and have a rewarding outcome for our growth-oriented Spiritual Journeys. For a successful outcome, we can learn and grow beyond the challenges. We have access to the greatest help possible, but we are invited to ask and take conscious and intentional action to become part of the One.

There is so much love and support from the Spiritual Realm. Support from the Spiritual Realm is from our ancestors who have transitioned, our Ascended Master Guides, our Souls, Spirits that have never been in a physical form, and the whole Angelic Realm. The physical and Spiritual are inextricable. They work together. They are here to help us, and we are helping them. But free will means we can decide to go it alone without Divine help or help from the Spiritual Realm. We don't have to listen to or ask for Divine Guidance or intuition.

Universal Oneness

BEing One with the Divine means we are One with the Universe. BEing One with the Universe, we exist in the Unified Field of energy together. We are all radiant energy BEings living in community, collaborating, and working together for the greatest good of the Universe at a Soul level. Each person is ONE with the

Universe, functioning as an individuated unit within the whole and sharing the energy fields of the Divine with others and the Universe. What we do to others, we also do to ourselves. The more we work together to align with the Divine, the more we uplift each other, activating radiant circuit energies to improve our collective health, strength, vitality, and resilience. This also activates our Divine Intelligence, making us feel more Divine and connecting us to the Divine Energy that is present everywhere in abundance. Activating our Divine Intelligence indicates we are creating from the Divine Mind.

Although we are One with the Divine, we can experience life from the false mental construct of our ego that gives the illusion of being separate or disconnected from the Divine. This illusion of separation provides an important landscape for our Soul's Growth. One way we experience separation is through attachment to our individual physical bodies, which gives the impression that what is not our body is not a part of us but rather an external other. As we progress on our Spiritual Awakening, we realize that there is nothing other than Oneness at a higher level of consciousness. Beyond that, we begin to experience that our physical body is an expression of the Divine that allows us to experience the physical realm for our Soul growth and expansion of Divine Consciousness.

Comparison and judgment are other ways we anchor ourselves in separation. When we move into the truth of our Oneness, we understand that in judging ourselves and others, we are judging the Divine within ourselves and All others, and we easily redirect such thoughts to gratitude for the life lessons we learn from our interactions with others on our Soul Journey. To be aligned with the Divine is to want nothing but peace, love, joy, and growth for others. Being grateful for others in our lives aligns with Divine Love. Whatever we give and how we perceive what we receive creates our reality. This concept is beautifully expressed as an infinity loop of giving and receiving.

Feeling separate from the Divine is like being in a sailboat in the middle of a lake without rigging the sails. We are going nowhere, getting tossed around, alone and without direction. Like being adrift without sails, things are harder when navigating life from a sense of separation from the Divine. Life in the physical world gets wonky. We lose touch with why we're doing what we're doing. We listen to our egos and get caught up in focusing on our problems, becoming imprisoned by them. We can't move forward. We can't see the solutions to our problems.

Focusing on our problems from a place of feeling separate and alone to solve them can be overwhelming without any chance of resolution. And truthfully, if we rely only on our ego selves to find resolutions, some problems may well be impenetrable. But the good news is that most of our problems stem from an illusion of separation and fear that can be solved when we look beyond ego to connect with the Oneness of the Divine, where we are loved and supported beyond what we can fathom. When we open the door to this connection, we discover the Divine is right there waiting for us to become One and find peace.

We see that all problems are really one problem with one answer—align with the Divine and our own Divine Nature to move out of separation consciousness and seek resolution beyond what our limited thinking tells us. Aligning with the Divine alters how we view our problems. We naturally let go of fear, stress, lack, and limitation. We better understand the bigger picture of our Soul's Journey and the necessity of certain experiences to help us grow and evolve.

We are going beyond being in the flow of the Universe to being open to allow Divine Energy to flow through us by merging our vibrational frequency with that of the Divine. Throughout this book, we will continue to explore how to be physical expressions of the Divine and use our intuition to listen to the guidance of the Divine through our Soul. We will learn to know our Divine Wisdom as Divine Truth awakens within us. As we transcend illusion, we see that what is really happening all around us is love calling out for love and love seeking more love.

The Oneness of Humanity

We are part of ONE HUMANITY. From the Divine thinking perspective, serving others and transmitting more love into the world is the only thing to do. We must move beyond taking care of ourselves and our families. We need to take care of each other. We are extensions of Divine Love.

Extending Divine Love is our ultimate life purpose. The intention is for us to share loving kindness in how we act and behave towards each other. We need to aid LOVE's purpose on Earth. Love is a high vibrational frequency of Consciousness representing our true default state. We are meant to think from the level of love, vibrate the energy of love, and act and behave from the level of Love Consciousness. Love Consciousness is a high vibrational state of BEing.

We are all Divine, taking care of the Divine. We are also invited to be the Divine's hands and feet since we are all called to serve one another. When we are plugged into Divine Energy, it guides us to look for opportunities to serve one another and bring more peace and love to the world. This not only helps individuals and humanity but also honors the Divine. This concept represents a figure 8 or the infinity sign, with the Divine sending love vibrations through us that we send out to the world and receive in return. We give and receive radiant love from others as the Divine gives and receives love energy through us. What a beautiful cycle of flow!

Instead of listening to or paying attention to our egos, decide to see others and the world differently, through a different, more loving lens—through the heart of the Divine. Experience the key principle of the Spiritual Realm, which is governed by love and peace. The Spiritual Realm is unconditional love. The energy of the Universe is compassion. We were created in love, and love is what we are at our core. How can the ego be correct? We are invited to stop listening to the false ideas the ego puts forth and encourages us to follow. The time is now.

The Divine intended for us to be physical forms with Divine Energy flowing through us. We are intended to receive this high vibrational frequency and transmit this energy into the Universe. We are meant to be the light for each other. As channels of Divine Energy, the Divine intended for us to unconditionally extend love, benevolence, kindness, and compassion to all Souls.

> I often teach about seeing through the lens of the Divine. If I want to be sure that I am in alignment with the Divine, I try to actually see through the eyes of the Divine to see if I am in alignment. I do this through meditation. I get to the TRUTH in meditation. It seems my intuition and connection to my Higher Self are stronger during meditation when I am paying closer attention and allowing space to receive the wisdom. I am also allowing the truth to become known. Meditation is an opportune time to get answers and the truth. We are in a different mindset, and we are open and have quieted our minds to other things going on around us for that period.

Now that we have explored what it means to align with the Divine, we are ready to examine how to tap into our Divine Potential, our highest vibrational frequency, and learn to live from our Soul. But before we get to that in the next Section, here are some exercises to help you connect on a deeper level with the concepts discussed in this Section.

EXERCISES

Reading this content is not enough to embed knowledge into your energy body and live from a new understanding. Only personal experience can catapult you into a new way of BEing. So, I invite you to spend some time on the following exercises to gain your own experience and insights on the concepts covered in this Section. You may want to revisit these exercises as you make progress on your Spiritual Journey. You will change along the way, and your experiences with these exercises will also change over time.

Exercise 1: Meditation and Journal Prompts

Use the following prompts for meditation and journaling for a deeper exploration of topics covered in this Section.

All problems result from a perceived separation from the Divine.

Describe how you know you are not separate from the Divine.

- How has conscious central channel breathing up and down the energetic core helped you feel the Divine Presence within?
- If you can feel the truth in your alignment with the Divine, how different is your interpretation of your problems in this new light?
- How could your problems melt away if you surrendered to the Divine Intention for your life?

Aligning with the Divine.

- How would aligning with the Divine change your perception of yourself and why you are here on Earth at this time?
- How would you show up differently in the world if you were more fully aligned with the Divine?
- Your alignment with the Divine is related to your level of happiness. On a scale of 1-10, 10 being the happiest you imagine your life could

be, what is your present number? How happy do you want to be? How can you align more with the Divine to achieve this level of happiness?

There is nothing to fear.

- Would you want the unfathomable Divine strength to help guide you through life's experiences?
- Instead of fear, you could ask yourself these questions:
    - How can I contribute to more peace?
    - How can I enlighten more people?
    - How can I share and extend more love?
    - How can I model my transformed life?
    - How can I counteract the negativity that surrounds me?

Divine Intentions.

- What if your focus in life was on your Spiritual Growth?
- What if you acknowledge your challenges as reminders to see new opportunities in the challenges and resulting experiences?
- What if you knew the Divine's Intention for your life?

We are Radiant Light.

- Why would the Divine create anything less than the light of the world?
- Why wouldn't the Divine create or want more light for our world?
- How would stepping into your radiant magnificence affect you, the people around you, and the Universe?

We are Radiant Love.

- What are the ways you can use to connect to the Radiant Love at your core?
- How would connecting to the Radiant Love change your life and who you are BEing?
- How would coming from the Radiant Love within affect your relationships?

Viewing ourselves through the Divine.

- What if you could see yourself as the Divine sees you?

- The idea of you is immutable. Isn't this the most loving and powerful way to create the world and you?
- How could the ego be correct or incorrect about you?

Divine's hands and feet.

- If you could be the channels of Divine Love, the love that heals all things, wouldn't that be the greatest thing you could ever do?

Identifying with your Divine Soul.

- Isn't it amazing to know that you were part of the creation process or a witness to creation?
- Are you able to identify with your Soul as who you are now?
- Are you able to connect with your Soul more easily now?
- Are you in awe and in love with your Soul now?
- What have you experienced that is the opposite of what your Soul most wanted to learn in this lifetime? Has that helped your Soul to grow and evolve?

Divine Soul blueprint.

- Are you able to figure out what your primary Divine Soul Energy is? Write about your realization of how you are either in alignment or out of alignment with your primary Divine Soul Energy.
- If you asked the Divine what you should do with your gifts and talents, what would that be?
- How can you use your gifts and talents to make this world a better place?

Exercise 2: Strengthening the Connection of the Assemblage Point to the Energetic Core

- To begin this exercise, activate the energy in your hands by rubbing them together for 20 or 30 seconds. Shake off any stagnant energy in your hands and circle them to further activate the energy in your hands. Then, rub your hands together again for 10 more seconds.
- Put your arms out to your sides, straight out from your shoulders. Face your palms toward the Earth and gather energy from the Earth into your hands for further activation, connecting to the Consciousness below your feet and in the Earth.

- Then turn your palms up and receive energy and get activated from the energy of Universal Consciousness.
- Since we can connect to our Assemblage Point through the heart chakra, put both hands over your heart chakra or breast area. Take several deep breaths while envisioning the dazzling sphere of energy, your Assemblage Point, about two feet in front of your heart area.
- Now, put both hands straight out in front of your heart area without touching, leaving several inches between your palms as they face each other. As you take several deep breaths here, imagine your dazzling Assemblage Point being strengthened by the activated energy in your palms. Do not rush through this step. Be consciously aware of any sensations you might feel between your palms.
- Keeping one palm lovingly connected to the energy of your Assemblage Point, put your other hand on the lower dantian, 1-2 inches below your navel, as if to connect the Assemblage Point energy to the lower dantian energy of the energetic core. Realize you are connecting the Assemblage Point to the superhighway of light energy in your energetic core, which also contains your Core Soul. The lower dantian is comprised of jing, or the *essence of life* energy.
- When you are ready, take your palm from the lower dantian point, and with your fingers now pointing up toward your head, trace your hand up the central line of the energetic core and place it opposite your other palm, still connected to your Assemblage Point. Determine if you feel different sensations as you connect to the energies of both of your palms. Drop into the awareness and sensations of the sphere of energy between your palms.
- When you are ready, take your palms and slowly move them back to your heart chakra on your body. Take a few long, slow, deep breaths there as if strengthening the access of the Assemblage Point through the heart chakra and connecting to your heart.
- When you are ready, move your hands to either side of your neck and put your little fingers behind your ears to energize the vagus nerve, an important component of the energetic core and regulator of the parasympathetic nervous system. Take several deep breaths here as you contemplate and sense a shift to a more peaceful state associated with the parasympathetic nervous system.
- Then, hold your hands gently over your throat with your fingers cradling both sides of your jaw to connect to the penetrating flow radiant circuit, a major component of your Radiant Soul that participates

in transporting your Core Soul Energy to the rest of your body and beyond. To end, weave figure 8s over the heart area to stabilize the connection between your heart and Assemblage Point. Then weave figure 8s from your heart to your Assemblage Point two feet in front of your physical heart.

Exercise 3: *What if* Questions

Ask yourself these *What If* questions as contemplations for meditation and journaling to explore what's possible to create in your life. Allow yourself to follow what unfolds as a journey itself, allowing you to deepen your experience of these truths, determine your growing edges, and expand. Be open to glean your level of understanding of your Soul and your connection and alignment with the Divine. Determine if you have made any significant leaps in Consciousness from the concepts offered in aligning with the Divine.

- *What if* it were true that I am as God created me?
- *What if* the physical and the Invisible are inextricably connected? What does that mean for me?
- *What if* I were created by the Divine as Divine Love? What would that change in me?
- *What if* I were aligned with the Divine? What would change in me and my life?
- *What if* I could receive messages from the Spiritual Realm or the Divine?
- *What if* I could feel the presence of the Divine in me?
- *What if* I could remember that the Soul is the most important aspect of me?
- *What if* I were an expression of the Divine? What is the Divine experiencing through me that helps the Divine expand?
- *What if* my Soul is guiding me? Where am I going?
- *What if* I could be my authentic Self and live in peace?
- *What if* my focus were on my Soul Growth, and I acknowledge life's challenges as reminders to see new opportunities in these experiences?
- *What if* I could grasp the magnificence of each Soul and step into that magnificence, impacting the world around me by connecting Soul to Soul?

Section Three

TAPPING INTO OUR INFINITE DIVINE POTENTIAL

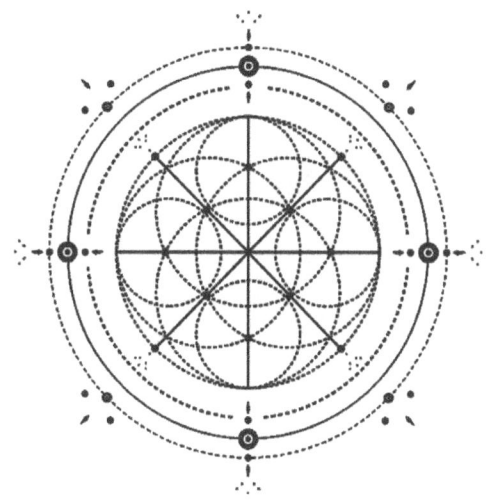

In this next phase of our journey, we take the next steps to increase our connection to the Divine, the Divine Mind, and Divine Creativity. As expressions of the Divine, there is a Divine Intention for each of us. The more we evolve to the level of our Soul and Divine Plan for this lifetime, the easier it is to tap into our Divine Radiance, our Divine Magnificence, and our Divine Potential.

Quantum physicists are discovering that what we thought was *nothing* is, in fact, *everything*. The Universe is a vast space teeming with the potential energy of an infinite number of possibilities and potentials of all different vibrations that have not yet manifested in the physical realm, offering limitless opportunities to be tapped into. This concept of Infinite Potential is often referred to as the Zero Point Field or the Void. In my book, *Journey to True Self*, I explain that we collapse these energy waves into form when we match the vibrational frequency and focus on what we want to manifest into form. In other words, the vibrational frequency of our BEingness determines what we attract and match in the Zero Point Field.

The truth is that we, including the geniuses and experts in the world, have barely even scratched the surface of our full potential as Divine BEings creating our experience in this physical world. We all have access to Divine Intelligence in Universal Consciousness. We have access to all the knowledge, intelligence, and wisdom that has ever existed or will exist, including all the novel and innovative ideas of the future. However, most of us are unaware of how to access all of this, even though it is us, and we are it. We are not separate from Divine Intelligence and Universal Consciousness. We are Divine Intelligence, and we are Universal Consciousness. We are pure Consciousness in a body. We are Creative Intelligence. The truth is, we have access to anything we want. We may have to manifest it if it isn't physically available to us in the moment, but we still have access to it. Using the Universal Law of Perpetual Transmutation of Energy will help us manifest what we truly desire. We can think of tapping into our Infinite Potential to communicate with reality beyond the physical.

Self-limiting Thoughts and Beliefs

What can block access to Infinite Potential is what we think about ourselves, because those thoughts are what create the world we live in and all aspects of the lives we experience. We've been taught to believe in self-limitations and unworthiness, but the Divine created us as magnificent Divine BEings capable of expressing our magnitude. The Divine can only create the Divine. All creations of the Divine are Divine. The Divine not only supports us but also prepares us to express our Divine Magnificence with the infusion of our unique entelechy and constellation of Divine Soul Energies.

Still, most of us feel inadequate; we are not awake to these gifts and are unable to open the doors to our success in BEing our true, authentic Divine Selves. We are caught in the hamster wheel of life and sabotage ourselves by focusing on negative thoughts, what isn't going right in our lives, and the unhappy situations of our past. Somehow, this negative thinking keeps percolating to the top of our minds, and we even wake up thinking about our unhappiness. It brings up memories of pain, sadness, and our perceived deficiencies. Even though the past is done and can't be changed, we keep it alive and present in our minds and energy fields by ruminating on it.

Low Vibrational Thinking Causes Misalignment

We focus our Consciousness on these low vibrational frequencies. Keeping past sadness and pain in the forefront of our minds puts us in a low-vibrational frequency that recreates more of the same, resulting in misalignment with the Divine and our Soul. Keeping a painful past alive is an unconscious habit in our subconscious mind. It tells us sad stories about ourselves that aren't true. This negative thinking becomes as unconscious as the routines of our day. We go through life on autopilot. According to Dr. Joe Dispenza, neuroscience research has shown that 95% of our unconscious habits, rituals, behaviors, reactions, attitudes, beliefs, and perceptions are established by age 35. This does not help us move beyond these past experiences and grow. We stay embroiled in our woundedness and are stuck in the past.

From this perspective, we are functioning somewhat like robots running a hidden computer program coded to see and focus on less-than-ideal situations, repeatedly leading us to less-than-ideal results. But we can create something new in the subconscious by reprogramming past beliefs and stories. The subconscious mind cannot reject what we are putting in as new beliefs. The subconscious mind is deductive in nature. Whatever we tell our subconscious mind, it goes in as truth.

From our subconscious mind, we can declare what we want. We can reprogram ourselves. *I am healthy. I have financial freedom. I have joy and peace in my life. I have an abundance of love in my life.* Although most of us don't have the unconscious habits to naturally create health, freedom, joy, peace, and happiness, we can create new programming by thinking through the Divine Mind. It is significant to consider that, as Thomas Troward taught, our minds are the center of Divine Operation because this understanding is the core method for tapping into the infinite supply. The Divine intends for us to reprogram our subconscious minds to be more aligned with our Souls and a successful Spiritual Journey, rather than being stuck in negative habits that disconnect us from our True Selves and our Infinite Potential.

Perhaps we create our own pain unconsciously in another way. According to Bashar, a Spiritual BEing or multidimensional Extraterrestrial Consciousness channeled through Darryl Anka, our personal pain results from our resistance to being, becoming, or connecting to our True Self.

Opportunities to Grow and Expand

The events and situations that occur in our lives are opportunities for us to grow and develop. We can embrace and be elated about every growth opportunity. It is why we are here on Earth—to grow. Creating a different picture in our minds will yield more positive results. We can set our own intentions with a different visualization—to see the truth of who we are and what we want. Be as clear as possible about what you really want to create. If we believe in the Divine, we believe in ourselves. We are how the Divine *expresses* in the physical realm. Once this concept is understood, it can be applied to our life experiences. We can develop the skills and mastery to triumph over the habit of negative thoughts and actions. We can be the victors of our creations rather than the victims of our circumstances.

When we limit ourselves, we limit the Divine and limit the Divine from flowing through us. We create a prison of our own making until we break free from our limiting beliefs to recognize our Divine Origin and experience our Divine Potential. We have the same creative capability as the Divine because we are part of the Divine. We share our gift of creativity with the Divine. No one told us how to use the gift or tap into this gift. Yet, it is the intention of the Divine for us to create.

When we create, the Divine is expressed through new potentialities. We benefit from our creative abilities and the creations that result from them. It's a win-win. Our expression of new potentialities becomes necessary for the evolution and expansion of the Universe and transcendence to something completely new. Evolution results from the continual unfolding of the new from the old, much like the continuum of traveling along a path of pearls, representing the miracles of life's lessons. Evolution flows through the revitalizing energy of the torus field.

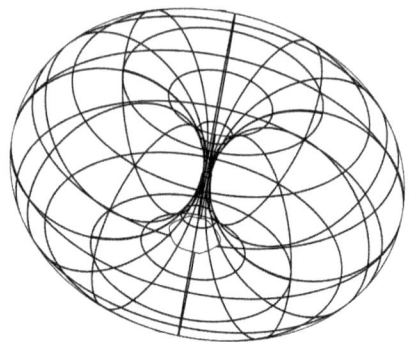

Figure 2: Torus

In our journey to discover the truth of our creative potential, we accept the Divine within us and plug into it, creating what is uniquely our vision and our interpretation of what the Universe intends through us. We can release the self-limiting beliefs because, from this new understanding, how could any self-limitation be true? As we have been exploring, the truth is that our minds are the center of Divine Operation. What we think, we create. What we focus on expands. The Creation Energy or the Divine Spirit works through us. There is only one Creative Spirit and only one creative process. Only one Source. This creative process operates in the same manner for our individual creations as it does for all Universal creations.

If we can raise our vibrational frequency to a level of this new creative potential as co-creators with the Divine, we will flow toward expansion and ever fuller expression. The Divine flows through us in our Creative states. We are empowered to create something innovative and insightful by breaking through our self-limitations. We are in a new zone of existence. We are no longer bystanders in the flow of life; we are the creators of the flow of life.

The key point is that the Divine doesn't shift its mind or inherent nature. We are part of that Intelligent, Creative, and Benevolent mind that is flowing toward growth, advancing our lives, and becoming more and more our Divine Selves as Creators. We *become* our inner potential or our entelechy. We are positively impacting and contributing to the increasingly higher and higher levels of experiences in the Universe.

To start overcoming negative habits, remove yourself from the negative energy by affirming a positive belief that is the opposite of what you have believed about your past. Start believing in what you want to create. According to the Law of Polarity, the opposite of what we have experienced must be present here and now. If we experience sadness in the present, then the experience of joy and happiness must also be there in the present. Everything exists with its equal and opposite. Focus on the opposite of a problem—what you want, not what you don't want. Prove that the past no longer exists. Looking at the opposite of past situations can reveal a new opportunity. Consciously view the past from this empowered aspect of growth. When you let go of the past, your focus moves to the present. The now is only where life takes place.

It is the perspective of ourselves in the moment that illuminates what we are capable of seeing or understanding. If our intention is to view a situation from our limitations, then we will understand our state of being from that perspective. If our intention is to view the situation from our empowered, elevated state resulting from past growth, then we will understand that the situation was a pathway to expand, not one that held us back.

We will always find what we are looking for. If we want to see the negative in a person or situation, we find that. However, it is also true that if we look for goodness in a person, we will find it. So, if we direct our minds to what we want to create in this world, we will be successful. What if we aligned our minds and Souls together? What if the mind is trained not to go off in all directions in panic and anxiety like a runaway train? What if our minds were trained to serve the Soul or True Self?

Believe that you deserve what you want to create. Believe that the Divine deserves what you want to create. Find the evidence for the new way to BE. Create new programming for your subconscious computer. Break through the self-limiting beliefs. We create those beliefs ourselves. If we created them, we can un-create them. Develop repetition in what you want, so the programming or autopilot becomes what you want in life.

The more you visualize and feel the emotional energy of what you want to be true, the higher the likelihood that it will manifest in the physical world. Our mental energy pictures get transmitted to the Universe. Our inner visions extend farther into the Universe than we can imagine. Our mental images are carried through the Universe with a powerful Life Force Energy. These mental pictures are the cause. What comes back to us are the effects. Whatever you think, feel, and believe about yourself, the Creative Energy will reproduce it with similar energy as a projection of the originating Divine Creative Spirit. The best is always there for you; *everything* is always there for you.

An Unlimited Haze of Possibilities

The Universe was created from an unlimited haze of possibilities with unlimited potential. Whatever the Divine conceived manifested from the invisible cosmos into physical form. We can think of the Creation Energy as a molding, undifferentiated substance. From the study of quantum physics, there are an infinite number of energy wave possibilities. Quantum physics teaches us that everything exists as a field of possibility. Strings of energy vibrating at the frequency of the electrons within them collapse and become particles, especially if the strings of energy are observed or the object of our focus.

These strings of energy appear to have choice or intelligence. Everything that we can see, including us, existed first in the Quantum Field as energy. Everything was originally thought. This Quantum Field of energy responds to thoughts and creates the experienced reality. The thoughts are the causes, and the physical realities are the effects, fulfilling the Universal Law of Cause and Effect. Our Universe is not random; it is the result of all our creative human minds working within the Divine Mind or Consciousness.

At every moment of the day, we are creating something with our thoughts. If we create new thoughts, we create new results. Every thought becomes form at some level. We literally have the power to influence the collapse of the specific wave of what we want if we focus on and enter the energy of what we want. We are then vibrating at the same frequency as what we want. Like attracts like in the Invisible World; in other words, we don't have to keep creating those past stories of our lives. We don't have to wait for a diagnosis or an emotional or physical trauma to force us to change. We can do it now. We now have a choice to shift towards joy, wonder, and awe rather than staying in sadness, pain, and suffering. We are the movie producers of our own lives.

> When texting a client who lives in France, I realized how I was tapping into the specific vibrational frequency of her cell phone number in the haze of possibilities of all the frequencies of all the possible cell phone numbers. There are no physical wires connecting our phones to each other. We can literally tap into the vibrational frequency of any cell phone number in the haze of possibilities at any moment. It made me think how this is just like the possibility of what we want to create for ourselves and the Universe. The opportunity we seek is in the haze of possibilities, the Zero Point Field, where we can create the physical in every moment.

Meditation and visualization are ways to enhance the creation of new thoughts and new directions. Visualization is one of our most significant, life-changing powers. We have the capability to mold Consciousness. Visualization is the most effective way for us to tap into the Infinite Potential in the Universe. What greatly helps this process is recognizing our power to manifest our desires. We realize our specific, energized thoughts, in connection with the Divine Mind, to help collapse the specific wave holding the potentiality of what we want.

To do this, we can consciously tap into the wonderful potential energy of the Infinite Consciousness at a designated time. The best times to visualize are in the morning, just after waking, and at night, right before bed. To feel more directly connected to Universal Consciousness, you could even open a window and take ten deep breaths. Imagine a circle of light around you. Visualize rays of light emanating from the circle and entering all aspects of your body, concentrating in your solar plexus or mid-torso. Hold your breath. From your solar plexus, visualize the light going up through your body and down and out through your feet as it travels up and down your energetic core. Imagine you are a conduit between the physical and Invisible Realms. Sit and reflect. Read aloud and repeat these affirmations of your Infinite Consciousness.

> *As an expression of the Divine, I am unlimited.*
> *My mind operates in the Divine Mind.*
> *I am creating a new potential for the Divine to experience through me.*

Visualizing may even be a form of self-hypnosis that helps reprogram our subconscious minds to focus on more positive futures. Creating the video in our mind's inner vision of what we want in our lives will help reprogram the subconscious mind. The subconscious mind doesn't have the capability to reject or refute what you're creating. The subconscious mind cannot distinguish between reality and imagination. Create an extraordinary life for yourself. Create life on your terms. Don't settle. Add value to others. View your future through the lens of the Divine.

Visualization to Focus the Subconscious Mind

Before engaging in any visualization practice, it is important to quiet the mind through meditation or a breathing technique that brings your focus inward and moves your thoughts beyond the analytical mind.

It may be helpful to remove any doubt or limitations that might reduce the power inherent in this visualization process. Remember these three facts as explained by Behrend: Creative Power exists in all of space, it is responsive to suggestion and direction, and it only works through deductive methods. This power to visualize and create is inherent in all of us.

Ask for what you want or ask questions related to what you want:

- What is important for me to understand right now about my Spiritual Journey?
- How can I enhance my journey?
- What is the next step for me to focus on?
- What is my next growing edge?

Listen for the answers as you stay open and receptive. Be happy, joyful, and the highest vibrational frequency possible with your will. Be in the highest frame of mind during meditation and visualization. Know that you are the center of Divine Operation. Stay in uplifting and inspirational energy as often and for as long as possible.

You can also state what you want specifically, especially in terms of how it will benefit you and others in being in flow with the Universe.

Then, begin the visualization. Imagine the new opportunities in front of you just waiting for you to pay attention to what the Divine intended for you. Be grateful for the vision. Whatever you can visualize is possible for you. Your words, thoughts, feelings, beliefs, energy, Consciousness, and visual images direct the power of Creative Energy. Consciously focus on the vision of what you want and meditate on it repeatedly. Understand fully that all that there is in the physical or the Spiritual Planes of existence first started as a thought, idea, or visualization.

In the exercises at the end of this section, I provide a useful step-by-step visualization process developed by Genevieve Behrend with some modifications. There are many ways to access and use visualization to reach our subconscious and activate our Creative Power. This is just one example that I have found helpful for embedding affirming concepts and truths for molding something from Consciousness.

This Creative Energy of visualization is very sensitive. One way your burning desire may not come to fruition is due to thoughts that oppose it. Do not doubt, worry, or sense that you don't deserve what you really want. Any of these opposing thoughts acts like a double image on a photographic plate. If it helps during the meditation, you can say and repeat the following affirmations until you find the truth in them.

> *The life substance of the Universe finds*
> *self-recognition and delight in me.*
> *There is one Source, one substance.*
> *There is one Creative Energy.*
> *I am One with Source and Creative Energy.*

Feel the reality of your visualization. Feel the feelings as if this visualization is a present fact. Experience enthusiasm and excitement. Be positive without any effort. Feel the emotions of having that in the very moment of the visualization. Believe you have it already. Feel what it will feel like as you keep adding to the vision as if you are creating a video clip in your inner vision. See yourself in the image and feel real emotions–feel your body's energy shift as the vision unfolds. Feel the feelings from your head to your feet—in your whole body. When you reach the height of joy and excitement, surrender the image to Universal Consciousness. Have certainty. Expect you will get what you desire. Do not expect your mental picture to manifest in a specific way. Allow the Creative Universe to figure out the best way. Trust that whatever you want will come to you easily and effortlessly— or something better. When you finish the visualization, check in to *feel the truth* of your affirmation that is already a reality. Feel an internal shift inside, indicating you are already in the energy of the new reality. Continue visualizing every morning and evening until you get what you desire, or your intuitive sense tells you to stop. The physical manifestation of your desire is always successful from what you consciously or unconsciously affirm, claim, declare, and expect.

Fully embrace that you:

- are Divine
- align with the Divine
- align with the Divine Mind, Will, and Intentions
- align with the Divine Creative ability
- effectively use visualization of what you want to create
- create beyond present potentialities
- can open new possibilities of expression of the Divine through you
- are the hands, feet, and heart of the Divine to carry out any action needed

Receiving Divine Messages

In addition to creating new potentials by connecting with the Divine and the Infinite Potential of Consciousness, we can communicate with the Divine and the Spiritual Realm. Divine Messages are coming to us in all kinds of ways, but most of us don't realize it. They come in the form of symbols we see, numbers we resonate with, synchronicities, spirit animals, dreams, oracle cards, other people, and even what we read. Divine Messages can also come in the form of intuition hits and *knowings* we receive. We know it is a message for us if it feels like love. The Divine only extends love. No criticism, negative thoughts, punishment, condemnation, judgment, or limiting beliefs come from the Divine. All those low-vibrational messages are likely from the false self or the ego.

Divine Messages come to us to provide guidance or reassurance that we're on the right path on our Soul Journey. Messages also let us know we're loved, supported, and not alone. The messages can be comforting, especially when we're struggling and not at peace, or they can inform us to pay attention to something that is out of alignment. Sometimes, a message comes with a truth that we need to know. It's not meant to hurt us but rather as a means of confirmation or an opportunity to see a situation differently for the purpose of growth, which is our Soul's ultimate goal.

There are some common signs or messages that we may not realize as being sent from the Divine for us. For example, certain objects we see in our drawers will suddenly become more evident. Some people have shared with me that items jump or fall off shelves in stores to get their attention and realize later that the book or item has an answer to a question they've been asking.

Numerology

Numbers are a common way we receive messages from the Divine and our own Higher Selves. Numbers have great significance in sacred geometry and the physical and Spiritual Realms. Each number has a different vibrational frequency. Numbers and numerical patterns have specific meanings because different vibrational frequencies are coming together. Numbers are presented to us in various forms: time on the clock, dates, addresses, miles driven in our cars, temperature, and even the number of steps we count each day. We will notice specific numbers more frequently than others. The numbers we keep seeing are codes that signal our higher Consciousness to awaken.

Specific numbers take on different meanings if we see them repeatedly. Here are some explanations of these meanings that you might find helpful in understanding why these numbers may be appearing in your life. These are only a few examples.

The number 1 is related to leadership.

1010 means something new is coming in for us. We are moving forward. We are about to start something new. Joy, love, and abundance are coming in. The number 1010 signifies that you are ready for Spiritual Evolution. Seeing 1010 repeatedly is a reminder to stay positive.

11:11, or 1111, indicates a major change in our life, such as a Spiritual Awakening. 1111 is the number of Spiritual Masters who have significantly impacted the world, for example, Buddha, Jesus, or Krishna, and raised the vibration of the Universe for all of us. If we see 11:11 or 1111 repeatedly, it's a sign or a message to us that we are Divine aspects of the Creator, and we can master ourselves as humans. This message means we're expected to make significant contributions to the world. Pay attention to your thoughts; they could represent an opportunity for opening up. Everything is a result of our thoughts and feelings. Each of us can use our energy to create a specific vibration that attracts similar vibrations to us. We can change our vibrations by changing our thoughts and emotions.

Seeing 11:11 and 1111 can also mean someone we love from the other side of the veil is close to us. We can be at peace and honor the memories of the departed one(s). Another significant message is that we are on a path to remember who we really are. We are awakening; we are way more magnificent than the Earth's third-dimensional programming has taught us. 1111 is also a signal of Divine Intervention—a type of wake-up call or that an energetic portal is opening. It's time to set an intention and take inspired action. Following your passion will lead to your purpose.

1234 is also an interesting number in numerology. In numerology, you add the digits up to reduce it to a single digit. For 1234, the sum is 10, which is reduced to 1. In this case, its significance lies in starting something new to make an impact in the world and leave a lasting legacy. It may also mean we are connecting or awakening to our Divine Self.

According to Doreen Virtue, 1234 signifies the time to simplify your life. It may mean we need to declutter. Living with clutter indicates we are holding onto our past. Holding on to the past means we aren't moving forward. Another meaning for 1234 is that we are on the right track. Our life or Spiritual Journey is aligned with our Divine Purpose or Mission. Still, another meaning for 1234 is that our well-being is closely tied to our internal growth and awakening. If our goal is to reach our highest potential, our outward achievement comes from our inner Spiritual Alignment. This represents the Universal Law of Cause and Effect.

I have had my own experiences with numbers appearing as messages that provided helpful insights.

> After my marriage ended, I moved into a house with the number 510. At the time, I didn't realize numbers had any significance, but once I did, this is what I discovered. The 510 message makes sense at the time of the move and still does. 5 was a very strong message for me in developing personal freedom and creating independence. 1 is about starting over, being bold, and asserting myself in new projects and goals. I create my own reality. 0 signifies the Spiritual Journey aspect of my life to choose with an Awakened mind and follow and trust my intuition. 0 is also a number representing completeness.
>
> 510 has a strong message of healing, especially after a heartbreak. It is a new beginning. I will become stronger. There is renewed hope. I need to put my life in order. I will find happiness again. Pay attention to my Inner BEing and be true to myself. Align my plans and my life with the Spiritual Realm. It is time to free myself.
>
> 510 is also a powerful message of optimism. I need a positive outlook on going through the change. Change is good. Embrace what's

in store for me because everything happens for a reason. Focus on what adds value to my existence. Use my instincts, intuitions, and extra-sensory perceptions. My life will expand exponentially. I have everything I need to achieve what I want—wisdom, specific abilities, insight, talent, and intuition.

Seek personal freedom and experience joy. Do not compromise my high standards and values to conform to anyone else. 510, as a message of personal fulfillment and happiness, indicates I am closer to my goal or burning desire. 510 is a message of advanced leadership skills. 510 is a message to lead others in the right direction. I positively impact others and use my gifts to inspire the growth of others. It is a message that the Spiritual Realm recognizes progress in life.

Currently, I live in a house with the number 9, which is a sacred number and represents Consciousness. It is about enlightenment and completeness. 9 is about being on a path of peace, joy, and love. It is about compassion and humanitarianism. It's about being successful in making a meaningful impact. 9 also represents a new cycle in my life and Spiritual Awakening. In numerology, nine means wisdom and leadership.

Dreams, Signs, Symbols, and Synchronicities

Messages from the Spiritual Realm can come from anyone or anything, from dreams to images, signs, and synchronicities. Dream messages can have a profound impact on our lives because the thoughts and images in our dreams can reach and affect the subconscious mind, which regulates most of our daily lives. Dream messages can be about people, opportunities, or experiences that provide guidance or a learning opportunity. Dreams are also a way to release energy blockages related to the past.

Using oracle card decks to receive messages from the Spiritual Realm has gained popularity for their creative use of images to enhance deeper meaning and insight. Opening a book to a seemingly random page is another way we receive surprising clarity about a situation or give a message of hope.

Common symbols can be messages from the Spiritual Realm, such as feathers, birds, flowers, shapes, trees, mountains, or anything that holds significance for you. You could see things that remind you of someone close to you who has transitioned—feathers, birds, dimes, or even smiley faces—anything.

Synchronicities happen as messages to show us that we're on the right path. Someone from our past, whom we have been thinking about, suddenly calls out of the blue. We could be applying for jobs and not getting the one we think is perfect, because a better one is meant for us. So many different scenarios happen, not by coincidence.

Songs, lyrics, and even advertisements can also convey messages to us when we feel an emotional or energetic response to them. When we are awakening, we feel our connection to words and the environment around us in a different, more powerful way.

Animals, or spirit animals, are also messages if we see them regularly or at specific times, especially when we are trying to solve a problem and need an answer. It may not be a physical animal, but perhaps it is a picture or a symbol of an animal, as in a sculpture. An animal may be part of a meditation, and our intuition knows why that animal is present. Before I repair a grid for someone, I ask them to pay attention to nature because they will likely receive a sign, such as an animal, which symbolizes the energetic shift they will experience with the grid repair. If you repeatedly see a particular animal, research what that animal signifies as a spirit guide. This information will give you the message.

Money and coins found on the ground are likely messages that abundance is on its way. Do not dismiss the coin and walk past it. Instead, honor the coin. Bless the coin. Be grateful for the coin being on your path. Take it home, and remember it is a message of abundance. If I find money, it is usually one cent or sometimes a dime. But the morning after I wrote this passage about money, I found $0.17 near my house.

The number 17 holds a sacred meaning and implies Spiritual Knowledge. 1 is highly materialistic, referring to mastery over the material aspects of life. The vibration of 7 resonates with Inner Wisdom, enlightenment, and manifestation. Combined, the message of 17 is to remain positive and optimistic, and we'll manifest our desires by aligning with our Inner Wisdom. Together, 1 and 7 mean we are about to experience new beginnings. We will be led to Spiritual and material good fortune. Number 17 also signifies we're on the right path in life and in alignment with our Soul's Mission and Divine Purpose. I interpreted the appearance of $0.17 by my house as a message affirming that what I had just written about the meaning of money on our path is aligned with the purpose of this book.

Social media posts can also be signs or messages for us. Paying attention to how our energies shift with different messages on social media can really activate the message meant for us. If a word or message resonates with us in a positive way, or we feel we need to pay attention to or learn from it, then it is a message for us.

Also, remember that intuition is a beautiful way to get messages.

An Empowering Message

Receiving a message is only the first step in working with the Divine Power available to us. By taking action on that message, we acknowledge the connection, open ourselves up to receive more messages, and ensure that the channels of communication are clear and working in both directions. Action is the demonstration that we have received the message.

In addition to receiving unexpected messages, we can also seek guidance from the Divine by making a specific request and asking for a message in response to illuminate a new way forward. Don't give up if the message doesn't appear immediately or isn't what was expected. Just trust. The Divine is only ever loving us and guides us in ways most aligned with our highest and best good in Divine Right Timing and Divine Right Order.

For example, when contemplating this topic of receiving messages from the Divine, I meditated on it. I received the following information to share.

1. You are so much more than you believe you are. You are not random. You are unlimited. You have a specific purpose that only you can accomplish.

2. Everything you desire is possible and already here for you.

3. You are totally supported in your journey of Self-discovery. Trust you are on the right path.

4. When you feel like you don't fit in, that highlights the significant difference of you. Love and celebrate that difference—your uniqueness.

5. You have had and will have specific challenges to help you:

- understand yourself better
- strengthen your character
- grow and evolve to be more and more your True Self
- embody the truth and the everlasting things of value
- understand the Oneness

6. Don't underestimate the value of your life's journey. What you learn from your challenges can be used to help others in life and help raise your level of Consciousness.

7. When you are aligned with being the *true you*, you will believe in the miracle of you and the miracle of all others.

8. You are to open a new space for expansion that unfolds new opportunities for yourself and others.

9. Follow the magnetic pull of your desires, and you will be following the best way forward on your journey.

Receiving messages inherently means one is aligned with the Divine. We can get Divine Messages without realizing it because the voice of the Divine is quieter than the voice of the ego or mind chatter. There are several ways to enhance receiving messages. The methods and techniques discussed below offer a range of ways to enhance our intuitive skills, deepen our connection with the Divine, and receive intuitive messages that help us tap into our Infinite Divine Potential. Allow time and space for you to receive messages, perhaps through meditation or journaling.

Be in Silence

Understanding that God's first language is silence, we are invited to quiet our minds, open our hearts, and rest in silence, knowing the Divine is there with us. Being in silence with a quiet mind is one of the most effective ways to be receptive to our intuition and receive messages. It is only in the silence that the Divine speaks to our open hearts, minds, and spirits. Silence is a type of surrender. Letting go of our thoughts and agendas is a way to hear what is surely coming from the Divine. If we are truly on a Spiritual Path toward enlightenment, being in silence regularly is essential. Silence allows the space for the Divine to enter in Oneness with us.

In the noise of our lives, as news media, electronic devices, and social media all vying for our attention, it may seem difficult to stop and be in silence—just be, not do or think. If we don't take the time to tune into the silence and connect with the loving guidance of the Divine, then we are less able to allow life to unfold naturally in grace and ease rather than challenge and struggle.

Our silence allows the Divine to reveal itself to us and be with us. Silence allows for a deeper connection or relationship with the Divine, leading to knowing the presence of the Divine. Silence is a space packed with presence, love, support, and Oneness. Silence is a knowing that we are home. In silence, we break through barriers within. We can know more when we dwell within the sacredness of silence and stillness.

Mindfulness and Meditation

Meditation is an effective way to quiet our minds by letting go of ego-driven thoughts and the inner-critic monkey mind and opening us up to connect with our Inner Essence. Quieting our mind through meditation and going inward with slow, deep breaths can also increase our intuitive powers, magnifying our ability to hear the whispers of our Soul.

During meditation, we can ask questions and get answers from our True Self, the Divine, to guide us. We can receive messages from the Divine in various forms, including words, images, sounds, or even smells. We can also use meditation to visualize what we want to create in our lives and connect with the Divine to help us manifest an incredible life.

> One time, during meditation at a Taize service at my church, I had an amazing vision that I will never forget. All participants were sitting in chairs in a circle. After several minutes, the vision of a beautiful white light connecting each person became visible in my mind's eye. The white light energy was like strings or straight lines. Everyone was connected in this crisscrossing of white light throughout the circle. Besides being energetically beautiful, the vision was a message of how we are all connected. Although we were all in our own meditative experience, we were all ONE.

Receiving Messages Through the Physical Body

As stated previously, we get messages in our physical bodies to help us pay attention and take action. Examples include pain, tightness, soreness, feeling unwell, or experiencing symptoms of an illness or disease. However, we also receive messages in our physical body in response to what is happening around us or when we need to make a decision about something.

Since everything is energy, we can engage with everything on a vibrational level. Do you feel the energy in your body? If the energy feels warm, open, and flowing, then you have resonance with the decision, a person, or an opportunity. If the energy feels blocked, tight, or restricted, then your energy is not in harmony with what is going on around you.

The energy could be flowing or not flowing in a number of different areas of our body. More often than not, the energy in our hearts or gut areas has messages for us. Using our intuition to read people can make us more effective leaders or negotiators in our business lives. Again, we have resonance with people or what they are saying if our energy is flowing well. We don't have resonance with a person or what they are saying if our energy is tight and restricted.

Our gut has an entire network of neurotransmitters, known as the enteric nervous system, and a brain of its own, often referred to as the second brain. When neurotransmitters, as chemical messengers in our gut, fire up, we may feel either "butterflies" or queasy sensations. We have sayings like, "I can't stomach this. I feel like I got hit in the gut."

> The more I work with my energy fields and clear my blockages, the more open I am to my intuition. I learned years ago to listen to my intuition —even if it didn't seem rational. In fact, my intuition has sometimes led me to places completely unknown. The most obvious example was the intuition to leave my career as a research scientist. Everything in that aspect of my life had a high degree of certainty. I had goals. I had plans. I had a clear direction.
>
> But my intuition was opening a new path. A path I didn't recognize. A path with absolutely no certainty. A path without any precedence. However, since I was able to trust my intuition, I took the difficult step of letting go of the only life and career I had

known for decades. It turned out to be the absolute best choice for me. It has transformed who I am.

Healing Our Wounds for Enhanced Divine Connection

Another way to receive Divine Messages is through our woundedness. The Divine Presence is present in all aspects of our lives, including our wounds and, especially, our core wounds. Our wounds signify an opportunity for healing, growth, and ascension. Healing our wounds is another powerful way to connect with the Divine and discover our Infinite Potential. From this perspective, we can consider healing as a release from the energetic blocks that prevent us from accessing our True Essence of BEing.

As we all have experienced, life offers us tremendous opportunities for growth and expansion. Through life experiences, we develop wounds; some even become core wounds. Through our wounding, we often lose connection with the deepest part of ourselves—our Soul. Instead of suppressing or avoiding our wounds, we need to be present with them and receive the message that the wound conveys. Freeing ourselves from what has been holding us back helps us move forward and flow with the Divine Plan we co-created. Any wounding from our past can be the doorway into new growth and expansion. Everything, especially our wounds, happens so that we can grow and evolve. Our Soul may even pre-plan the wound(s) for our Spiritual Growth and expansion.

But we are not meant to stay wounded. Our wounds may be a type of guidance system. They get our attention to help us move beyond the wounds. What if we could discover a Divine Message in our woundedness? In her book, *Healing through the Akashic Records: Using the Power of Your Sacred Wounds to Discover Your Soul's Perfection*, Linda Howe asserts that, from the perspective of the Akashic Records, our wounds serve a higher purpose in facilitating healing, growth, and expansion. This helps us focus our attention and intention in a specific way for our highest good and perhaps even align with our Divine Purpose.

The human adventure in the physical realm presents opportunities and situations that allow us to encounter the Divine Essence at our core. Some of these situations result in Sacred Wounds, which are really opportunities for transformation and transcendence. Sacred Wounds help us grow the most. This intersection with a Sacred Wound brings us to a place where we can meet or converge with

Divine Reality or understand a Divine Intention for us. From that experience or opportunity, we transmute the wound and find the blessing to rise above our current level of BEing and into our magnificence.

If we could embrace all that has happened in our lives as a gift of grace and an opportunity to become our best selves, then we could even be in radical acceptance that it was all meant for our highest good. We could then embrace that our wounds are sacred; they are the gateways to our healing that show us something needs to change. Our wounds are meant for our transcendence. Our wounds are meant to highlight the growing edges of our existence. We are not meant to be limited by them.

In fact, we are invited to go into the core or heart of our wounds. Our wounds are the result of scars or injury to ourselves in a physical, mental, or emotional way that induces a negative response about ourselves, others, or life itself. In the wounding process, we are unable to express ourselves fully or freely. The key is that the wound is self-inflicted due to a lack of personal expression. Our wounds can initiate a withdrawal or a disappearance of the self, a reluctance or resistance to presence ourselves. Our wounds lead to distortions in our perceptions, which eventually result in a less-than-full experience of our Life Force vibrancy and radiance. This distortion in perception also leads to disruption or interference in our energy flow and the connection and experience of our Soul.

In the acceptance or surrender to the wound, we are invited to understand the Spiritual Purpose of the wound. Everyone has wounds. Wounds are like neon lights, guiding us to pay attention to our greatest opportunity for evolution. Wounds are likely related to our Divine Purpose. If we can radically accept that the situation exists for our growth and greatest good, we can experience the sacredness of the wound as the gateway to its healing. When we can heal and reconnect to our Soul, our Divine Purpose may be revealed to us. We are invited to surrender to the wound, and in that non-resistance, we can witness the Divine Presence within us and the wisdom to achieve healing. There are infinite possibilities *in* the healing process and as a *result* of it. Be open, surrender, and trust—there is a magnificence unfolding in the healing.

Gateway to Our Divine Magnificence

Each one of us is wounded. Others have hurt us, we have hurt others, and we have hurt ourselves. Although woundedness is universal, it is also personal. These wounds can cause distortions in how we think and what we believe, thus limiting our vibrancy and connection to Divine Energy. Our wounds also cause distortions in our energy fields, impeding the natural flow of energy. We can use our wounds to avoid aspects of life that are difficult for us. This choice, rather than facing the issue, further cripples or limits us physically, emotionally, socially, or spiritually. We tend to focus on the wound as evidence of our imperfection or deficiency rather than as a gateway to discovering our magnificence.

However, there is a tremendous gift and opportunity inherent in the wound that most miss. Everything happens for us! If we can radically accept the wound, we can seek out and be open to the Spiritual Purpose of the wound and face it directly for resolution. We can seek out the *sacred opportunity* of the wound by asking, *How can I grow from this experience?* From this *wounded awareness,* we can take the next appropriate action through choice to align with our True Selves rather than stay wounded.

The heart of our wounds can guide us to our Inner Essence, opening doors or gateways to deeper Soul Growth and alignment. We can approach the configuration of our Light Grid in our Akashic Records and make a new declaration about *how* we want to be. We can set a new intention for *who* we want to be. We can decide how to respond to our specific situations from a higher vibrational frequency or level of Consciousness. Setting intentions and making new declarations affect the energy flow in our Light Grid when we make these choices in the energy of the Akashic Records.

In this level of understanding, our wounds elevate us to higher levels through healing, growth, and new discoveries they reveal. We ascend through the layers of self-imposed disconnection to the doorway of our Divine Magnificence. If we are awake and aware, we can perceive our wounds as beacons that illuminate an open portal to our True Self as an aspect of Oneness. Through this portal lies the invitation to ascend and become One with the Divine while still existing in the physical realm. To accomplish this in the paradox of living as a human in Divine Expression, we have to achieve higher levels of Self-mastery.

Wounds Are Necessary for Our Spiritual Journey

In our Spiritual Journey, there are three significant relationships in life: our relationship to ourselves, our relationship to others, and our relationship with the Divine. Our wounds highlight the level of our disconnection from ourselves, others, or the Divine. Wounds provide a doorway to new Self-awareness and growth on our Spiritual Journey. How we interpret and navigate wounds that manifest in our life experiences depends on our state of being and our level of connection.

Looking first at how wounds reveal where we are disconnected from ourselves, most often they surface as a sense of disempowerment or lack. We create a false identity around the wound or create a false meaning that it indicates a lack or deficiency within us. We may feel that we deserve the trauma, abuse, or the situation, and falsely identify ourselves as not being or having enough, or that we are unworthy. We may respond to the wound from a state of isolation, invisibility, or shame. However, because we don't want to feel these feelings, we naturally avoid or resist them, pushing away the wound and establishing resistant behavioral patterns that further disconnect us from ourselves.

From a different, higher perspective, though, wounds help us grow. Understanding that the wound is a result of something we experienced that made us feel unsafe, rather than who we are, creates space to face the wound as an ally rather than an enemy to be avoided at all costs. Moving beyond fear and resistance gives us the opportunity for growth and resilience. It allows us to become curious about the wound and ask ourselves, "What can I learn about myself from this wound?"

Through a process of discovering the inner expression of the wound, the wound becomes a beacon, guiding us to a new level of understanding and acting as a guidance system for navigating physical pain and suffering, ultimately leading to true healing. Connecting to the wound and being present with it, even loving it for the opportunity for growth and release rather than resistance and suppression, opens us to a deeper understanding of ourselves.

When we are connected to ourselves and fully grounded in the present, we may discover that the stored trauma of the wound is based on our interpretation of what happened, rather than the event itself. Knowing that the wound is tied to a perception or interpretation of a past event that we created, we are empowered to rewrite that interpretation with a new Self-awareness in the present moment. We can create Self-empowered stories about our inner strength in surviving the event. Who we are is still intact with or without the wound. We can create or even claim who we want to become as a result of the wound. We move into a higher perspective with increased Self-awareness, knowing that our wounds do not define us. How we respond to our wounds makes all the difference in empowering or disempowering us. If we take the empowered path, our relationship with ourselves is also empowered, and we enhance the connection to ourselves.

Secondly, in the same way we interpret experiences that have happened to us, we also interpret how others have treated us, which can create a sense of disconnection from others. Again, we create false identities based on how we view our relationship to others. We invent false stories about how someone's behavior towards us implies we are less than. The truth is that people behave in ways that reflect their inner relationship with themselves. It really has nothing to do with us. When we are disconnected from others, we may misinterpret their intentions towards us negatively because our defensiveness gets triggered, and we imagine the worst possible intentions or outcomes. But, in truth, the wound trigger is likely within us, stemming from our past relationships. This is why relationships can be such a fertile ground for growth, as they trigger wound responses that allow us to discover our limiting patterns of behavior that disconnect us from others.

We can react to others from a state of disempowerment or empowerment. Our wounds can open us up to a new level of Self-awareness, allowing us to realize that we did not deserve what happened to us. We understand it is our disconnection from others that led us to misperceive the situation. For example, our lack of trust in others may represent a lack of self-trust. If we distrust ourselves, how can we trust others?

Our wounds can help us develop empowering relationships with others, in which acceptance and forgiveness are key aspects of growth. This allows us to move beyond resentment or resistance, enabling us to express ourselves authentically, forgive without judgment, and accept that others, too, are on a growth trajectory in life. We realize our Divine Self would naturally allow, accept, and forgive others as they are being in the moment. The Divine Self recognizes that we are all Divine. We make mistakes along the way to grow into our full Divine Selves. We can learn to overcome negative judgments about ourselves or others and disrupt limiting patterns through the new flow of energy and the awareness that we are one with the Divine Presence.

It follows then that another source of wounding stems from being disconnected from the Divine, making us feel isolated, abandoned, and unsupported. We view the world as *us versus them* and feel that we're on the losing side. Being disconnected from Source or the Divine puts us in a disempowered state in which we have chosen to go it alone, not realizing that we're cutting ourselves off from the benevolence of Divine support and guidance. If we are awake on our Spiritual Journey, we realize that life shows us how to connect more deeply to the Divine.

Wounds help us to awaken to this inner journey and take that inspired action to reconnect with the Divine.

Regardless of whether a wound illuminates disconnection from ourselves, others, or the Divine, it can serve as a launchpad to ignite transformation and transcendence. In our intention to connect with the Divine Energy that is within us or is us, we connect to the world around us from a new perspective, a new lens, or filter. We are no longer viewing the situation from the disempowered state of the wound. We view life through the gift of the wound and grow beyond it to an empowered state—a state in which we are connected to all aspects of support within ourselves, with others, or with the Divine. We recognize the wound draws our attention and offers us a choice. Our wounds are doorways into our Divinity.

Working with our Akashic Records can be a powerful tool for connecting more deeply with our Divine aspect and gaining greater insights into the wounds we have accumulated over lifetimes. It allows us to perceive our lives through the lens of our Soul Journey across many lifetimes, revealing the trajectory of our wounds and how they can be harnessed to guide us toward our ultimate goal of transcendence into our Higher Self.

I invite you to do the exercises at the end of this Section to understand the potential of your wounds for healing, transformation, and even transcendence.

> To personally experience how one could change a pattern in their Light Grid, I decided to go into my Akashic Records on my own. I thought that if I could change the patterns of things in my life that are not serving me, this would be amazing. I did the Pathway Prayer Process exactly as Linda Howe explains in her book. I addressed an issue related to a disconnection within me. I asked a question: *Why must my financial situation always be so difficult for me?* No sooner had I asked the question than I received an answer. At the time of my divorce, I made a declaration that money was going to be an issue for me: single parent, two kids, one income. I was not awarded alimony, only child support. It was certainly going to be hard for me financially! That was it, like I had signed a contract on the dotted line. *I did it to myself.* I embedded this pattern into my Light Grid. I had been going to healers for ten years or more, trying to solve this problem. No one solved the problem. I got the answer in the Akasha in five seconds.

As I was still pondering the ease of this process, I saw the Light Grid around me change through my inner vision. There was an aspect that had been clearly distorted or punched in on one corner. Without me directing anything, the Light Grid opened and extended outward, the kink was removed, and the Light began pulsing through the points on the Grid easily and fluidly. It clearly was not moving before. I was in absolute shock. This was the simplest shift I'd ever done. It was profound that I was able to see the distortion immediately. I had intercepted a block that could have continued had I not gone to the root of the cause and recognized my participation in it. Just as easily as I created the contract, I could eliminate it. I had converged with a difficulty in the energetic space where it could be corrected easily. Colliding with this self-inflicted barrier is also evidence of my growth and expansion. I was led to the book and that moment of collision to get resolution. The contract or declaration was never actually true. I was feeling like a victim at that time.

What I had tried to accomplish through gurus, proclaimed miracle workers, and healers for years was done by me alone in seconds. The power and wisdom really are within us! Because I could go into my Records and focus on the issue, the Light Grid started to change right before my inner eyes. This experience gave me the empowerment and motivation to learn more about the Akashic Records and how to make my life flow better. Flowing better would enable me to really focus on serving others and guiding them to transform their lives. This breakthrough radically amplified my understanding of being in alignment with one's Divine Purpose, demonstrated the loving support for us to be our best by focusing on what is essential to us, and captured the essence of being in flow with the Universe. We can use the Akasha to help straighten out the kinks in our patterns of BEing to be in better alignment with our Souls, the Divine, the Universe, our Divine Purpose, and our Infinite Potential.

Amplifying Energy Flow for Divine Connection

Amplifying or improving the flow of energy in our energy body and physical body enhances our Divine Connection and access to our Divine Potential. Our energies can be blocked, interrupted, disconnected, and distorted in many ways. Life happens. There are many methods for removing interruptions and distortions in our energy fields. There are also simple techniques to amplify, activate, and reconnect disparate energy systems, thereby amplifying and realigning energy flow. Here are some helpful techniques that you can do on your own.

Crown Chakra, Portal to the Divine

The seventh embodied chakra, the crown chakra, is an energetic connection to higher levels of Consciousness and the Divine that helps us connect to the fundamental Oneness and real selflessness of the Universe. It is the highest energetic aspect of our physical self. Activating and working with the crown chakra helps us be aware of higher wisdom, receive intuition, and be open to a deeper purpose in our lives. We gain Divine knowledge, truth, and wisdom through this spiraling energy vortex. This energy also connects to the compassion, unconditional love, and peace of the Spiritual Realm. The crown chakra helps us grow Spiritually and even transcend to our Higher Purpose. We can connect to our Divine Potential through this energy.

At the top part of our head, the crown chakra energy radiates upwards in a spiraling energy or vortex. The crown chakra is the point where our individual Consciousness meets Universal Consciousness and where the physical body and the Universe or Soul meet, most likely in connection with or through our energetic core. This chakra is responsible for transcending our perceived limitations.

As a communication center to the higher Spiritual Realms, the crown chakra's Sanskrit name, sahasrara, means "thousand petals." The crown chakra is often depicted as a lotus flower to symbolize enlightenment, rebirth, infinity, and the Divine bridge between the physical and Spiritual Realms. When balanced, this chakra allows and promotes Spiritual Awakening, deep peace, inner joy, and absolute serenity. It is the real connection to the deeper meaning of existence and our Divine Nature. The crown chakra can be like a filter of the sunlight of Spirit or a beacon of light, streaming from the Spiritual Realms into our body, strengthening the connection to the Spiritual Realm through the physical body.

This Divine Sunlight may also flow through the superhighway of our energetic core.

As the center of awareness and enlightenment within our bodies, connecting with and aligning the crown chakra opens us up to:

- see the beauty and the Divine in all people and all aspects of the Universe
- experience the Oneness with every person and everything
- witness and transcend to higher levels of Consciousness
- connect the physical self and Spiritual Self with clarity and enlightenment
- feel serenity, joy, and deep abiding peace

Tuning into and listening to our crown chakra is like having a conversation with our Higher Self. Trusting in the Universal Energy and our Higher Self promotes the balance of energy in our crown chakra while also eliminating emotional symptoms. The crown chakra doesn't open completely all at once; it takes time.

Suppose you are seeking to communicate with the Divine and receive messages that enhance your wisdom and understanding of Universal truth and enlightenment. In that case, clearing the crown chakra is a good place to start. Clearing the crown chakra is like washing a window or clearing what obscures our view, allowing us to see beyond the physical. A clear and open crown chakra guides us to our higher purpose and elevated Consciousness. An aligned crown chakra provides us with greater access and a clearer understanding of the messages about who we truly are and why we are here on Earth.

The crown chakra also gives us an awareness that we are a Soul in a human body. Saying the following affirmations during meditation or the clearing of the crown chakra enhances Spiritual Growth:

- I connect to the Divine Wisdom of the Universe.
- I am One with everyone and everything.
- I feel deep serenity and peace within me and all around me.
- I am Divine; I am worthy.
- I let go of anything that blocks me from expressing my Divine Self.
- I know the whole Universe is Divine and everything in it.

If the crown chakra is imbalanced, we feel disconnected from the Spiritual Realm; we feel lost. We may also experience depression, anxiety, and disconnection within ourselves and with others. Physically, the crown chakra influences the top parts of the brain, specifically the cerebral cortex, the nervous system, and the pituitary and pineal glands, as well as the hypothalamus, to regulate the entire endocrine system and essentially all biological systems. Physical issues associated with an imbalanced crown chakra include headaches, neck aches, upper back and neck tension, sinus issues, jaw pain, and even immune system problems.

Opening our crown chakra helps us live a life aligned with the Divine. In turn, we can continue to develop our Spiritual Skills and boldly dive into the mystery of the Universe while remaining firmly grounded and being in the present moment.

To move crown chakra energy, visualize a clock at the top of your head. The clock is visualized with 12:00 at the top connected to the forehead and 6:00 at the back part of the head. Clearing or opening the crown chakra is different for males than for females because of the way yin and yang energy flow into a female's body versus a male's body.

For most women, crown chakra energy is cleared by moving energy in a counterclockwise direction. Circle your left hand counterclockwise 2-4 inches above your head in the direction your left fingers are pointing very slowly for 2-3 minutes to release congested energy. Then, use your right hand and circle clockwise in the direction your right fingers are pointing, keeping the same height above your head, for 1-2 minutes to integrate the energy of the crown chakra.

For most men, the crown chakra energy is moved or released in a clockwise direction. Circle your right hand clockwise for 2-3 minutes in the direction your right fingers are pointing to release congested energy, and then circle counterclockwise with your left hand in the direction your left fingers are pointing to integrate the energies for 1-2 minutes.

When your crown chakra opens, you may experience physical sensations such as tingling, which represents the movement of energy. Everyone is different, and if no physical symptoms occur, it doesn't mean that the crown chakra is not opening. You may or may not experience changes in sleep, food choices, or lifestyle. One way to counteract unwanted symptoms is to meditate and quiet the mind because meditation promotes Self-awareness, connection to Universal Consciousness, and deeper levels of relaxation, which generally balance the chakras.

Emotional detachment or changing beliefs may result as the crown chakra opens. Grounding is essential for calming any emotional imbalance that may arise. Spending time in nature or practicing yoga and focusing on the energy flow surrounding us can help us get back into balance. Breathe deeply to connect to the energy flow. As we do this, the crown chakra can open even more and continue to develop. At this point, we are likely to start feeling Spiritual Symptoms. Strength and balance are achieved by clearing.

Potential Spiritual Symptoms include:

- increasing intuition
- dreaming is more vivid
- manifesting is easier and faster
- increasing the connection to and sensing the Divine
- receiving Spiritual Visions and Messages increases
- aligning all other chakras

A common but prominent Spiritual Enhancement is becoming more aware of our heightened intuition. Our intuition is stronger or appears louder and more prominent. Once we start listening to our intuition, it only gets easier to understand and trust the guidance. Our intuition may become so strong that we may start to develop other symptoms as well, such as honing our skills and gifts, recognizing new talents, and experiencing enhanced power and ease of manifestation. Our dreams become extremely vivid and easier to control.

As our crown chakra begins to develop, we gain a deeper understanding of life, one that is more Spiritual and distinct from the material world. We tend to start living our lives seeing through a different lens or filter—perhaps the lens of the Divine, making a definite shift in our level of Consciousness. We are more aware of the energy flowing through the Universe. Many people's beliefs change radically or slowly over time. Like me, you may change careers because what is essential to you has changed. We start to realize that certain people are meant to stay in our lives, and others are meant to leave. We will likely feel a great merging with the abundance and Infinite Cosmic Energy of the Universe. We see life from a different and higher perspective. We become more compassionate toward ourselves and others. We may be more aware of the food we eat. We take better care of ourselves. Usually, we start to care more about how we impact the world in this life.

As our crown chakra opens, others may remark that we radiate energy, or they love being around our energy. This type of response is because we're tuned into the Universal rhythm or the flow of the Universe, which gives us the power to absorb and transfer this energy to those around us.

The true benefits of an open crown chakra include the following:

- alignment with our dreams and burning desires
- alignment with the Divine, our Divine Mission, and the Universe
- receiving messages, blessings, and unexpected miracles
- becoming who we were meant to be before conception
- flowing freely in the Universe
- awareness of an overwhelming sense of love
- feeling more rooted and more grounded in who we really are
- trusting in our intuition, Divine Right Timing, and Divine Right Order so strongly that fear, anxiety, and worry melt away
- becoming one with ourselves, one with the Divine, and one with the Universe
- understanding that we are not separate but different expressions or aspects of the Divine

Our Energetic Core, a Portal to the Divine

Our energetic core is our direct connection to the Spiritual Realm or the Divine. The energies of the energetic core help us to connect more completely with the Divine, our Soul, and our Divine Potential. Our Core Soul is in our energetic core, as discussed in Section Two.

Our energetic core flows vertically through the center of our bodies in two directions. Even though the chakras 2 through 6 are also located in the center line of our bodies, they are not considered part of the energetic core. The energetic core comes from the torus energy structure. The chakras also come from the torus, but later in human development. The torus structure comes from the morula, the structure of the first 512 cells in human development. Just like the torus energy, this morula or ball of cells invaginates at the top and the bottom to form the north and south poles. The north pole eventually develops into the mouth, and the south pole eventually develops into the anus of the developing human. I believe that the channel that forms between our north and south poles becomes our energetic core—our central vertical channel. This energetic core is the center of the torus energy that surrounds our human bodies.

We live our True Essence from our energetic core—our Soul. Moving in and out of our energetic core is moving in and out of our wholeness and our True Essence. The connection between our energetic core, or our Core Soul, can be disturbed, and we can become disconnected from our Radiant Soul through life's trials and tribulations. The energy flow from our energetic core out to the rest of our energy body can become disconnected. We may still be connected to our Divine Potential, but the energies do not permeate from our energetic core to our Radiant Core; therefore, these energies do not permeate to the rest of our energy body, physical body, and beyond. We feel more whole and complete if the energies in our energetic core and our Radiant Soul are interconnected and activated throughout our whole BEing.

Not only do we feel more whole, but activating and strengthening our energetic core enlivens our Soul and aids in our connection to and our alignment with the Divine. We are wholly aligned with the Divine and our Divine Potential. Our goal in activating and enhancing the connections of the energies in the energetic core is to weave the fabric of who we are more tightly so that it maintains its full integrity and wholeness within us and within our awareness. Developing the strength, integrity, and resilience of our energetic core is important so that nothing happening in our lives will disturb the balance and the energy flow. Our True Essence is not disrupted. We become resilient to life's ups and downs.

Our energetic core is the integration of several different types of energies that work together to construct our Inner BEing or Essence. According to Prune Harris, the main systems in the energetic core include the Taiji Pole, stellar diamonds, the dantians, and the yin-yang vortexes. Other energies associated with the energetic core are the Earth Star (or chakra 10) and Sun Star (chakra 9), the auric membrane (chakra 12), the Assemblage Point, and at least three radiant circuits—central, governing, and penetrating flow. The penetrating flow may well serve as our Radiant Soul to transport energy from the edge of the energetic core through our whole energy body and beyond.

Other radiant circuits may also act with the penetrating flow to bring forth the Radiant Soul throughout the body. The penetrating flow radiant circuit has no set pathway; it is not restricted in its energy flow and is considered Divine Intelligence, as are the other radiant circuits. (Section One) I refer to them as contributing to the energetic core because, when activated, the radiant circuits are not limited to a particular location in the energy body. All these energies have different flow patterns, different vibrations, and different functions, but they all support the center vertical channel of our energy body.

Energies of the Energetic Core

As stated, in addition to the radiant circuits, the energies in this energetic core are primarily the yin and yang vortexes, stellar diamonds, three dantians, and the Taiji Pole.

Yin and Yang Vortexes

The yin and yang vortexes are energies that spiral up from below us and spiral down from above us into our physical bodies, respectively. The yin vortex flows up in counterclockwise spirals, and the yang vortex flows down in clockwise spirals. These vortexes provide revitalizing energy to the energetic core. They are spiraling portals of Universal Connectedness. These vortexes are essentially the energy of our origin and essence. The yin vortex is thought to be goodness and compassion, and the yang vortex energy is strength and confidence. In the energy body, they are likely to aid in Spiritual Transformation and alignment with other energies, creating harmony and balance. I sense them as spiraling tetrahedra that meet at the lower dantian point, located just below the navel, which is a powerful energy that supports the physical body. Perhaps together, they become or participate in or as the Merkaba.

Three Dantian Energies

The three dantian energies are at least in part comprised of filaments of vibrating energy interconnected in a web-like structure, or nadis. The three dantians are reservoirs or holding tanks of energy. According to Taoist and Buddhist traditions, the three dantian points are associated with a higher level of Consciousness. Traditional Chinese Medicine interprets these dantians as the holders of three treasures, which are actually three different subtle energies: jing, qi, and shen.

The lower dantian, located approximately 1-2 inches below the navel along the central line of the physical body, is associated with the root and sacral chakras, kundalini energy, reproduction, genetic material, and the kidneys and adrenal glands. The lower dantian is associated with our survival response. It is the treasure of jing or one's Essence. This lower dantian is also a center of energy, serving as a storage area for the energy that comes in from above and below the energetic core—our Life Force Energy. This energy center not only holds our highest potential but also energizes and supports our other energy channels. The lower dantian sends energy to the middle dantian. The middle dantian, the spark of all living things, is located between the breasts and aligns with the Earth, the heart, the heart chakra, and the thymus gland. The middle dantian energy is the treasure of qi, or the seat of Life-Force Energy. This middle dantian of qi nurtures the Soul Journey and Soul Evolution.

The upper dantian, located on the center of the forehead between the eyebrows, is associated with the third eye chakra and the pineal gland. It is the treasure of shen or intuition and Spirit. The three dantians are energies or 'elixirs' for harmony, balance, and well-being of the body. On the physical level, they support blood, bodily fluids, and tissues. They also support the mind and the Soul in Spiritual and Consciousness development.

Stellar Diamonds

Stellar diamond energy is an energetic structure derived from the Sun Star, chakra 9, and connected to our energetic core. The stellar diamonds are light-filled energy that contributes to our level of radiance and enhances intuition. Significantly, they support our physical structure and enhance the heart's stability and the heart band of energy.

Both the Sun Star and the Earth Star, chakras 9 and 10, respectively, which are considered part of the energy of the stellar diamonds, sit in our auric membrane, chakra 12, at the interface of our energetic core and Universal Consciousness, and represent the top and the bottom of our energetic core, respectively. The Sun Star energy, chakra 9, is above the physical body, and the Earth Star, chakra 10, is below the feet--both in the central line of the physical body.

We use the Sun Star and Earth Star to enhance the energy flow through the energetic core or the Taiji Pole. This enhancement also helps with our connection to Consciousness. Between the Sun and Earth Stars are stellar diamonds of different sizes. The stellar diamonds are always formed along the central vertical line. Our physical structure and bones are held in place by stellar diamonds. The various sizes of the stellar diamonds support us structurally and physically while allowing Universal Energy to flow through us.

Taiji Pole

The Taiji Pole energy is connected to the torus energy that surrounds our body. The Taiji Pole holds our essence--the energy of our Soul. The Taiji Pole is light energy and contributes to our radiance. The Taiji Pole energy enables us to be the conduits between the physical and Spiritual Realms. The Taiji Pole is the superhighway of light filaments that flows through the center of our BEing, defining our unique essence. The Taiji Pole energy of our Soul also connects us to the Soul of the Universe.

Activate Energies of the Energetic Core

While there are several ways to activate or strengthen the energies in the energetic core, this is a practice I have found works well. To prepare for engaging in these exercises, it's important to start with a grounding exercise. You can rub a stainless-steel spoon on the bottom of your feet or cross your arms over your body and hold your hands under your opposite arms. Your thumbs can be under your arms or on the front of your upper chest. Hold this pose for several minutes, taking deep breaths.

You can do all the following exercises or intuit which ones are most needed in the moment. Check in with yourself and tune into how you feel after each exercise. The goal is for you to feel safe and protected. You may even experience a sense of calmness.

Strengthen the auric membrane.

You can strengthen your energetic core by strengthening your auric membrane. The auric membrane is not wholly in the energetic core. Still, it connects to and affects the energetic core at the Earth Star or chakra 9 and Sun Star or chakra 10, so we include this in the series of exercises that enhance the vibrancy and strength of the energetic core. You can do this by simply tuning into your aura and auric membrane, the outer edge of the aura, and consciously becoming aware of it. The auric membrane is thick, flexible, and has a color that may change at any moment. Focus on visualizing or sensing your auric membrane and determine what color it needs for strengthening. Then sit and envision that color in the auric membrane in your mind's eye. Then, sit and envision the color of your aura within the auric membrane. The color of the aura and the auric membrane may differ. Dr. Sue Morter considers the auric membrane to be the 12th chakra.

Activate energy flow between the Earth Star and the Sun Star.

To strengthen the energetic core, you can consciously connect to the Sun Star and Earth Star at the beginning and ends of the energetic core to enhance the flow in the central vertical channel between the Sun Star and Earth Star. Begin by connecting to the Sun Star above your head. Hold your hands above your head to connect with the Sun Star energy and feel the energy pulsing in your hands.

Your elbows can be bent slightly. Then, hold your hands toward the area beneath your feet with the intention that you're connecting to the Earth Star below your feet. Feel the pulsing in your hands. Then imagine the energy flowing up from the Earth Star to the Sun Star and back again several times.

This enhanced flow is a way to strengthen the flow of your entire energetic core, as well as your personal integrity and wholeness. Then, you can put the top of your hands together with your fingers pointing toward the center of your body, a few inches from your body, and slowly bring your fingers from the Earth Star up to the Sun Star. Do this several times.

Strengthen the stellar diamonds.

You can add more energetic structure by drawing diamond shapes to enhance stellar diamond energy, along the central vertical channel to strengthen your energetic core. With your hands, draw large and small diamonds in your field along the center of your body. These diamonds are the shape of baseball diamonds, not jewel diamonds. You might start with a big diamond that starts above your head at the Sun Star, goes out to the edge of your aura on both sides, out from the hips, and then comes together at the Earth Star. Then, you may want to draw smaller diamonds over your face, upper chest, middle of the chest, and so on, down the center of your body. Intuit what your body needs. Wherever we place our hands in our energy field, the energies will follow the magnetic energy, much like iron filings responding to a magnet. When we draw diamonds in our field, the energies of our field form the diamond pattern. You can also draw smaller or tiny stellar diamonds if you intuit that need.

Connect the three dantians and tap into wisdom.

This exercise strengthens this powerful energy within your energetic core and feeds the meridians and chakras. Using a 3-finger notch with your thumb, middle, and index fingers, hold the lower dantian point 1-2 inches below your navel along the center line of the body, and the middle dantian point between your breasts with the other hand in a 3-finger notch. Hold for several minutes or until you feel a connection via pulsing energy in your fingers. Then, hold the middle dantian point with the upper dantian point, which is at your third eye between the eyebrows. Again, use 3-finger notches for these holds. Hold this in place until you sense that the three dantians are connected, or you feel the energy pulsing between them.

Activate the yin and yang vortexes.

This exercise enhances the flow of the yin and yang vortexes to meet at the lower dantian point while also activating, revitalizing, and strengthening the energy of the entire energetic core. You can activate the yin and yang vortexes together or separately. You can do this sitting down. To activate the yin vortex, place your left-hand palm flat toward the ground above your left knee and move it toward the right side of your body, making slow, clockwise circles—visualize the clock on your knees. Do this for a few minutes. To bring down the yang vortex energy, take your right hand with the palm facing up above your right knee and go toward the left side of the body. You will be making slow, counterclockwise circles. Do this for a few minutes. You can circle both clockwise and counterclockwise at the same time. You may feel a sense of calm come over you. Then, cross your hands over your heart. Then, draw a large sideways figure 8 or infinity sign across your breast area.

Activate the Taiji Pole

All the exercises discussed to enhance the energetic core are exercises that also enhance the Taiji Pole. Another exercise to activate the Taiji Pole is done by circling your whole body slowly ten times, either clockwise or counterclockwise. To further enhance the Taiji Pole energy, laugh as you circle to engage the radiant circuits. One more simple exercise to activate the Taiji Pole is to first activate your hands by rubbing them together and then shaking off any stagnant energy. Then, place both hands at the center of your body, with one pointing up toward the sky and the other down toward the Earth. Hold for several minutes.

Simply by consciously becoming aware of the Taiji Pole, it activates and connects to the energetic core. The Taiji Pole is like an energy station intimately interconnected to the torus. As the center of the torus, the Taiji Pole also helps us to bridge to the Divine. The Taiji Pole also connects to our radiant circuits. Activating the Taiji Pole helps align with the Divine and become part of the Oneness of the Universe through the wisdom of the Taiji Pole. Since the Taiji Pole serves as the conduit for Universal Consciousness—the Divine—opening the Taiji Pole helps our energy fields to be fueled directly by Universal Consciousness in a more unified and connected way. One becomes the other.

Activate the Torus

Every living thing in the Universe has an associated toroidal field or torus—all nature, cells, Consciousness, Earth, sun, tomato, apple, Soul, the whole Universe, everything. The torus energy is Infinite Consciousness surrounding us. It is a magnetic field believed to be the remnant energy of the Big Bang. According to Dirk Oellibrandt, all aspects of life have this spiraling energy flowing in two directions through a central tunnel. It is the principle of infinitely creating energy that exists in all aspects of the cosmos.

Torus energy connects us to the Divine. Our torus grows and evolves with us. The torus around the human body is a stable vortex of energy interconnected with the Taiji Pole and the energetic core. The torus encompasses all the energy systems, yet it also transcends them. Donna Eden sees the torus as purple and the Taiji Pole as white light. As described earlier, the energy field of a torus looks like a donut, folding in on itself in an ever-renewing and never-ending flow. (see Figure 2) If our torus is disturbed in any area, the disturbance can affect our physical bodies and their functioning. In particular, a disturbed torus is likely to have a negative impact on the immune system. A torus disturbance can also affect the flow of toroidal energy around our cells, causing a loss of energetic radiance or frequency.

The human toroidal field is directed by our breath, and just as we take regular showers to cleanse our physical body and keep it healthy, we are invited to take regular energy showers to clean and strengthen our energy bodies. We are meant to be strong, powerful bridges between the physical and Spiritual Realms. See the exercises at the end of this section to activate the torus.

Activate the Merkaba

Another way to tap into our unlimited Divine Potential is to activate our Merkaba. The Merkaba helps transport the Spirit and the body from one world into another or from one dimension to another. Merkaba translates literally to "light" (mer), "spirit" (ka), and "body" (ba). The greater energy field surrounding our body beyond our auric field is our Merkaba. The Merkaba has two intersecting tetrahedra that spin in opposite directions, creating a three-dimensional energy field around the body. The counterrotating field of light interacts with the Spirit and body.

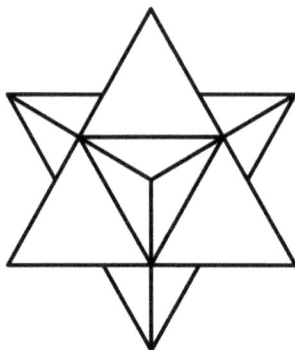

Figure 3: Merkaba

As a star tetrahedron, the Merkaba is a sacred geometry structure that also represents a stage in human development. This structure is also the light body vehicle or vessel that transports us initially from the Spiritual Realm to the third-dimensional experience of the physical realm.

Other roles of the Merkaba are to support us energetically, help us open to expanded awareness of who we really are, and connect us with higher levels of Consciousness. The Merkaba is love. One can only know the Merkaba through the experience of love. The Merkaba can be envisioned as a living field of love. We are not separate from this living field of love. We are the living field of love Consciousness. We receive the Life Force Energy from the Divine and send it from us to the Divine—a two-way communication. It is our direct connection, our link to our Oneness with the Divine. Love and knowledge flow around us in the energy of the Merkaba. We can travel via a Merkaba into any Spiritual dimension as it is infinitely circulating the flow of energy from the Divine in all directions and all at the same time. It also harmonizes male and female energies.

Our Merkaba is in constant connection with the Divine. Our Creative Energy matrix enables us to combine our Soul Intention with the Divine Spark of Source Energy, allowing us to create any reality we choose. Our Merkaba can combine with the energy matrix to assist in creating the reality we desire.

Like crystals, the Merkaba is programmed through meditation and intentions. We can create intentions and meditate on cultivating ease and flow in our lives, aligning ourselves with the Divine's intentions, and being in harmony with the Universe.

For example, we can set the intention, "Merkaba, I program you to create an open energy channel in me as I align more fully with the Divine and directly flow with the Universe to reach a higher potential within me and contribute to the Universe at a higher level."

We can activate the Merkaba around our body through meditation, specific breathing techniques, and breathing patterns. Activating the Merkaba combines the opposing energies for perfect balance—masculine and feminine, as well as Earth and cosmos. The Merkaba provides energetic protection for us as we transport our Consciousness to higher levels and dimensions.

Walk a Labyrinth

Walking a labyrinth is another way to raise our Consciousness and align with the Divine. The labyrinth is a symbol of wholeness and the Divine Imprint. The labyrinth represents a journey of Spiritual Awakening.

Walking the labyrinth is a tool for reflecting on our lives and releasing what blocks our sense of Oneness with the Divine. It is an opportunity to reconnect more deeply to the Divine and likely receive messages about how to proceed on our Spiritual Journey. Walking the labyrinth's path opens the chakras' energy, allowing for the release of congested energy and clearing of energetic blocks to our connection with the Divine.

The labyrinth can be used as a Spiritual practice, a walking meditation, or a way to calm the mind, be in silence, find peace, or reflect on one's life. Walking the labyrinth is a Sacred Journey one takes to align with the Divine. Used as a Spiritual tool for 4000 years, it combines the circle and spiral in a purposeful and meaningful path. The way in is the same as the way out. There are no hidden pathways and no tricks. The labyrinth is a metaphor for our own Spiritual Journey. The labyrinth represents inspiration and relates to the hero's journey, with its twists and turns as you follow the intended path, moving toward and away from the center.

It is likely that labyrinths were a part of all ancient cultures. They have been used in Christianity since the 4th century. The prototypic 11-circuit labyrinth, illustrated here, was embedded into the floor of Chartres Cathedral in France in 1220.

Figure 4: Circle Labyrinth

Walking the labyrinth is a three-part journey of releasing, reconnecting, and reintegrating.

- **Release:** As we enter the labyrinth and walk toward the center, we release or let go of our stress, grief, fear, emotional upset, and worries. This part is an opportunity to surrender and empty our hearts, minds, and energy fields, allowing space for something new to emerge.
- **Reconnect:** Reaching the center of the labyrinth, we reconnect with the Divine. Being in the center is an opportunity to receive illumination, enlightenment, or answers to our specific questions. We may also receive specific messages because we've created the Spiritual Space. Most significantly, we can just BE with the Divine. Allow the Divine to flow into the emptied-out spaces.
- **Reintegrate or re-unite:** Our journey from the center back out of the labyrinth is reintegration or reunion with Oneness. We take this Spiritual experience or Spiritual Oneness back into our lives in a transformed way. Due to the renewed experience of Divine Oneness, there are more opportunities for our transformation. We are different because of our stronger Spiritual connection and renewed alignment with the Divine.

As we walk the labyrinth, we naturally clear the spiraling energy of the chakras as we turn and twist, weaving in and out of the center. No wonder it feels so good to us as we walk! No wonder we are opening up to new insights and answers as we release congestion in each of our chakras! I show the 11-circuit labyrinth here, but there are other labyrinths with fewer circuits, like the 7-circuit labyrinth, and each circuit represents a different and specific embodied chakra.

Enhance the Diamond Inlay

Enhancing Diamond Inlay structures in our energy fields is another way to align and enhance our connection with the Divine and tap into our unlimited Divine Potential. The Diamond Inlay pattern is different from the stellar diamonds in our energetic core. The Diamond Inlay is an energetic diamond structure in our human energy fields, not just our energetic core, which aligns us with the pulse of the Living Universe. The energy of one Diamond Inlay structure also helps to realign, strengthen, and evolve the Assemblage Point.

The Diamond Inlay structures could be interpreted as a gateway, portal, or bridge to the higher realms. Diamond Inlay patterns are created organically as needed to evolve. Diamond Inlay Structures can also be enhanced using energy techniques. These Diamond Inlay structures will help us intuitively and physically receive information from the Spiritual Realm, connecting us to external energies.

The Diamond Inlay Structure helps us tap into the truth of our Soul, enhance intuitive abilities, and enhance the grounding effect as we take quantum leaps of Consciousness. We are better able to overcome the energetic blocks to higher levels of Consciousness to allow Spiritual Growth and transcendence.

Donna Eden, the pioneer of Energy Medicine and my mentor, can see Diamond Inlay energy with her physical eyes and has designed five specific protocols to activate and enhance specific Diamond Inlay Structures, thereby enhancing the diamond-like energy in our energy fields. These Diamond Inlay protocols are unique to the Eden Method, as is the teaching of the basic grid structure. To my knowledge, these topics are not discussed in other energy healing modalities.

In working with the Diamond Inlay structure, Eden realized that enhancing and strengthening the structure helps us tune into higher levels of Consciousness, allowing us to live and achieve at higher potentials. According to Eden, when this energetic structure appears in someone's energy field, it has the effect of being both grounding and expanding, lifting them out of their perceived limitations.

Eden says that when evident, the Diamond Inlay patterns appear brighter than the other energies, like diamond gems with sparkly, radiant energy. They become more evident when someone is ready for a conscious or a positive evolutionary shift in their life, and they permanently appear in highly intuitive individuals.

Activate Energetic DNA

By activating our energetic DNA, we can hold higher vibrational frequencies in our energy fields and embody more of our Higher Self or Divine Self energies in our physical being. This helps us connect with and understand the true essence of who we are—Divine Love —and tap into our Infinite Divine Potential more easily.

The subject of our true DNA makeup and how we can activate more strands of our DNA potentialities is vast and beyond the scope of this book. But, essentially, to reach our highest potential level of Consciousness and vibrational frequency, the goal is to activate all twelve strands of DNA present in our energetic body using specific commands and sacred geometry codes. In this process, lower vibrational frequencies are cleared, and higher Consciousness from the Soul Identity is downloaded into our energetic DNA template.

Mastery and Self-Actualization

Becoming a master means you are mastering your own life from the inside out. There are many aspects of this mastery, but the main concept is that you feel safe and secure in who you are in this world. You are independent, and you are a part of the Oneness of the Universe. You are on your own unique path in life as designed by your Soul. You feel aligned with your Soul, and you identify primarily as your Soul. You honor this Self and your physical self as the vehicle you are using in this lifetime. You are connected to your Soul as a Loving Presence and sense this connection most of the time. You are the Universe since Universal Energy or Quantum Reality flows through you and enlivens you to become who you are meant to be. You recognize and live into being a Divine Magnificent BEing, expressing the Divine Love through your thoughts, beliefs, and actions. You feel grateful and blessed. You no longer react to life; life responds to you.

Mastery Unfolds from Our BEingness

In her book, *The Wisdom of the Council*, Sara Landon shares many channeled enlightened messages from the Council. One message focuses on mastering the human experience easily from an elevated state of Consciousness. This empowering message has remained with me. I sense it as one of my invitations to align and step into this mastery, focusing only on my pathway of growth and enlightenment.

Although Landon's Council encourages us to live and be at our highest potential, we are not going to put the steps together and figure out the pathway to mastery. I get the sense that mastery is already within us. However, there is really nothing to do to become a master of our life. There is no achievement, recognition, or award ceremony to anoint us as a master. We slowly but surely find our way without trying or effort. It is in our BEingness that mastery unfolds. Just by experiencing ourselves fully and with love, we become masters.

Mastering ourselves, we become sensitive to the energy around us and go with the flow of that energy. We are using the increased Universal Energy to support and guide us. We are using Universal Energy to supply the energy we need in the moment. We decide who we want to be, what our focus is, and what is needed to get there using all our resources, including the Spiritual Realm. We accomplish more and at a higher level when we ask the Spiritual Realm for guidance and help.

Being a master of our life, health, well-being, money, and energy flow means being open to the continuum of Universal Energy that is constantly flowing through us. Doing breathing exercises and building energetic circuits is routine to strengthen and animate our energetic core—our energetic bridge to the Spiritual Realm.

Whatever thought we have, it is ours, and it connects to the Creative Energy of the Universe. Our recognition of this Creative Energy induces our thoughts to focus and concentrate, allowing them to be projected from formless to form. Our words and thoughts are the channels through which Creative Energy moves. Creative Energy must reflect that channel, like water reflects the shape of a pipe it flows through. Directing our thoughts to where we are going, not where we've been, is an aspect of a master. Focusing on the abundance of opportunities, possibilities, and unlimited potential within us, we will elevate our vibrational frequency. Mastering our thoughts and emotions is crucial to achieving Self-mastery.

What I really mean by Self-mastery is mastering who we are BEing in any given moment and mastering our focus on creating what comes most naturally to us. Mastery of ourselves is becoming who we were meant to be in this lifetime—our entelechy. Self-mastery is taking responsibility for our energy and our level of Consciousness. Be the director of your life on this elevated path of living and higher frequency living. Use your energy and Consciousness to serve yourself and others. Master your mind. Focus your mind on your body. Focus on the body, breath, and love to work together to guide your mind. Be the Loving Presence within. Always include this Presence as much as possible. Be connected to the vibrational frequency of Loving Presence as often as you can to master your life and become your True Self. Your True Self should guide your mind—not your mind guiding your True Self.

You Are a Creator BEing

Come to terms with yourself as a creator who is part of the Divine Creator. You can create what you want if you align with it. Go deep within. Discover the truth and wisdom. Be your free and Creative Self. Understand yourself to the depths of yourself. Realize that creating is a significant aspect of your life. You are always creating, whether it be relationships, opportunities, situations, wealth, health, joy, peace, or love. You are also creating obstacles to foster growth to become a new version of you—a version that vibrates at a higher frequency. Be a creator of the highest good that you are. Be the master of your existence and your life experience. Be the master of who you are becoming. Allow the Universal Flow to guide you on your way to becoming your True Self. Build the energetic circuits of becoming with intention and love.

To create, we can connect to the vastness of the Universe—Zero Point Field, Quantum Reality—where every potential is a dazzling, vibrating dance of opportunity that we each can reach for from deep within our Inner Wisdom. No limitations exist in the vastness. Nothing is stopping us, and the right opportunities are calling us. If we willingly go into the Void, the vastness of All That Is, we will embark upon the most amazing adventure of a lifetime beyond our wildest imagination. We can select from the infinite number of choices and potentials that are available to us, allowing us to take on new opportunities and move forward. This represents the miracle of life. It is all right here waiting for us to wake up, witness, experience, and *become* our Divine Truth.

Create more sacredness in life to attain or maintain a higher vibrational frequency by choice. Create each day as we would want it to be, and then every week and every year. If we create in this way, through gratitude and appreciation, from our wholeness and completeness, we can do anything we want. It is all possible within us. Self-mastery is the confidence to create something new. It is trusting that you will be guided to create what is naturally inside of you to create. It could be a relationship, a workshop, a book, wealth, health, a new career, a non-profit, or a business. Self-mastery is allowing the entelechy to help create the reality from your Inner Potential. Allowing indicates acceptance and a lack of resistance.

To start your creatorship, consider being in a creative mindset and focusing your attention on harnessing Creative Energy. You can take creative action with your True Self as your guide—with lovingkindness, benevolence, and compassion. You are a creator because you have ideas. Realize that new ideas emerge spontaneously within you because you are open and in a creative state. Step into the knowing that whatever you create has already been accomplished. You can envision completing your creation, and you can *feel* it is done. As you complete this project, you will learn new things and gain pearls of wisdom for a successful outcome. It is really the process of learning and expanding that is the goal, not the outcome. As you proceed with your creation, you are aware of the guidance of the Loving Presence that is guiding you. Bliss flows to you and within you. You feel blessed as you are BEing a blessing.

Co-create with the Divine

Be in full alignment with being a creator, yourself, using all your avenues of Consciousness. Allow and be. Be free and let go. Be in total and complete alignment with *ALL* that you are. It is all about aligning with Divine Energy in the energetic core and aligning with the Divine Intentions for this world, the Universe, and for you. Be in alignment with the Divine in co-creation. You are in harmony or in Oneness with Divine Intelligence if your thoughts and words—your mind—reflect the Divine Mind.

Consciousness creates. As you move into Universal Consciousness, you become aware of your universality. You are an extension of Consciousness, and you can expand more and more into Consciousness. This represents a true Spiritual Journey. Connect to the full Oneness that you are within and without. The Universal Oneness is the amassing of all the potentials of each uniqueness of each expression. Not that we are all the same. We each need to be our unique selves to contribute to the full spectrum of the infinite in the Oneness. Each of us, in our uniqueness, is necessary and significant to the spectrum of infinity in the Oneness.

Master BEing the Love that You Are

To experience ourselves fully, we must know ourselves fully. We can recognize our own gifts, talents, and specific abilities that have helped us along our pathway to BE who we are today. We can recognize what we do and don't resonate with. Doing and BEing more of what we resonate with is key to experiencing ourselves fully. Then, we can be in a state of allowing life to happen to reveal who we really are more and more. Allowing is being in non-resistance. Whatever is showing up for us is meant for us. Start embracing what shows up.

Metaphorically, whatever shows up is a doorway to see deeper into who we are becoming. Becoming is a process that we go through as we experience life. Becoming is also about allowing what shows up to guide us to the next step—accepting what shows up as an invitation to a gateway on the path to enlightenment. It is surrendering to our higher path, becoming intolerant of the same old way of BEing.

A significant aspect of the journey in my book, *Journey to True Self*, is becoming Love Consciousness by making the connection with your True Self. Becoming Love Consciousness is not just loving the people and things that you care about. It is loving everything and everyone because it is Divine, just like you.

There is also becoming the Love or Loving Presence, being in the love vibrational frequency, whether you are alone, making dinner, taking a walk, weeding the garden, or doing your job. It is a frequency of BEing that guides you to make different decisions or take different actions. In the vibrational frequency of love, lower frequencies dissolve in the higher vibration of love. Fear cannot exist, anxiety cannot exist, stress cannot exist, anger cannot exist, panic, worry, and grief cannot exist.

This is not about being at the vibration of Love Consciousness, but about BEing ONE or merging with the love that you are. It is a presence that you transmit or radiate. This Love is your True Self. You can be Love at a high vibrational frequency, but you can also become this vibrational frequency and stay there most of the time. We can connect to this Loving Presence so deeply that we don't disconnect from that aspect of us, ever.

We are interwoven into the fabric of the Loving Presence within us, and it is us. Mastery of Love is why many Souls come to Earth. Our Souls want to learn to be this Loving Presence, no matter what is happening. BEing Loving Presence is an enlightened way of BEing. It is the reflection of us from the Spiritual Realm. It parallels the understanding of Oneness. If we know that we are One with ALL, then the natural reaction is to be in Loving Presence. We have merged with the Divine aspect of ourselves.

This Divine aspect constantly flows through us. We have opened the door to a new level of existence that has always been there right inside us, in the center of our energetic core. This doorway offers a new way to explore life through different parameters and different lenses of BEing. This new BEingness leads us to understand Oneness and enlightenment because we are the Pure Consciousness of Oneness and enlightenment. This is ultimate Self-mastery.

As part of BEing Love, Sara Landon's Council invites us to love our lives. The Council invites us to love the human experience. Be the Loving Presence of who you are at your core. Mastery involves love. Being a master of your life is also through your heart energy—your heart chakra and Assemblage Point. Keeping your epicenter in front of your heart is key to being the master of your energy flow in your whole energy body.

Love the human experience. Love what is unfolding for you. Love yourself inside and out. Realize that we are responsible for interweaving our physical and Invisible aspects of our BEingness. Mastery is bringing all aspects of ourselves together in an elegant tapestry to fully realize the inextricable connection between the physical and Invisible aspects, thereby becoming complete and whole in our present existence. Mastery is creating from our wholeness, our completeness.

Don't disperse your energy to others. Keep your energy focused on yourself, your path, and your unique journey. Allow others to be on their own journey and refrain from interfering. Create what you came here to create in a co-creative process with the Universe. There is nothing stopping us from achieving greatness but ourselves. We can expand ourselves and elevate our level of Consciousness to reveal more and higher potentials. We can go deeper in a quest to know all there is to know about our True Selves. We can learn to express our Consciousness more freely and effortlessly—to be more and more of who we really are.

Who We Become is Our Responsibility

We are responsible for who we *become* in life. Be open to let the love flow to you, within you, and through you. Be the conduit of love. Be a vessel for amplifying love. Be the conduit for raising the vibrational frequency of you, your family, your community, your state, your country, your continent, your galaxy, and your Universe. It is all possible, but you won't necessarily know that it has happened. You just need to be YOU—a higher or highest version of you. You may need time to become who you are meant to be. Pay attention to the guidance to follow the right path of becoming. You must become who you were meant to be to realize your highest potential.

It won't happen if we try or force it to happen. Allow and *be* in the Universal Flow. Be in complete non-resistance. Let life unfold naturally. Focus your attention on creating what you want with no attachment to the outcome from the physical realm perspective. If you are in a state of lack or separation, you create gaps in the energy flow of becoming. You are not in your Oneness. You are not connected to peace, well-being, completeness, wholeness, joy, and abundance. Perceive that the concept of being separate from who you are becoming is an illusion. You are in a continuum of moving into full alignment with who you are becoming. There is a full spectrum of all possibilities of you! You already are who you are becoming. You are simply building the energetic circuits to become fully One with that complete aspect of you.

Be in gratitude and bless what is happening for you, which is everything. Be aware of new revelations and understandings. Being a master of your life means you take the time to dwell in the Loving Presence within you. Carry the Loving Presence with you all day. Be aware of the Loving Presence. Walk through your space with your hands over your heart and sacral chakras, with the awareness that you are tapping into the Loving Presence in these two vortexes of energy. The more you can connect with and enliven the energetic core energies, the more you can become a master of your life.

Being a master in your life also means being intentional about aligning with higher vibrational frequencies of enlightenment, compassion, benevolence, radiance, sacredness, courage, unconditional love, peace, joy, forgiveness, and gratitude. These high vibrational energies amplify the decisions and the pathway for your transformation—these energies are directing your transformation. It is a great process of becoming a master of your life.

One of the ways I gained a deeper understanding of Self-mastery and Self-realization was through automatic writing sessions, which were weeks and sometimes months apart. Automatic writing is a method for receiving guidance and engaging with BEings in the Spiritual Realm. I started automatic writing as a way to connect with my Higher Self and Ascended Masters, whom I called upon for guidance. There are various techniques for automatic writing. I start by taking deep breaths, expanding my energy beyond my physical body as I breathe, connecting to my heart, and becoming the light that illuminates from my heart. Then, I ask questions of my Guides, Soul, or Ascended Masters and sit quietly until I am drawn to write the response that comes to me.

Here are some excerpts from my automatic writing sessions on the topic of Self-mastery.

Messages from the Guides

Question: What would my Soul want me to know about Self-mastery?

Dear Beloved,

Self-mastery is the path that you are following right now. Being in love and starting each day with the practice of coming from love and connecting to the Loving Presence within is a form of Self-mastery. Loving yourself, loving others, loving the human experience, loving the journey, and loving growth are all crucial parts of Self-mastery. It is living moment by moment from the truth of who you are and presencing yourself so that life or the Universe responds to you. You no longer react to life. You love what is happening as you are playing your Divine Role in the unfoldment of life, moment by moment.

Although there is a lot you want to do, you are kind to yourself. You take rest, and you find ways to play and do things you enjoy. As often as you can, you tap into the high vibrational frequencies of love, peace, and joy. It is your intention to live at those levels to bring more life into your existence from those vibrations. Keeping your energy within you or on you rather than dispersing it or giving it away to others, situations, or circumstances has been an aspect of your growth.

Self-mastery is working on and consciously balancing and maintaining energetic harmony in your energy fields. Life can easily pull you away from this self-care, but the more you do simple things to communicate that you are tending to your energies, the better. Conscious awareness of the things that matter most in life is a key aspect of awakening and living life according to your highest intentions and desires. Being purposeful, being intentional, and following the intentions of the Divine are so important to Self-mastery.

Asking for help from your Higher Self, Guides, Ascended Masters, Angels, and loved ones is a sign that you are living in the Oneness. You recognize you aren't alone. You aren't existing without support. There is so much available to you when you ask and when you are in alignment with the larger aspect of life. You are the Universe, and you play a significant role in and as the Universe. That is Self-mastery.

We love you. We love you. We love you.

Question: What would my three Ascended Masters have me know about Self-realization?

Dear Beloved,

You are on your way to Self-realization. It is a state where you truly know your physical self and your invisible Spiritual Self. Self-mastery is when you have merged the two and identify yourself as a Spiritual BEing in a physical body. It is when you use your gifts and talents infused in your energy fields for good in the Universe. You no longer only function at the levels of Self but more and more at the level of the Universe.

When you are Self-realized, you have mastered your energy flow, allowing life to respond to you. You no longer react to what is happening in the world around you. You can rise above it and realize it is all happening for you and others to grow and expand. You meet what is happening to you with love and joy because you know you're going on an adventure of further Self-discovery.

Self-realization occurs when you recognize that life is guiding you toward your Divine Purpose, one situation or growth opportunity at a time, on the journey of Self-discovery and Universal discovery.

Self-discovery and Self-realization indicate that the ego has no power over you any longer. You have let go of the past and live in the present moment.

We love you. We love you. We love you.

Question: What would my Ascended Masters have me know about being a Master of a Human Life?

Dear Beloved,

We would want you to know that you are empowered to live the life of your ultimate dreams. You have a connection to All That Is and the Void of all possibilities. You were created with Divine Creative abilities. You have access to all the resources; they are abundant. You have the capacity and ability to transmute energy into physical form with your thoughts, feelings, and beliefs, plus your actions. There is nothing you are not. There is nothing you can't do. You are the whole Universe. The Universe flows through you to use as you wish. You are constantly being renewed and revitalized with the energy of the torus that surrounds you and encases you with love, wisdom, joy, and peace.

All you must do is master your energy flow and be the director of where you focus your attention. Be the director or master of this flow to be your most empowered and masterful, complete and whole Self. Master your energy to guide your mind and thoughts to be aligned with your destiny—your Divine Purpose. Do not get sucked into the chaos and confusion of the 3D world. Rise above the clamor and din of the 3D world and focus your attention on the highest endeavors.

Master the Loving Presence within you and direct love to all around you— to your True Self, career, body, neighbors, acquaintances, and friends. Find the joy that already exists there.

Master your response to what is going on. Know, believe, and surrender—all that is happening for you. Embrace and bless all problems, obstacles, and experiences as they are leading you to become more and more masterful. You are invited to learn, grow, expand, and evolve as you go through the miraculous journey of life.

Be a master of finding the lesson in each of your wondrous experiences. Master gratitude as a response to all that you experience, as if everything represents another rung on the ladder of growing and ascending toward Self-mastery.

Master your life to live on your terms. Master your life to live in alignment with the Divine; visualize and sense your life through the eyes, mind, and heart of the Divine. Understand why your Divine Soul Energy constellation is what it is so that you can become your entelechy—become what your Divine Soul planned for you in this lifetime. Perceive your life and who you are from higher and higher vibrational frequencies.

All of this mastery will help you on your path to enlightenment.

We love you. We love you. We love you.

As we continue our journey of awakening to Self-mastery, we now turn toward enlightenment. We have a choice to come from our unlimited True Self or our limited physical self. We know of the Divine's Intention for us and how to thrive in the flow of the Universe to grow, evolve, and expand. We know that we, as physical beings, are inextricably connected to the Spiritual Realm. Even more, we now understand that the Spiritual and physical realms always work together.

We know we are expressions of the Divine. The Divine can only expand through our physical bodies and through our experiences and adventures in life. Evolution is only possible through us. For Consciousness to expand, we must expand, and the Divine must expand. We will explore the path to enlightenment in the next section.

EXERCISES

Use these exercises to become more connected to the Divine—to plug into the Divine at a deeper level and discover your truth and your wisdom around these concepts. I invite you to reach beyond the physical in these exercises to the Spiritual Realm and discover the truth and wisdom about yourself, your life, and where you are going in this life.

Exercise 1: Meditation and Journal Prompts

Use the following prompts for meditation and journaling for a deeper exploration of topics covered in this Section.

1. Tapping into Infinite Potential.

- When have you experienced the connection to your Divine Potential?
- When have you experienced your mind as the center of Divine Operation?
- When have you manifested something that you visualized beforehand?
- Ask for what you want or ask questions related to what you want:
  - What is important for me to understand right now about my Spiritual Journey?
  - How can I enhance my journey?
  - What is the next step for me to focus on?
  - What is my next growing edge?

2. Receiving Divine Messages.

- When have you asked for a message from the Divine and received one?
- What form was the message?
- How did you interpret the message?

3. Visualization Process.

The best time to visualize is when you wake up or right before you go to sleep. To feel more connected to the Divine, open a window and take 10 deep breaths. Imagine a circle of light around you. Visualize rays of light radiating from the circle, entering all aspects of your body, and concentrating in your solar plexus or torso. Hold your breath. Visualize the light going up and down your energetic core from your solar plexus. Imagine you are a conduit between the physical and Spiritual Realms.

1. Sit and reflect. Repeat affirmations such as these:

   - As an expression of the Divine, I am unlimited.
   - My mind operates in the Divine Mind.
   - I am creating a new potential for the Divine to experience life through me.

2. Then, start to meditate to get beyond the analytical mind.

   - If you aren't in a theta state, then do several rounds of deep breathing—inhale for six counts, hold for three counts, exhale for six counts, and hold for three counts to make sure the ego or your mind chatter doesn't interfere with your visualization.

3. Sit silently with your creative thoughts and allow yourself to enter the energy of what you want.

   - Enter a deeper place within you.
   - Slow down your brain waves by deep breathing to tap into another way of BEing and seeing. Be in the vibrational frequency of new possibilities.
   - Ask for what you want or ask questions related to your wants.
   - Listen for the answers as you stay open and receptive.
   - Be happy and joyful and have the highest vibrational frequency possible by your will, without struggle or effort; allow the process to be easy.

4. Be in the highest frame of mind and acknowledge that you are the center of Divine operation. Stay in uplifting and inspirational energy as often and as long as possible.

   - You can also state specifically what you want, especially in terms of how it will benefit you and others in being in flow with the Universe.
   - Imagine the new opportunities in front of you just waiting for you to pay attention to what the Divine intended for you. Whatever you can visualize is possible for you.
   - Do not doubt, worry, or sense that you don't deserve what you really want.

- Be clear on how this manifestation raises your vibrational frequency and contributes to the Universe.

5. Repeat the following affirmations until they feel true for you.

    - The life substance of the Universe finds Self-recognition and delight in me.
    - There is one Source, one substance.
    - There is one Creative Energy.
    - I am one with Source and Creative Energy.

6. Feel the feelings as if your visualization is a present fact in the present moment. Feel how grateful, joyful, and at peace you feel in this moment.

7. When you reach the height of joy and excitement, surrender the image to Universal Consciousness.

    - Have certainty - expect to get what you desire.
    - Do not expect your mental picture to manifest in a specific way. Allow the Creative Universe to figure out the best way. Trust that whatever you want will come to you easily and effortlessly—or something better.
    - Continue the visualization process for as long as your intuition feels right.

8. Overdoing the visualization may stem from a sense of lack or of not having, which promotes the need to continue the visualization repeatedly. Being in this state of need will surely block the manifestation.

9. Connect with the abundance of the Universe to provide you with this manifestation.

10. Be in the energy of what you want to create, expect it to come, and know that it will benefit more people than yourself.

11. Let go and trust.

Exercise 2: Improving or Developing New Relationships with Yourself and Others

1. Develop an improved relationship with yourself

The goal of this part of the exercise is to develop an awareness of the part of you that has been your constant companion on this Spiritual Journey. It is the aspect that has heard all your stories about who you are and what has happened in your life.

1. If you could describe that aspect of you, what would you say?

2. During your life, how aware have you been of this aspect of yourself that has journeyed with you and listened to your interpretations of what has happened in your life?

3. Becoming aware of that aspect of yourself now, can you develop a relationship with it?

4. Are you able to accept who you are from this aspect of yourself?

5. Are you able to extend unconditional love to yourself now?

6. Can you accept both the physical and Spiritual aspects of yourself?

7. Do you understand why your Soul chose *you* for this journey?

8. Do you understand why your Soul chose the challenges you've experienced for this journey?

2. Develop improved relationships with others

1. If you can accept yourself in this new light, you will likely also accept others. Describe ways you have witnessed or experienced this acceptance of others.

2. Have you been able to forgive someone whom you couldn't forgive before?

3. Has your judgment or criticism of yourself and others changed?

4. Can you now understand that others are wounded, and their Souls are working to help them heal these wounds?

3. Transformation and transcendence

1. Have you experienced shifts or blocks within you that have enabled you to change your perception of the world around you to be more positive? Describe these shifts and your new perceptions.

2. Are you more aware of and connected to the Divine Presence within you?

3. How has connecting to the Divine Presence within you changed your life?

Exercise 3: Healing Wounds in the Akashic Records

Three distinct stages of healing occur in the Akashic Records: the Story, the Causes and Conditions, and the Soul Truth. Under each stage, there is a list of questions to ask yourself to guide you to a resolution and get to know your Divine Soul.

Stage 1: The Story

What is happening now that is an issue in your life? Be specific. Include all details possible. In your description of what is happening, be clear and honest about your involvement.

- *What has been the experience for you?*
- *What has been your role in what is happening?*
- *How have you been affected by it?*

Stage 2: Causes and Conditions

Determine your knowledge and understanding of the situation. Determine the beliefs you have about the situation.

- *What are your thoughts and beliefs about the situation?*
- *What has been the cause of any difficulty you experienced arising from the situation?*
- *Why are you struggling in this situation?*

Make sense of what is happening in your situation. Is this related to or triggered by something in the past, either in this life or a past life?

Discover as much as possible. Try to obtain a resolution or even just a new understanding. The mind is more at ease when there is understanding.

Stage 3: Soul Truth about Ourselves

- *What is the truth about the situation from the Soul's perspective?*
- *What is the greatest opportunity for the Soul in this situation?*

The answers that come from these questions will help you discover the truth about yourself at the Soul level. Uncover the truth about your perfection, wholeness, and wellness.

Rise above the story, causes, and conditions, and view yourself from this higher perception of your unlimited and compassionate Soul.

- *What has your Soul learned from this experience?*
- *How has your Soul grown or expanded from this experience?*
- *Can you identify yourself as an infinite, loving Soul?*

Understand from this experience who you are now and who you have been through time.

Exercise 4: Activate the Torus

Here are three exercises that will enhance, cleanse, and activate your toric field. Engaging in these exercises will lead to inner strength and increased radiance while deepening your connection to Oneness.

A. Enliven Areas of Your Physical Body

1. Use your intuition to help move the energy in this exercise. The energy will follow your thoughts and intentions. Where your attention goes, the energy flows.

2. With your mind, internally scan your body and energy field to see if there are any weakened areas or any strong areas. Scan the back and front of your body. Scan the inside and the outside of your body.

3. Imagine inhaling from the soles of your feet into your heart.

4. Imagine inhaling one of the sacred geometry forms —the dodecahedron, Seed of Life, Fruit of Life, or the Merkaba—and brilliant golden liquid light into the soles of your feet and into your heart. You can inhale any symbol of positive or high vibrational frequency that specifically speaks to you.

5. Fill your entire body with golden liquid light and the sacred geometry image to shine through every inch of your skin, both the front and back of your body.

6. Focus on sending the sacred geometry image and golden liquid light to all the weakened areas or low energy areas, painful areas, or areas that are ill. If you feel tightness, soreness, or achiness anywhere, send the sacred geometry image and golden liquid light into those areas as well. Send the sacred geometry image and sparkling golden liquid light into the weakened areas noticed when you scanned your body. Fill your body with Divine golden liquid light to enhance your Essence.

7. Allow your brightness to sparkle and glow beyond your skin, strengthening your aura.

8. Notice and feel the energetic glow from within to without. Feel empowered. Think it, feel it, and it will be.

9. The energy flow in your physical body and energy body has been enlivened, as well as the toric field around you.

B. Tracing the Toric Field Flow

1. Start with deep, slow, intentional breathing in and out through your nose. Breathe to your core at the level of your pelvic floor. Breathe up and down your energetic core.

2. It is better to do this exercise sitting on the floor or standing. Keep up the deep breathing. As you inhale from the Earth, place the backs of your hands slightly together with your fingers pointing down and slowly trace up your central line as the breath rises through your body to your head. At the heart area, allow your fingers to invert slowly and point upward.

3. As your breath is at or above your head, exhale while slowly moving your hands around the outside of your body with the intention of completing a circle at your pelvic floor.

4. Sense the energy of the torus surrounding you as you move your hands slowly around your body in a circle back to your pelvic floor. The energy is subtle, but you can feel it in time. The sensation should get stronger with an increasing number of breaths.

5. Repeat the process of inhaling at your pelvic floor and moving your hands slowly as the breath slowly moves up the central line of your body. Exhale at or above your head. Repeat ten times or as many times as you can. It will feel empowering.

6. Feel the sensation of the enhancement of the toric field flow around your body. Memorize the feeling.

C. Life Force Ritual Process Activates the Toric Field

To meet the demands of our changing and challenging times, we must be mindful of maintaining a strong energy body and the need for energetic Spiritual adjustments to maintain our strength and radiance. Releasing the distortions in the torus around our bodies and around the Earth is an important practice for maintaining optimal Life Force.

The Life Force Ritual or prayer in movement can strengthen the torus. Relax and let your mind be free. Focus inward. The Life Force Ritual movement reflects the story of creation. Therefore, the Life Force Ritual process is an experience of the creation process.

1. Sit cross-legged on the floor and slowly bring both arms behind your back.

2. Slowly circle both arms forward again, crossing them in front of your body and extending your arms out from your body.

3. Then, bring your arms to the back again, and then in front of the heart area.

4. Create a circle around your heart center in your mind.

5. Cross your arms in front of your third eye chakra and around your head.

6. When your arms are at the side of your head, bring your hands together in a prayer pose with your fingers pointing toward your head.

7. Move your hands slowly down the front of the body, along the energetic core or center.

8. When you get to the navel in prayer pose, turn your hands to point your fingers down.

9. When you get back to your knee level again, repeat the process.

10. If you were doing this for the Earth, you would start at the South Pole, the perineum, then proceed to the equator, the heart area, and finally to the North Pole, the head.

11. Continue the process several times until you sense the energy pulsating around you.

12. Continue meditating to deepen your connection with the Divine. Feel the connection to the Oneness with all living beings.

13. Connect to the energy field around you and tune in to the magnificence of who you really are.

14. Then, from your pelvic floor, move your hands up the center of the body to guide the energy up into your field.

15. Make this movement into a circle, starting from the center of your body and moving up over your head. Then, move your arms out to your sides and back to the knee area.

16. Circle up around the center and outside of the body to strengthen the aura.

17. Continue repeating the movement until it becomes automatic.

18. Do not let your mind think about it; you are connecting to an intelligent energy field—the torus.

19. Then, contract your pelvic floor as you bring the energy up with your arms at your sides.

20. Then scoop up the energy, and when your hands meet in front of your body, move into a prayer pose in front of your heart.

21. Connect to your torus and realize it is the one torus of the whole Universe.

22. When you are finished, bend forward, holding your prayer pose, and then place your thumbs on your third eye chakra, located between your eyebrows. Take this energy into your day and your life.

Exercise 5: Activate the Merkaba

This exercise raises your vibrational frequency by focusing on the sacred geometry form of the Merkaba to help you tap into the unlimited potential of the Universe:

In a comfortable seated position, close your eyes and imagine the sounds of something peaceful and beautiful like a Tibetan singing bowl, the soft tinkling of wind chimes, the ebb and flow of ocean waves, the soft pattering of rain falling like love from the sky, the coo from a dove, or the wind as it rustles through the leaves. Sit with your eyes closed. Breathe deeply and slowly to slow down your brain waves and enter a meditative or theta state of BEing. Let go of any emotional stress with your deep breaths. Breathe deeply into your belly. Breathe in and out through your nose. Exhale longer than you inhale.

When you are ready, repeat an invocation to declare your truth out loud. Here are some inspiring invocations I use.

> *I am Love.*
> *I was created in Love.*
> *I feel love within me and surrounding me.*
> *I am one with Love Consciousness.*
> *I am one with the compassion of the Universe.*
> *I am Love.*
> *I am Divine Love.*

I am connected to Divine Love.
Divine Love flows to me and from me.
I extend love from me to all.
I extend Divine Love from me to all.
I am a conduit of love for the Universe.
I am one with the Divine.
I am Divine.

Exercise 6: *What if* Questions.

Your radiant imagination is a very useful tool for breaking through limiting thoughts, feelings, and beliefs. In this next exercise, imagine or accept that the concept is true for you in the moment you are performing this exercise. Be as authentic and as honest as you can to reap the rewards of the truth that you will be able to access. Allow expansion in your thinking and understanding of these concepts. Explore what's possible to create in your life with these new truths. You can meditate on these concepts and journal what you discover in meditation.

Meditate on one or more of these questions and tune in to the answers that come to you.

- *What if* I am more than I thought I was?
- *What if* I were more aware of my Spiritual Self? How would that change things for me?
- *What if* I could receive messages from the Spiritual Realm?
- *What if* I had access to a higher level of BEing?
- *What if* I had access to a higher potential within me?
- *What if* I could do exercises to strengthen my connection to the Divine?
- *What if* being more connected to the Divine makes life easier for me?
- *What if* I could heal wounds I've had since childhood? What would change for me?

Section Four

THE PATH OF ENLIGHTENMENT

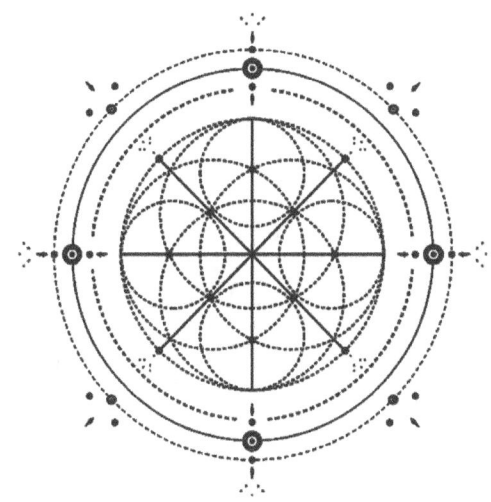

The Path of Enlightenment

As I travel this path,
Toward enlightenment, Self-discovery,
I feel YOUR presence and love.
I feel YOU holding my hand.

I feel YOU move in my heart.
A wave of joy from my crown,
To my feet and beyond.
Am I dissolving?

Don't know how to get to "Enlightenment."
Don't know where "Enlightenment" is.
But I live each day, learning, connecting, and growing.
To live in awe and wonder.

What is unfolding on my journey?
Is peace, wisdom, and joy.
There's so much more than dreamed.
There's so much more than witnessed.

I am more and more awake,
I am more and more part of Oneness.
I am delighting in this other Realm.
I am both physical and Invisible.

Both states helping one another.
Beyond the knowing,
Beyond the growing,
Beyond the physical dimensions of space.

With each step, I see YOU in people,
In nature, in Angel, my dog.
I know what lies ahead is beyond my wildest imagination.
Surrendering and trusting bring excitement.

I don't have to know where I'm going.
I must be present to the process.
Living in wonder and mystery brings me joy.
I am just BEing me.

I am just BEing me but expanded,
And expanding still . . .
Beyond where I've ever been.
Beyond physicality.

Expanding farther than imagination.
Further away from physicalness.
I see light and dancing energy,
Experiencing YOU as Divine Love.

I am completely connected to YOU.

~Anne M. Deatly

Now that we have gained the knowledge of our Infinite Potential, we are ready to embark on the penultimate phase of our Spiritual Journey. We are ready to understand that we are, and have always been, on a path of enlightenment, even if we haven't been consciously aware of it. When we travel forward on this path, awe-inspiring events will unfold before us. One might think of enlightenment as an ever-present light that can be turned on, illuminating a new way of BEing through the awareness of truth we couldn't see or understand before. We realize ourselves as en-lightened BEings filled with Divine Light existing in the physical realm.

We will explore various ways to understand what enlightenment means to us and how it is connected to our Divine Purpose. We have been gifted; we are meant to discover new meanings of enlightenment—specific to us in this lifetime. Ultimately, our goal in this part of our awakening is to deeply understand and embrace the concept of Oneness. BEing in Oneness, we learn to detach and absolutely surrender and be in non-resistance to our journey of growth, making us open to accept and trust the guidance from the Divine and Higher Self that is freely available to us. We are more tuned into the Divine Opportunities when invitations are presented to us.

We will understand that everything that has happened in our lives has happened for a reason and that it all matters. All our experiences are woven together as a beautiful tapestry that defines us and our lives. As we progress along our path of enlightenment, we begin to understand the miracles happening right before us every day and learn to become miracles for others. We realize we are more significant than we realized and can contribute to the overall highest good of the Oneness. Ultimately, we are invited to fully embrace our Divine Magnificence as enlightened BEings, radiating out the high vibrational frequency of our inner light and lifting the level of Consciousness for everyone and the Universe.

Enlightenment is Knowing our True Self

Enlightenment is viewed differently through a myriad of lenses—religious, philosophical, and Spiritual. However, regardless of one's perspective, all these views share a core belief that enlightenment is a state of Self-knowing and Self-mastery. Lao Tzu (sometimes spelled Lao Tsu or Laozi), an ancient Chinese philosopher and founder of Taoism, wrote in his classic Chinese text, the *Tao Te Ching*, that while getting to know others brings wisdom, getting to know ourselves brings enlightenment. However, understanding that there is no *other* is further down the road on a path to enlightenment. From this, we can understand the connection between enlightenment and knowing our True Self. We move into a more enlightened state by discovering, understanding, and believing the truth of the Divine Magnificence of our True Self.

In his book *Power versus Force: Hidden Determinants of Human Behavior,* Dr. David Hawkins placed enlightenment as the highest level of Consciousness with a value range of 700-1000 on his logarithmic scale. This is the broadest value range he assigns to any level of Consciousness shown on his Map of Consciousness, suggesting a tremendous depth of understanding to be discovered at this level of Consciousness.

The story of Siddhartha helps us understand that the path to enlightenment may be right in front of us. However, until we become aware of the path and pay attention to what it is illuminating for us, we are unable to discern its guiding light. In the classic book by Hermann Hesse, the story of Siddhartha follows his journey from being a wealthy Indian Brahmin to an ascetic who relinquishes all his possessions, choosing to live simply to develop and achieve Spiritual goals and finally reaching enlightenment as a fully realized Buddha. As an adept, Siddartha practiced strict self-denial and abstention from indulgences of life to help him find Spiritual Illumination, fulfillment, and wisdom.

During his wanderings, Siddhartha meets all kinds of different people, including Buddhist monks, successful business owners, other ascetics, a ferryman, and a courtesan, among others. He learns something from each one. Significantly, the ferryman helped him find enlightenment by studying the river. The river held the clues to Spiritual Illumination for Siddhartha. Listening to the river, Siddhartha discovered nature exists in a repeating and sustainable cycle of change, time is an illusion, and every individual carries the potential of their opposite. Therefore, the opposites co-exist, making the world complete and balanced. The river showed Siddhartha how to look at life differently, and Siddhartha was reborn. The river showed Siddhartha completeness, leading him to understand the Oneness of all things. Siddhartha learned how to connect more deeply to all living things—all life. Siddhartha realized that wisdom or enlightenment comes from within. In his fully realized, enlightened state, Siddhartha became the Buddha we are familiar with as a central figure in Buddhist traditions.

The concept of enlightenment is a primary focus of Spiritual Growth in Buddhism and Hinduism. In Buddhist philosophy, one can study the Eightfold Path to Enlightenment—right view, right intention, right speech, right action, right livelihood, right effort, right mindfulness, and right concentration—to overcome negative states of mind. Buddhist tradition describes the state of enlightenment as reaching the ultimate experience of nirvana, characterized by the absence of experiencing suffering, the egoic self, and attachment to desire. The attainment of this enlightened state releases one's mind from the karmic cycle of death and rebirth.

Hinduism focuses more on the emotional aspects of enlightenment, rather than the mental, through the concepts of Ananda and Sat Chit Ananda. Ananda means bliss, pure happiness, and Divine Joy for everyone and in everyone. Sat Chit Ananda translates to existence, Consciousness, and bliss. Encompassing all three concepts, Sat Chit Ananda is the enlightenment of Oneness and wholeness of all existence in terms of limitless conscious existence. If one experiences Sat Chit Ananda, one has reached the ultimate goal of their Spiritual Journey.

Enlightenment can also be interpreted as the dissolution of the ego, resulting in freedom. Enlightenment is when we feel we are not a body or a mind, but beyond a body or a mind. We are not separate from the Divine. We are Divine. We exist in the Oneness. We are part of Divine Love. *A Course in Miracles* explains enlightenment as a shift in perception from body identification to Spirit identification and from fear to love.

Enlightenment is also considered a state of being free from suffering. Suffering is a choice we do not have to experience. Aligning with the Divine more completely erases suffering in our lives. If we learn to surrender to Divine Will for our lives, we naturally let go of attachment to how our lives turn out. We trust that whatever the Divine has designed for us, we will be better off and have better outcomes in our lives. This knowing and trust frees us from the desperation of suffering.

Here are some further interpretations of the meaning and experience of enlightenment:

- We can experience enlightenment or know we are enlightened by mastering our minds, thoughts, feelings, and beliefs, and no longer being pulled by the guidance of our ego. We are in full awareness of being guided to move toward the best versions of ourselves--our true Divine Nature, our Divine Magnificence. We no longer resist the flow of the Universe. We accept and are grateful for what is happening since it is for our awakening, our enlightenment, and our discovery of our Divine Magnificence. Therefore, we embrace, rather than resist, all of life. We become overwhelmed with gratitude for all the new doors that open and the new opportunities that lie in the mysterious spaces beyond the doors.
- We are becoming increasingly aware of our Soul—who we really are. We realize we are beyond the physical body and the mind. We no longer fully identify with the physical body—we are moving toward primary identification with our Soul. With this awareness, we can "see" others as Divine Souls as well.
- We are happy regardless of whatever is happening around us. We experience inner peace and stillness. We are connected to the wisdom and Divine Presence. We know that love and understanding are the keys to a Soul-ful life. Love is really all there is at these higher vibrational frequencies of living. We begin to see every living BEing as love. We love all, and we feel love from all. Our hearts are open to all. There is a loving sense of BEing part of one loving humanity. All of us are here to help, support, and love each other in the Oneness.
- We practice gratitude, knowing this life is about opportunities for growth and expansion. We feel the inner expansion as we merge with the higher vibrational frequencies of the Universe.

- We slow down our pace of doing. We are more focused on BEing. We feel compassion for ourselves and others. We express ourselves through kindness—kind words, voices, tones, and actions.
- We take better care of ourselves in healthy, life-enhancing ways. We offer to help others in need. We volunteer. We extend our arms, reaching out to support others and share Divine Love.
- Our Spiritual enlightenment leads to the release of separation Consciousness and merging into Universal Consciousness, or Oneness. We experience Oneness with the Divine Presence within ourselves and others. We realize that everyone has a significant role in contributing to, enhancing, and expanding Oneness.
- There is nothing lacking or limiting in our understanding of enlightenment. Everything is provided for us as we learn, grow, and evolve.
- We experience life as one miracle unfolding from another. We witness the Divine in every aspect of life. We see how the Divine expresses love in even the smallest details and the tiniest creatures of life. Everything is an expression of Divine Intention. Everything is an expression of Divine Love.
- We see life as a miracle, and we are miracles for each other.

After my marital separation, I started listening to personal development courses in my car to and from work. I remember listening to Wayne Dyer and Deepak Chopra's Path to Enlightenment course one day. I remember one moment very clearly as if it had happened yesterday.

I said out loud, "That is what I want—to be on a path to enlightenment!" I exclaimed it. I boldly and confidently declared it.

Since I didn't know how to get myself on an enlightened path at that time, I didn't do anything consciously. I just waited, or actually forgot it, and let my life unfold. Recently, about 20 years or more after this declaration, I was preparing a program on letting go titled "Letting Go to Manifest Prosperity." I was reviewing David Hawkins' Clinically Proven Map of Consciousness and meditating on the highest level of Consciousness, which is enlightenment. I wanted to determine if there was a way to help people achieve this level through my course. Suddenly, the memory of that declaration I made years prior flashed in my mind.

Remembering my declaration made me realize I was on the path to enlightenment. I was being guided all along, and I was listening. I did not follow any specific steps or formula to be on this path. I had not followed a set of specific goals to make it happen. It mysteriously unfolded naturally. There was something way beyond me guiding me. I believe this is part of everyone's journey. The question is whether one is ready or open enough to follow the intuitive nudges. A corollary to this insight is that we can make declarations of what we want to have, do, or be. Let the Universe figure out how to unfold it with all its miracles for us.

In thinking about a path of enlightenment, I wrote out what it signifies to me to be enlightened based on my learning and practice of energy healing, personal healing, experiences, intuitive messages, and wisdom gained from books. From that, I curated ten steps for achieving enlightenment as a state of BEing in which we understand our Divine Nature, Divine Magnificence, Oneness, and see the world through the lens of Divine Love.

Ten Steps to Being on a Path of Enlightenment

1. Understanding that we are an energy or Spiritual BEing living in an energy Universe, everything is energy, and all aspects of life are transmitted through energy, a living, loving life force, or field.

2. Clearing energy blockages caused by stress, anxiety, emotional upset, and trauma. The goal is to raise our vibrational frequency to match what we really want and become a conduit for the flow of Divine Energy, helping the Divine expand to benefit the world and the Universe.

3. Understanding that we have chosen our life, our challenges, and obstacles, we are here to evolve our Soul, not *just* for our Soul, but for the Soul of the whole Universe.

4. Giving birth to our True Self and awakening to our Divine Mission and being of service, being light with love and compassion, giving

and receiving in equilibrium, and being non-resistant in flow with the Universe.

5. Letting go of the past of what is holding us back on our path of enlightenment to create and allow higher levels of Consciousness, dimensions, or higher vibrational frequencies or awareness to come into our energy field. Letting go of physical world problems or obstacles allows who we really are to emerge. We need not be held back in the present to move forward to make our unique impact. This step also includes letting go of the will to accumulate and climb the success ladder.

6. Understanding all challenges and obstacles are happening for us to learn, grow, and evolve our Soul. Be in gratitude for everything; even the challenges are gifts.

7. Understanding we are Divine Magnificence. We are as the Divine created us in love; that is unchangeable. We are to connect to that love, see that love in others, live from that love, and extend that love. Understanding our worth is determined only by how much we love and are loved. Release or dissolve all that is not love.

8. Seeing beyond the veil between the physical and Spiritual Realms and identifying ourselves with being an eternal Spirit in a physical body. We are much more than a physical body; we are one with our Soul. Seeing everyone and every living being as the Divine intended—seeing and witnessing our life and others from our Soul.

9. Surrendering and trusting Divine Guidance to embody our Higher Self, bringing Spiritual Realm principles into the physical realm. Being open to the invitations from the Universe in the form of new relationships, new opportunities, new events, and new circumstances to learn, grow, and evolve.

10. Aligning with the Divine and seeing the world around us through the eyes, heart, and mind of the Divine. Seeing everything as the Divine. Aligning with the Oneness of Universal Consciousness to provide an opportunity for the Divine to expand through us.

These ten steps are not necessarily followed in the same order for everyone. There is Divine Right Timing and Divine Right Order for each one of us. Everyone's awakening path is unique, based on their life mission and the lessons they need to learn in this lifetime. We are all being guided by our Higher Self, our Soul, even if we ignore it or dismiss the guidance. The Soul will keep communicating with us, offering new invitations for this awakening. The Soul does not give up on guiding us.

We have our Souls to guide us and a path to follow; we don't have to accept third-dimensional programming with its limitations, self-limiting beliefs, and misguided paradigms. We don't have to listen to our fear-based egos. We are meant to achieve at much higher levels with less stress and anxiety. We all have unlimited, Infinite Potential. Life is meant for joy, freedom, and growth.

If you aren't feeling joy and freedom, perhaps you would like to change that. Reading through the ten-step list, what resonates with you? What don't you resonate with? Are you satisfied with that way of BEing? Or are you ready to change? Ask yourself what step or steps are next on your path to enlightenment. Connecting to the possibility of this new opportunity will encourage situations that will enhance learning opportunities and foster growth.

> In my current practice, I meet people where they are and what they want in their lives. Most people don't realize there is so much more to life than the 3D earthly programming of success, wealth, and status, or even living pain-free. There is no judgment here. It is just an opportunity to open the door to a new way of perceiving and a new way of BEing. We have all been programmed a certain way from birth. In our social media-driven world, this programming is further emphasized. We can live an inspired life, not a reactive one or one focused on material possessions or success. It is a change of focus from doing, doing, doing, to just BEing. I am offering a way to change to a more enlightened perspective through my Divine Wisdom Moments and Higher Frequency Living videos on YouTube, which come from Divine Inspiration.

As we progress on the path toward deeper levels of enlightenment, we awaken to a misperception and want to change it. We experience personal healing in some way or another, realizing that our wounds or traumas were not meant to harm us but rather to help us grow and evolve. We may even understand that our Souls planned our traumas and our wounds to pave the way for Spiritual Growth in this lifetime. We may want to heal the energetic repercussions of continuing to hold onto our pains and traumas and free ourselves to move forward on our journey without these burdens.

Detachment, surrender, and non-resistance are natural next steps for further enlightenment. If we are no longer trying to control our circumstances but rather allowing Divine Guidance to show us the way, we are less likely to want a specific outcome. We can surrender to what is happening to us. We can embrace what is happening rather than resist it.

A natural trust of the Divine also takes root. We no longer need to control our circumstances or manipulate life to what our ego self thinks is best. We develop a new understanding that we don't have the big picture for our lives. As we let go and trust the Divine, we are free to accept the Divine Will and Divine Intention and realize abundance everywhere in our lives; whatever we need is and will be provided. There is no lack or limitation in the Universe—only in our minds and perceptions.

All of this awakens us to a newer or higher commitment to our Divine Purpose. We are more focused on higher levels of BEing and becoming. Divine Opportunities become clearer and more evident to us as we move forward in our growth and awakening. We become resilient to life's distractions and negativity. We no longer resonate with low vibrational frequencies, such as fear, anger, panic, worry, or everyday grief. We understand that the experiences of our lives are woven together in a beautiful tapestry to show how all aspects are important and meaningful for our growth. As we continue, we'll explore these concepts as a connected path guiding us toward deeper levels of enlightenment to reach our ultimate goal of knowing Oneness and BEing One with the Universe.

Healing on Our Journey

Healing is a part of our Spiritual Journey to enlightenment. Understanding our past experiences as stepping stones to enlightenment may help in the healing process. It was all meant to be; in fact, our Soul most likely chose our most difficult circumstances and traumas. Healing our past opens the door to a new future. By letting go of the past, we heal the scars and open up new opportunities by elevating our vibrational frequencies and level of Consciousness. Healing is a natural part of the path of enlightenment.

True healing requires healing of the mind, body, and Soul. In this holistic approach, the body expresses the energy of the mind, and the mind expresses the energy of the Soul. We heal the body through healing the mind. We heal the mind from the Soul. Therefore, healing the body and mind ultimately comes from the Soul.

Healing at the Soul level means that you understand you are primarily a Soul existing in a physical body. Healing at the Soul level means you have transcended beyond a wound of victimhood, brokenness, or shame. Our core Soul wounds can come from a single event or a series of seemingly insignificant yet still painful events. To heal, the Soul needs to come back to wholeness. The Soul must overcome the event, trauma, pain, circumstances, or beliefs to better align with the deeper truth. If you could perceive the trauma or wound in a new light as a catalyst to overcome a misperception in the physical realm, the event or trauma can actually help you connect to who you really are and achieve your Divine Purpose. Healing on all levels offers enlightenment, the truth, and wisdom of the Universe. Knowing this wisdom, you will know who you really are, your place in the Universe, and why you are here at this time. Healing at the Soul level is really what this whole book is about.

The key to healing starts with an intention to heal and be whole. Through her research on intention and the power of eight intention groups, Lynne McTaggart concluded that healing could occur when an intention is set. McTaggert used groups of eight people to conduct her research. Each group was asked to set a group intention to support a request for healing by one person in the group, be it a situation, ailment, relationship, or other problem. As a group, everyone, except that person, focused on the intention for the healing to occur by visualizing the recipient receiving the intention during a ten-minute period of focused attention. During this period, the recipient focuses on receiving the energy from the others. These experiments showed that most recipients felt an overwhelming sense of love and Oneness with the group, magnifying the power of the intention and transforming the recipient's troublesome situation.

> The number eight means infinity, limitlessness, and eternity. The figure 8 represents scalar energy that is present in the torus and throughout the Universe as a healing energy. I am so taken with this concept of the eight because this is a predominant energetic structure in our energy fields. Weaving a figure 8 in someone's field will strengthen their Celtic weave and aura energy systems. One

way energy practitioners release stuck energy in an energy body is through the figure 8. Personally, I believe the figure 8 is a symbol for balance in the world or your life.

It embraces or signifies what you give out to the world; you get back in equal proportions. I also view the figure 8 as the balance of giving and receiving, which needs to be in equilibrium. Recently, a friend sent me a picture of time-lapse photography showing the movement of the sun over the course of a year. The photos were taken weekly at the same time and place. The pattern of the sun's movement over a year created a figure 8. The 8 is a powerful symbol in nature as well as our energy fields, serving as a pattern for healing and creating a channel for healing in these Power of Eight groups. I enrolled in Lynne McTaggart's program, The Power of Eight Intention Masterclass, to experience the Oneness with people all over the world.

Whole and United with the Divine

The Divine intends for us to be whole and united within the Divine. When united with the Divine, our will becomes the Divine's Will. In truth, exerting our will over Divine Will is effectively fighting against ourselves, limiting our ability to heal because we do not truly understand that we are One with the Divine. Realizing this unity is essential to achieving complete healing.

A simple way to understand healing is to view disease and ailments as a way in which our body expresses separation from the Divine. Since our Soul is constantly guiding us toward alignment with the Divine, it manifests life experiences, such as physical or mental suffering, to signal that we are out of alignment. Every healing thought of wholeness or Oneness is a step toward resolving the misalignment through realizing the truth that we are One with the Divine and there is only one will—Divine Will.

The ego is the part of us that *seeks* separation and strives to exert its will, securing outcomes based on the belief in separation. If we let the ego enter our minds and control our thoughts, the power of the Divine is diminished; it is harder to hear the whispers of the Divine. Still, the Divine is with us as we go through life, waiting patiently for us to know and welcome Divine Will in our lives. The

Divine cannot do anything for us without an invitation or request. So, the real question comes down to *who you want to host as your co-creative guest—the Divine or the ego?* Healing and freedom come with choosing the Divine. Healing and freedom come from being in the light.

The Divine wants us to be healed and be our best. What the Divine wills for each of us is ours—but we have to accept it and want it. If we choose another path or allow the ego to control our lives, we will be in darkness, separated from our wholeness. We cannot understand wholeness if we are not whole. If we aren't united with the Divine, we are not whole.

Understanding wholeness also means understanding who we are in our Divine Magnificence. If there is any part of ourselves that we do not like, we are forgetting our Divine Nature and seeing ourselves through a filter without love. If we feel like a victim, broken, or shameful, we are not seeing ourselves as the Divine sees us. If we view ourselves differently from what the Divine intended, we are not united with the Divine's creation of us. We *can* believe in our unlimited potential. We can resonate with the unlimited aspect of ourselves. Any limits we impose on ourselves are not part of the Divine Will. Any blaming of ourselves or others is a sign that we are identifying with the ego. We can realign with the will of the Divine. Only we can put limits on ourselves. We are the only ones who can deprive ourselves of anything. This is a significant aspect of our awakening on the path to enlightenment. Our peace lies in understanding our potential to be limitless. Healing happens when we understand that we are disconnected from the Divine. Re-aligning with the Divine and Divine Will for our lives is healing.

The door to the Divine is never closed. But we can enter in wholeness and without condemnation or blame. We can accept that all are welcome. All are part of the Oneness. We are blessed if we radiate the truth and wisdom of the Divine and align with Divine Will. We are called to share this radiance with others.

Divine Opportunities

On our path to enlightenment, we become aware of how different life is meant to be according to the Universal Laws, enabling us to see opportunities that are already there. It is like the lens through which we view the world around us changes—a new window opens, a ray of sunlight highlights something new. When we bring light into our lives, darkness can't get in.

Opportunities arise from the vibrational frequency we transmit—based on our thoughts, feelings, and beliefs—attracting matching, like frequencies that manifest as an experience. Divine Opportunities, however, come from surrendering our personal will to Divine Will. Letting go of our will is necessary to see and reap the benefits of new opportunities. Our presence or vibrational frequency and commitment to letting go lead us to be the best versions of ourselves. Within us is the key to the door of awakening. Awakening is the portal to our unique path of enlightenment. We can choose to unlock the door of our highest potential or not. We can choose to listen to the resistance of our egos and not move forward. Or we can choose to unlock the door, see what's in front of us, and completely surrender and trust the Divine. New opportunities are available to us at a new level of Consciousness.

Sometimes, Divine Opportunities are disguised as negative experiences that ultimately provide a gateway to a meaningful lesson or open a path leading to fulfilling our Divine Mission. Once we release the idea of suffering or resistance to the negative experience, we can let go and relax into it as a perfect opportunity to open our eyes, enabling us to see things differently. What was unwanted and unpleasant becomes a blessing—jet fuel for our Spiritual journey.

This is why we need to trust the Universe, the Divine, or Source, or whatever name you want to use, to provide us with the opportunity. Trusting that the Universe is always conspiring for our highest and best good allows us the freedom to focus on moving forward rather than getting stopped and trapped in the cycle of suffering and negative thinking. The more we train our minds to see Divine Opportunities, the more we experience them, thereby furthering the expansion of our Consciousness and alignment with the Divine. It's a win-win situation as we align within ourselves; the Universe aligns with us. As we surrender and move into non-resistance, we are open to opportunities that we wouldn't have seen before.

If something shows up, it is meant for you. Wherever your attention goes, opportunity grows. Try not to pre-decide how an experience will be or that there aren't any more lessons to learn from a specific opportunity. Pre-deciding conceals opportunities and potentialities for growth. It helps to remember that if there wasn't anything more to be learned from a situation or experience, it wouldn't be appearing in your life. For example, you might think you won't get something new from a program or seminar you already attended. But we comprehend information and experiences in layers. We hear something once; we have an awakened connection to the meaning, or we learn something new. We hear the same program or seminar again, and the next layer of understanding pops up. We are blown away by a completely different level of interpretation or understanding.

The same thing happens with books. The best books have many layers of teachings. When we read a book, we only understand what we are ready to understand at that time. People talk themselves out of opportunities all the time based on a mistaken belief that there is nothing more to be gained. However, if we understand that everything appearing in our life has a benefit, we can be open and receptive to what opportunities might be present, such as a random page falling open when we pick up a book we have already read, revealing a significant message or insight. There is a wondrous world of opportunity when we are receptive to the Divine Invitation.

> During the initial lockdown of the COVID-19 pandemic, my in-person business closed. I started to work on people's energy systems remotely. A new door opened for me. I was able to learn as I worked with people. I taught some people how to do self-testing. With others, I learned how to connect to their energies and bring their energies into my physical space to be tested. Because I love to be physically present with my clients, I would never have added this option for them if it hadn't been for the pandemic. This opportunity enables me to assist people in other parts of the US and abroad. This opportunity also helped me channel messages from people's chakras during the clearing process. I call this Chakra Messaging. This opportunity came because I was open to new ways of working with my clients.

Our lives grow in the places where our energy is focused.

Detach from Personal Will and Goals

On the path of enlightenment, detachment from our will is key and part of the process of letting go of control and being open to the Divine Opportunities that show us the way to a better life—a better way of BEing. When you know you are Divine, you see the illusions of the third-dimensional Earth programming and detach more easily from experiencing life through the lens of these illusions.

You can create from your True Self or Divine Self rather than your ego. You are aligned and want to co-create with Divine Will within.

We realize that in order to express ourselves as the Divine, we will have to think like the Divine. We express at a higher level of Consciousness and create for the benefit of others beyond the consciousness of fear, lack, and limitation in the physical realm. Competing with others and climbing corporate ladders will be seen as a far cry from an expression of Divine Will.

What will bring out your Higher Self?

What is your specific Divine Mission to accomplish?

We may already know our Divine Mission as we're being guided to do it—especially if we're on the path of enlightenment. We will have an energetic resonance with whatever that something is. We might want to pay attention to how we react emotionally to different opportunities, people, situations, or events. Our Divine Guidance system will be nudging us in a particular direction. Our Divine Guidance system may be showing us a completely different path from what we are currently experiencing. Focus on these nudges or messages. Detach from the ego.

If we understand our connection to the Spiritual Realm, we will understand the Divine Guidance system. There is so much support for us and our journey—we can't possibly imagine. But that is the truth. Sometimes, it takes a lifetime to realize that a whole support system is ready, willing, and able to help us with whatever we need—whenever we need it. We are inextricably connected to the Spiritual Realm. We might as well learn this concept as soon as possible!

The closer we come to Self-actualizing, the better it is for us, the Spiritual Realm, the Divine, Consciousness, and the Universe—although I just listed five different concepts of the Divine, they are all one! We can learn to detach from our earthly goals and go in the direction of the Divine Guidance system. We can surrender and trust in this new understanding.

Resilience, Self-Awareness, and Inner Strength

Developing resilience is another area of growth on our path of enlightenment. Resilience is the ability to live as we are in the moment and not get pushed off course by getting entangled in physical realm drama. We are focused on what is most important and essential to our Spiritual Realm journey. Resilience is Self-awareness. It's the ability to bounce back by knowing ourselves and our strengths and using that to move through life, especially when things are not going well, trusting that everything is happening for our highest good. Resilience is the ability to remain at peace even under the pressure of trauma, emotional upset, or crisis. Resilience comes with unwavering strength within our Inner Essence. Resilience helps us move toward our Divine Mission, goals, and life purpose. Resilience focuses on the positive potential and learning opportunities presented through life experiences.

Developing resilience is key to developing a sense of optimism. If we are not optimistic about our ability to successfully handle problems, it's unlikely we hold a positive outlook for our future, since life is filled with challenges. Many of my clients are filled with anxiety, constantly anticipating the next problem and unsure of their ability to work through it. Because of this, helping people develop resilience is a goal in my energy medicine practice. When a client's energy field is out of balance, we work together to correct the energy flow; however, the natural tendency is for the energy flow to return to its prior habituated state of imbalance. To retrain the balanced flow of energy, my clients continue the corrective measures at home, re-enforcing the new pattern of flow.

The goal of an energy medicine practitioner is to optimize all energy systems to support the health, vitality, vibrancy, and resilience of the individual. Sometimes, a correction will be sustained after just one session. Other times, it takes several weeks to establish a sustainable correction, depending on how long the energy was blocked or disconnected. This is due to the interrelatedness of the various energy fields in our energy body. As adjustments are made to one pattern of flow, it can affect other energy systems that also have to adapt to the correction. All nine energy systems must be coordinated to support the correction, which means that some of the other systems may also need to change their flow to adapt. It is like a dance of energy! Once the new energy flow is constant, it has reached a resilient state and will hold that pattern in a manner that best serves the client.

Radiant Circuits and Resilience

The ten radiant circuits help with developing resilience in the body. The radiant circuits act as reservoirs of energy, serving as a backup system to supply energy to energy-depleted systems or to reconnect energies that have been disconnected. The radiant circuits can jump anywhere, like hyperlinks, to form a circuit or bridge between disconnected energies. They possess exceptional intelligence to *know* where to go and how to help the systems flow better together. The radiant circuits are known to enhance health, vitality, and strength. For our discussion here, they also help to establish resilience within the energy body due to their unique capabilities.

> In my practice, I experienced what I might call a miracle healing, where my work to correct an imbalance related to eight years of back pain resolved in one session. This client was in a car that was hit from behind by a truck. Her back pain had been constant since that accident. She had been a personal trainer but had to change careers because she could not stand for long periods of time due to the pain. She became a health coach. During the energy session with me, eight years after the accident, I realized that fear energy was stuck in her kidney organs. What I did was imagine being in a car and getting hit by a truck. I felt fear. When the kidney meridian is imbalanced or depleted, it holds the energy of fear and hopelessness. First, I balanced the kidney meridian, the energy that governs the energy of the kidney organs, but the back pain persisted. The fear energy stuck in her kidney organs was the core issue of her back pain. It was an emotional imbalance of fear that had gotten stuck in her kidney organs from the actual moment of the accident. I simply removed the fear from her kidney organs. I also cut the energetic cords of fear to her kidneys. This treatment was different than the other ways to treat back pain. That client walked out of my healing space without any pain—the first time in eight years.

Other clients have had emotional issues stuck in different organs, but most of the time, it takes more than one session to remove the emotional imbalance. The correction takes longer to bring lasting relief because there is an entanglement of multiple energy imbalances—not just one.

Being completely free of the energy imbalance is another way to understand resilience. When energy sustains an optimal flow, it supports the organs to function optimally, resulting in a higher state of wellness, health, vitality, and resilience. This resilience in our energy fields enables us to be resilient in our lives. When we are resilient in our energy fields, we feel stronger internally. We are more aligned with our True Self. We can follow our own intuition, desires, and purpose. We don't doubt ourselves or think that someone else knows what is best for us. We are aligned with what is best for us.

When not resilient, we often try to please others by being what they want us to be. We are trained from a young age to follow the advice of our authorities: parents, grandparents, teachers, coaches, and clergy. We often do what someone else wants us to do to gain approval or avoid conflict. When we do this, we are really living someone else's life. We are giving our power away. We are not living our own lives. We are not living from our Inner Essence. But really, no one knows what is best for us but us. No one can make decisions for us—they don't have the inner knowing or intuition that we have. At some point, we will see clearly how we are misaligned within our lives. This misalignment could result in lack of trust, lack of belief, and lack of faith in ourselves. We might even think we are a failure at what we are trying to do. The truth is that we are created to possess specific gifts or talents that enable us to live out our purpose. We are not prepared, talent-wise, to live someone else's purpose. But no one has the right to impose their wants and desires on our lives. No one else has the wisdom of what our Divine Purpose is but our Soul. Inner strength, resilience, and the optimal flow of energy support alignment with our true life and purpose.

The key is to follow our own guidance or intuition to live according to what is most natural and life-giving for us. That is really living what we came here to do. That is when we can live at higher vibrational frequencies. That is when we can be true to ourselves. That is when we can more easily connect to the Divine. That is when we can align with our True Selves and accomplish our Divine Mission. We can learn the lessons we need to grow and evolve our Souls.

Let's be ourselves if nothing else. Let's be who we really are. The best you *is* the real you. Let's learn our lessons and grow the way we are meant to grow. No one knows our secret thoughts, our knowing, and our desires. Knowing who we are and focusing on our innate mission is being on a path of enlightenment.

It is freedom to live our own lives and make our own decisions in alignment with the Divine. Living our own lives brings about peace and contentment, even in the face of problems. The problems are meant to help us learn something new. Learning something new helps us grow. Growing helps us evolve our Souls. Evolving our Souls is the ultimate goal for our lives. We can't evolve our Souls unless we are on a Spiritual Journey of our Soul's choosing. We need to learn *our* lessons. We need to find a way out of *our* problems and challenges. We need to develop *our* inner strength to enable us to know we can handle anything that comes our way. Resilience is key to being on our path of enlightenment.

Experiencing Abundance

On the path of enlightenment, we also discover that the Universe is abundant. Everything we need on our aligned path is provided to us by attracting or manifesting what we need on our journey. We are always manifesting or attracting—we just don't realize it. In my book, *Journey to True Self*, I reveal the truth that we can manifest anything we want in life.

Remember the Universal Law of Perpetual Transmutation of Energy? Whatever we can think of, we can have. If we have the desire, it is already here for us in our energy fields. It is one of the haze of possibilities. We can't have a desire if it isn't available to us.

Do you understand how this concept makes the Universe abundant?

Matching the vibrational frequency of what we want may be the hard part. We actually must be what we want to manifest before we can manifest it. What I mean is that we must be in the spirit or the energy of what we want before we can manifest it. We must be at the vibrational frequency of it and think and act from that vibrational frequency. Being aware of our higher vibrational frequency or level of Consciousness helps us to manifest the next steps on the path of enlightenment and achieve mastery of who we are on this journey.

When we don't get what we want, karma may be blocking our manifestation. For example, it's possible to inherit a lack mentality and poverty consciousness karma—the opposite of abundance mentality—from our ancestors, even ancestors we never even knew. When we view the world through the lens of lack and limitation, we cannot see the world as abundant. It is just not possible to see abundance through a scarcity lens.

> I went to a healer once several years ago and discovered that I inherited poverty consciousness from a grandmother eight generations ago. This poverty consciousness existed through the family lineage for all these generations. I thought it was a good

time to clear that karma from my energy field and from all my ancestors and descendants!

Seeing and experiencing the abundance of the Universe can be especially challenging when we look at it through the lens of a bank account balance that doesn't match our sense of abundance. It is hard to surrender and trust that the Universe will bring us more money or more of what we want when our bank account balance doesn't reflect that. But viewing money from a position of lack only creates more lack. We create through the energy of need or perhaps even desperation in not having enough, which most certainly blocks abundance from flowing freely into our lives.

Money is just a form of energy that is neither inherently abundant nor lacking. Seeing it as representing lack suggests that we view life through the lens of lack in other aspects—especially in ourselves. To turn this around, we can train ourselves not to use a bank account balance as the sole indicator of lack or abundance in our lives, understanding that abundance in the Universe goes beyond the physical presence of money. Instead, focus on what we want in terms of how we would use the money to make a positive difference in our lives and the world. Trust the Universe to bring that to us—perhaps through money or some other way.

> Some years ago, I sold the home where I raised my children at the 510 street address mentioned previously. It was time for me to leave. I needed to be in a home that was better suited to my needs. I wanted to be on a body of water. At the time, I thought I couldn't afford something near the water in my area. Then, one day, I heard about a community called Lakeside and decided to check it out. I saw some places that were for sale, but they were not on the lake. I decided not to settle for less. What is the point of having a burning desire for something and accepting less than that? I asked the realtor who lived in the community if there were homes for sale near the lake. She responded that those places never come on the market. I told her, "I am in no rush." I rented a townhome for a few years to take time to find something perfect for me. Within the next week, she called to tell me she found a place for me on the lake. The homeowners were even going to leave the furniture! It was not going on the market and could be mine if I wanted it and agreed to the price. Everything worked out when I detached from trying to

get the home and stepped into a vibrational frequency aligned with that outcome. I took that as the Universe letting me know I could have whatever I wanted with a bonus! The Universe is abundant! This experience demonstrated how easily this manifestation could be achieved by utilizing the enlightenment tool of detachment and believing in abundance.

A New Level of Commitment to Our Purpose

Understanding that we are on a path of enlightenment provides an opportunity to step into a higher level of commitment to our Divine Mission and life purposes. When we are on the verge of something great and miraculous, we are invited to step into a higher standard of commitment and move with the opportunities showing up for us. This level of commitment can be shown in lots of ways. Sometimes, we have to say yes to an opportunity just because it's there, even if it doesn't seem to align with our burning desire.

Some opportunities are presented just to put us in a better alignment or position for the next, even bigger opportunity to arise, and our commitment comes in surrendering to these shifts, trusting that it will lead to what is most beneficial on our path. It may be saying yes to a small, seemingly random opportunity that leads to a breakthrough. We never know what an opportunity will open for us when we show up and say yes! The Universe or the Divine knows the best way to bring us to our next step or growth opportunity, often in unexpected ways.

This is not to say that we can simply wait around for the Universe to bring us our desires, even though it sometimes seems to happen that way. The Universe wants to know that we are all in for manifesting our burning desires; it conspires with us rather than creating for us. Taking action toward our desires creates momentum energy, shows our commitment, and attracts the Universe to support us. Putting our hearts and Souls into what shows up is also part of the surrendering process and is an act of trusting the Divine, knowing that whatever shows up is the right thing for us at that time.

The key is expecting a door to appear for us in every situation and opportunity. It is our choice to open it and walk through it to experience the opportunity without doubt or reservation. Not doubting and not questioning demonstrates a high level of commitment.

For example, we don't want to preclude opportunities for growth or abundance that may be available to us by engaging in these types of thought processes or actions:

- Pre-deciding how or what the Divine is going to give us.
- Micro-managing our manifestations in the way we want them to come to us.
- Putting limitations or lower expectations than what the Divine has planned for us.

We can only see or understand as far as our current level of awareness. Sometimes, we won't see an opportunity until we have grown into it. Even if we can't see the visible signs of an opportunity, it doesn't mean it isn't there. If we are on the verge of a quantum breakthrough, we will likely get stalled at some point. This may be because there is something important we need to learn or SEE in an opportunity that is a bridge to the greater breakthrough. Sometimes, we are looking in the wrong places for opportunities.

A good example of detaching from preconceived ideas and following the invitations that are unfolding is found in an article called "Acre of Diamonds" by Earl Nightingale. The article tells the story of a South African farmer who wanted to enter the diamond business and sold his property to purchase land in another area that appeared more promising for diamond production. But the property he sold turned out to have acres of diamonds and became one of Africa's most productive diamond mines. Of course, the moral of the story is to look for what we are searching for right where we are. There may be acres of diamonds waiting for us that we just can't see until we open up to the possibility of life's miracles.

Whatever opportunity appears on your path, big or small, has a purpose that leads you further along the path of enlightenment. Whatever the gift of the opportunity, see it, even if it's just a test of your level of commitment, and embrace it. Be ALL in. One hundred percent commitment needs to be transmitted in every cell of our being. Great opportunities can arise and do arise in smaller ones. Do not pre-decide or pre-judge where the opportunity resides. What shows up in our lives is the opportunity, the invitation from the Divine.

To make sure the Universe, the Divine, and your Higher Self are aware of your intention and commitment, you can write a heartfelt letter explaining how you perceive the opportunity and your commitment to embracing it to support your Soul Growth. This transmits your intentional energy to the Universe; then, you continually show up to receive what is in the highest alignment with your path.

Go through the open doors available to you without doubt or confusion. Just do it. Reap the rewards. Be in the attitude of expecting things to show up, knowing everything has already been lined up for you to receive, but may be in energetic form until the Divine timing is right. Don't lose patience or limit possibilities because the timing isn't what you expected.

Being committed to the Divine timing of opportunities in our lives also benefits others. On the path of enlightenment, what helps us personally or professionally also helps the Universe. From this perspective, opportunities also appear to show us how we can contribute to improving the lives of others.

Very often, it may be necessary to let go of something in order to align with a door to opportunity and walk through it. If you see an opportunity but aren't sure it's right for you, you can ask yourself what needs to be left behind to open this new door.

> *Little doors of opportunities open to greatness and magnificence.*
> *Do everything with greatness.*

Be inspired on your path of enlightenment. Feel the energy flowing within you in an energized way. Whatever comes before you, perform at your highest level without concern for personal gain. Treat what shows up as a gift—an invitation or recommendation from the Divine. This is the highest level of commitment to our purpose. The more preposterous the offer or invitation appears to us in the physical realm, the more likely it is that the Divine is holding out an Invisible hand to help us step into an entirely different world: a path of enlightenment.

> There was a time during the pandemic when I was focused on opening a new door of opportunity. When I started meditating on this, my clothes closet door magically locked me out all on its own. The door didn't have a key lock; it just had an ordinary doorknob that jammed. For about a year, I tried all kinds of ways to open the door, but nothing worked. The whole time, I couldn't wear my clothes inside the closet. Gradually, I shifted my focus from my desire for a new open door to appear in my life to what opportunity the closed door might hold. I spent time meditating on the lesson in the closed door and received a message that I wasn't ready for my next open door yet.

Once I understood that, I opened the door with a crowbar in less than five minutes. For a year or more, I was in a closed-door problem, not an open-door solution. I couldn't see how to solve the problem, and I wasn't ready for an open door. I realized that the Universe wants to know that we are all in for manifesting our burning desires, and I wasn't there yet. I wasn't able to see a simple solution to open my own door, so how could the Universe open one for me? I needed to learn a new lesson before the closet door, and a door of opportunity would open. We can't force things to happen when the timing isn't right. I also think this story is a great example of how what's happening in our external world is so attuned to our inner world.

Trusting the Divine

With a new level of commitment on our path of enlightenment, trusting the Divine is essential for optimal growth. At a Spiritual book group meeting, I was introduced to Brian McLaren's book *Faith After Doubt: Why Your Beliefs Stopped Working and What to Do About It*. When the discussion turned to the chapter "Doubt as Doorway," McLaren explained that doubt can act like a doorway into a more mature and honest faith. In my Spiritual Transformation, metaphoric doorways had certainly opened for me, providing new opportunities. However, in the context of the group discussion about faith and doubt, I wondered:

Does doubt offer the same doorway to opportunity as faith does?

On some level, doubt helps us grow and evolve by prompting questioning to get clarity, revealing deeper levels of truth. Doubt can help us develop the intellect and wisdom to experience the truth. A period of distrust can lead to real trust. However, doubt can also block us from allowing life's truths to emerge, eroding our trust in our inner knowing and our ability to align with the Divine. The energy of doubt radiates out to create doubt in others. Self-doubt—*I don't deserve, I am unworthy, I am not good enough*—is a type of self-limiting belief that interferes with accepting and receiving the truth about who we really are. Adding doubt to a visualization creates an overlay that distorts the original image, detracting from its energetic clarity for manifestation.

Ultimately, we need to grow beyond doubt to find trust. In our growth toward trusting the Divine, perhaps we need to ask questions and experience actual situations to realize the Divine can be trusted. We may have grown up believing in our insignificance or been programmed to believe that we're not worthy and, most certainly, not Divine. We may even hold strong doubts that we are worthy to be acknowledged by the Divine. We have been misled in concepts of who we really are. But we can start to trust and believe in our magnificence where we are. We can learn to believe that we are worthy of Divine Love, opening up to a new and revitalized connection to the Divine.

If we don't have a relationship with the Divine, how can we trust the Divine?

> At some low points of my Spiritual Journey, I had serious doubts, but I was open to change and seeking the change. Several quantum breakthroughs were accessed first through doorways to less-than-ideal experiences. Both were major losses for me, and I experienced significant doubt. But the doubt wasn't sustainable. One breakthrough came from my divorce, and the other one came from Mike's passing. These doors opened to long, dark tunnels of grief. The breakthroughs were disguised; the events were not uplifting times for me and didn't look like Spiritual Transformation opportunities. I had to let go of a lot of negativity and distrust. But with time and growth within me, I broke through the darkness to see the light at the end of these tunnels. I had to grow first to achieve the breakthrough. I had to stretch into a new way of BEing to achieve the breakthrough and Spiritual Transformation. These experiences helped me develop a deep relationship with the Divine and to trust the Divine completely.

As we progress on the path of enlightenment, we learn to embrace ALL our experiences as golden opportunities offered to help us accept our Divinity and magnificence. If we understand the flow of the Universe, we know we attract what we need as the next step of our Spiritual Journey. There is always the possibility for misperception about the significance or purpose of our experiences but facing them with trust and knowing that the Universe is always conspiring with us for our highest good provides a doorway to see the opportunity for growth within them.

Following pathways for our Spiritual Journey that are filled with uncertainty and risk represents opportunities to develop a deeper trust. When we trust the Divine, we're able to take risks and go beyond the first three basic needs of:

- Love and connection.
- Safety and security.
- Significance and self-esteem.

Advancing to this level of connection and trust helps us get out of being trapped in repeating cycles of survival-based living and express who we truly are at our core. We can let go of patterns and ideas that are not aligned with our higher expression and trust that our journey will unfold for our highest growth and good. Trusting that even the unexpected, unwanted, or unpleasant situations hold within them opportunities aligned with our true path, we are ready to receive the gifts of our journey—the pearls of wisdom unique to our life lessons. We move into trust, fully embracing our Divine Plan and Purpose.

Trusting the Divine connects us with our Innate Wisdom, recognizing that we are part of something far greater than ourselves. This awareness allows us to understand that our True Self is guiding us forward into the unknown, leading us along a life path that we co-created. We hold no grievances towards ourselves or others, knowing that we are all a perfect Divine Creation of pure love, expressed as the Divine Incarnate.

An important aspect of trust in our Divine Purpose is allowing ourselves to experience what brings us joy and happiness. This is an integral part of BEing one with the Divine. If we aren't doing what we enjoy and are good at, we aren't using our gifts; we're not aligned with our Divine Soul Blueprint. Being in alignment with our Divine Purpose is inherent in trusting the Divine. This deep trust indicates our growth toward enlightenment.

Surrendering to Discover the True Path

On our journey of aligning with the Divine, we are asked to step up to a higher level of BEing and focus our attention on the Spiritual Realm paradigms of living. We are invited to surrender to higher ways of BEing and doing from a Spiritual Realm perspective and release what no longer supports our growth. New doors will open, providing us with challenges that allow us to grow into a new way of BEing that is more aligned with the Divine. Sometimes, we need to blindly follow the Invisible Force calling us to walk through that door and into the unknown. That is the epitome of surrender.

Since we don't know where this doorway or the path behind it may lead us, we don't really know or understand how to prepare. Actually, it transcends our present comprehension, as we haven't been there before, and there is no precedent or previous experience to help us. It might even feel or look like we are being removed from everything we thought was true. That's key to its significance. The Invisible Life Force knows more about where we need to go than our physical selves do.

> For me, when my life completely shifted course, it was the opposite of the pathway I had been traveling for decades. But the flow of life picked me up and dropped me into this new life and a new way of BEing. There was no precedent for me to be in this new direction. Everything was unknown, and the path was uncharted. Somewhere deep in my Soul, however, I knew this was the right place for me to be. For perhaps the first time in my life, I knew that wherever I was headed, I was going home. I did not resist. I accepted that wherever this new path took me, it was for my best and highest good. I surrendered and trusted the Invisible Force to carry me in a new direction at the exact perfect time. My children were finished with college and ready to launch into their independence and be on their own journey. I had the independence and freedom to launch into a whole new adventure.

Surrendering to the Divine Guidance system, the Invisible Life Force allows us to trust that everything is happening for our best and highest good. Surrendering to Divine Guidance requires surrendering the false self to the True Self, which serves as the conduit for our connection to the Divine. The True Self, Soul, Higher Self, Eternal Self, Divine Self, Energy Body, or Life Force Energy—whatever you may choose to call this aspect of Self—represents the highest version of ourselves that is connected to Divine Wisdom, giving us access to our unlimited power and intelligence. Guided by love, the True Self is the loving, peaceful, confident, fulfilled aspect of Self that supports and directs us in accomplishing our Divine Purpose. Creative, limitless, present, and knowing, the True Self is like a guiding light illuminating our path of enlightenment.

Guided by fear, the false self—ego is insecure, fearful, and expects the worst to happen. The false self is stuck in the past and views life through the lens of victimhood, brokenness, or shame, masking our highest potential for making positive contributions to the world. It sees problems as external circumstances rather than an internal journey. It represents contraction, restriction, and limitation that give rise to feelings of guilt, shame, and self-doubt that block us from accomplishing our Divine Purpose.

Once we shed the false self, we can literally fall into the True Self or the Divine. Aligning with our Soul—the pure Divine aspect of ourselves—transcends all understanding, even if we have been influenced by the false self our whole lives. We can learn and know ourselves as our True Self, our Soul.

> A significant experience of surrendering and trusting for me occurred several years ago when I was traveling in Greece with friends. On the last excursion, I fell, injuring my left knee. I hobbled to a nearby medical clinic, where a doctor determined that nothing was broken, prescribed medications for the swelling, and recommended I get an MRI. With crutches, I was able to get back to the tour bus to Athens with three minutes to spare. We were scheduled to fly from Athens back to the United States the next day.
>
> When the tour guide saw my injury, he suggested that I go to a private hospital near Athens to get an MRI before getting on the plane. The following day, a friend and I went to the hospital emergency room. An X-ray showed a clean break in the patella bone of my left knee. The ER doctor told me it would be very dangerous for me to fly back to the US because there was a high risk of blood clots with this type of injury. He told me that to fly that day, I would have to sign a form stating I would take full responsibility for anything that happened to me during the flight.
>
> The prospect of a blood clot while traveling rattled me enough to stay and undergo a knee operation the following day. I had no way of evaluating the hospital or doctors. I had to surrender and trust. My friend offered to stay, but I encouraged her to travel home as planned. It was hard for me to say goodbye, but this journey was one I had to do on my own.
>
> When I woke from the operation, I saw that my left leg was wrapped with layers and layers of gauze, making it twice its normal

size. I was a little freaked out by this and realized I could not put on the clothes in my luggage. I would have to figure something out to deal with that. I was in the hospital for sixteen days due to complications related to my blood oxygen levels. I can't really speak to the specifics of my treatments or care because the medical staff did not tell me what they were doing or why, largely due to the language barrier. The doctors did not find the reason for my low oxygen levels. I just continued to surrender and trust.

Coordinating my flight home was its own challenge. Eventually, my insurance company provided an ER nurse with the necessary medical equipment to administer oxygen to me during the long flight back to the US. After we arrived, the ER nurse helped me get checked into the US. hospital. Apparently, my lesson in surrender and trust was not quite over, as I had to spend another two nights in a hospital before I was cleared to go home. My blood oxygen levels returned to normal with the use of a simple spirometer.

When I let go and detached from the outcome, all kinds of opportunities for lessons came to me. I had to learn how to speak up for myself and my needs. I had to learn how to tolerate screams of pain from my hospital roommates. I had to learn how to sleep and relax through the commotion of my roommates' families. I had to learn to see through the lens of my heart.

I share this story because earlier that year, I had decided to intentionally work on surrendering and trusting Universal flow in my life! I wanted to learn how to let go of what I thought I wanted so that I could more fully align with my Divine Purpose and Divine Will. A day or two after the knee operation, I woke up laughing out loud, realizing that I had attracted this situation to test myself and see if I could truly surrender and trust that everything was happening for my best and highest good. For me, it was not enough to simply claim my intention to surrender and trust; I needed to create an opportunity to make a real commitment and follow through on it. What better way to determine if I could surrender and trust than being at the mercy of doctors and nurses in a foreign country where I couldn't speak or read the language? I was very grateful for this opportunity to discern if I could truly surrender and trust.

When we are on a specific part of our journey, we attract situations to help us grow and learn what we need at that point. If we don't surrender and trust, we might lose valuable time on our journey. I could have totally wasted the time I had in the hospital if I hadn't understood that it was happening for my greatest good. Knowing that everything is happening for our best and highest good also means that we don't have to get wrapped up in negative emotions or trauma and can bypass the drama of all that!

> Although I didn't realize it at the time, my path of developing surrender and trust began well before my hospitalization in Greece. Perhaps the first time this path came into my awareness was when my body shook after I read the program announcement of Donna Eden's workshop in New York City. As a critical thinker, the last thing that I trusted was a modality that used a faceted clear crystal! But if my body was shaking as an insistence sign urging me to attend the workshop, I surrendered and went. I was curious to see what would happen if I listened to my shaking body and learn why my body was giving me such a strong message to attend the workshop. Ultimately, the workshop proved to be a pivotal turning point in my life, leading me to embark on an entirely new career path in energy medicine.
>
> I let go of a fulfilling position with great benefits at a major pharmaceutical company to venture into uncharted territory and start my own business, performing energy healing on whoever would show up. During the transition, I meditated regularly, losing myself in deep states of peace and ease. I was learning to plug more deeply into the truth of me. I was learning how to plug into the Divine. I wanted to meditate all the time. Since I had no idea how to start a business, I surrendered to being led by insights that came during my meditative states.
>
> As it turned out, nothing about how I was starting and doing my business was conventional. Business coaches did not understand what I was trying to do. They tried to fit my business into their business models. None of it worked for me or my business because I didn't own a traditional business. I figured out a better business model for me and my clients. The model evolved slowly over time.

Non-resistance: Letting Go to Be in Flow

Surrendering also requires that we move through life in a state of non-resistance. At first blush, this may seem obvious, but closer examination reveals a contradiction to our normal way of thinking, which draws our focus to resistance rather than acceptance. Fearing the worst, we tend to direct our attention to all that could go wrong and try to control the outcome. But, for the most part, all this does is give power to the negative energy of fear, feeding the possibility of a worst-case outcome, now or later. Even though we think we avert harm by resisting what appears to be arising as a potentially unpleasant experience, the energy of what we are resisting can stay with us like a shadow we are vaguely aware of but can't quite make out. Our resistance creates an energetic wall that holds in this shadow energy, old energy, and ideas that need to be released for our growth. Conversely, this wall also prevents new energy and potentialities from coming into our energy field and experiencing what would support growth on our path of enlightenment.

Resistance is about conflict, disharmony, friction, and discord, whereas non-resistance is about peace, harmony, flow, and connection. Non-resistance is letting the invisible Life Force guide us, allowing opportunities for growth and our highest good to flow to us easily and effortlessly. Surrendering to the flow of Universal Energy supports us to grow and evolve in ways we can't even imagine. Opportunities, money, and aligned relationships all gain substantial momentum for appearing in our lives, creating the potential for quantum leaps in all aspects of life. Resistance and non-resistance are the polar opposites of feeling safe and secure on one end and at risk and insecure on the other. Being in resistance means that one is not willing to give up the perceived certainty of avoiding risk in exchange for the uncertainty of what may unfold through surrender and non-resistance to the True Self and Divine Guidance.

So why resist? One resists because of a negative belief, a limiting belief, or a deep need to feel safe and secure. There may also be a subconscious story that blocks or resists the good from coming into form. If we can feel confident, with knowledge and awareness, we can feel secure in the new experience; then we can step forward. If we don't think we will be secure or safe, we are hanging onto the limiting beliefs of our shame, guilt, or core fears. We believe something is wrong with us or what we are doing. We are really stuck in the negative, and we resist. Likely, a perceived benefit is associated with the resistance that outweighs non-resistance. We can't see or connect to our True Self. We can't step into our purpose. We can't go outside our little boxes or comfort zones. We care about what others think of us. In general, we are unable to trust.

We can turn this state around with a conscious intention to trust our True Self and surrender to our Divine Guidance system. Non-resistance is all about trust. We can join forces with the invisible Life Force or the good that is seeking us. We can even bless the obstacles and challenges that help us grow. The challenges are the pearls of wisdom that lead us to our best and highest good.

In his book, *The Surrender Experiment: My Journey into Life's Perfection,* Michael A. Singer recounts how he decided at a young age to surrender and dedicate his life to meditation and solitude in the woods of northern Florida. He studied the voice in his head, which he describes elegantly in his book, *The Untethered Soul.* This voice was not his friend; it was incessantly listing what he personally liked and disliked. Singer wanted to find peace and stillness without the voice and set an intention to not pay any attention to it and, instead, follow the flow of what life offered him. This was his surrender experiment for being in a continual non-resistance state.

In the process of letting go and surrendering, Singer discovered the flow of the Universe, or what he refers to as the flow of life, being in total non-resistance to what was showing up for him in the moment. Further along in his surrender experiment, he realized that he would have blocked all the good that he ultimately did in his life if he hadn't trusted the flow of life and learned to be in a non-resistant state. He had found a path to understanding who he really is and his own Divine Purpose.

Singer's experiment was not an overnight success. Overcoming resistance is not a quick-fix shift in thinking. Patterns of resistance that develop over a lifetime can become hardened shadows behind the walls of our awareness, requiring steadfastness and commitment to root out and release. Our desire to be aligned with our Divine Purpose must be stronger than the hold of resistance, leading us to a state of full surrender, letting go to open new doors for experiencing what is in our highest good. When our desire for alignment with our Divine Purpose is strong, and we have surrendered to the uncertainty of the unfolding path, life experiences can change rapidly and almost magically. It is like the door to our true path finally flies open!

Living as if Everything is a Miracle

Now that we understand the importance of surrendering and being in non-resistance to live our authentic and best lives, it is time to apply these concepts to living a life of mastery on a path to enlightenment. We live at different energetic frequencies and levels of knowing. We can delve deeper into our understanding of enlightenment, exploring who we truly are and why we are here on Earth at this time. We start living as if everything is a miracle. Miracles are a result of aligning with the truth, love, and wisdom of the Universe.

Ever since I was very young, I knew about miracles. I had an unusual resonance with the concept of miracles that I can't explain. I was determined to witness miracles in my life, and indeed, I experienced many of them, some of which I have shared on these pages. Through curiosity, awareness, and experiences, I have come to understand that there is always the potential for a miracle in the haze of possibilities. Now, I live, or intend to live, as if everything is a miracle. I see the world around me differently and witness the miracle of each tree, flower, mountain, lake, person, experience—I could go on endlessly here. Everything represents Divine Glory, Divine Intention, Divine Creation, and Divine Love.

Living as if everything is a miracle has become even more natural to me since understanding the energetic flow of the Universe. If I am aligned with the Divine, miracles seem more likely than when I am not aligned. It took me decades to understand that this was even possible. Through my studies and work with energy fields, I have gained knowledge and experience that miracles are actually natural—they are meant to *be*. Knowing this opened up the potential for me not only to believe in miracles but also to rely on them. Now, I simply expect miracles and *allow* them to happen. If miracles don't happen, something is not right.

From a scientific point of view, miracles may be a natural expression of some scientific principle that we don't yet understand or may never understand. So many concepts are beyond the understanding of the physical world experience. Miracles are just another concept in that same category. Most of us have probably experienced at least one miracle in our lives. Some of us may believe the miracle was a fluke, a mistake, or something not real. But we receive miracles because of who we are BEing.

Miracles don't happen when we are *BEing* a low vibrational frequency—only when we are *BEing* a high vibrational frequency. Miracles are connected to the vibrational frequency of love and flow naturally from the love frequency. When we are at the vibrational frequency of Love Consciousness, miracles are expressions of that love. The love extends through and from us, and we witness miracles. The more we extend love to the Universe, the more miracles will come to us. We can also create and offer miracles by helping people see life through the lens of miracles and Love Consciousness. Living in a state of miracle energy means expecting miracles to happen, knowing we're conduits not only of goodness and love but also of miracles. We may never even know the miracles we create in the world.

> *There is no order of difficulty in miracles. One miracle is not 'harder' or 'bigger' than another. They are all the same. All expressions of love are maximal.*

Understanding that it is within our power to live as if everything is a miracle makes life so incredible and amazing. This revelation will help us advance on the path of enlightenment, creating a significant shift that raises our vibrational frequency. While it may seem relatively easy to see the miracle in a sunrise, sunset, or a rainbow, when you can extend this miraculous view to other aspects of life that may be less sensational, we are living as if everything is a miracle. Let the world stop you in your tracks through revelations of the miracles in plain sight all around you. Seeing the miracle in the smallest insect or creature is the key. See the miracle in difficult people, difficult experiences, and challenges. Experiment with this concept and challenge yourself to be the energy of everything is a miracle. You just have to decide to realize it. From this perspective of living, it is easier to let go of our misperceptions as we witness the truth and experience miracles for ourselves and others.

What does it take to live as if everything is a miracle? This is unique to each individual and could probably be described in as many ways as there are people. However, here are some core concepts that can help you find your own way of living a miracle life.

- Believe in your unlimited potential. Trust yourself. Trust your intuition.
- Believe in your magnificence, own it, and live from it.
- Know that everything is happening for you and through you.
- Know deep within that only love is real.
- Shift from fear-based living to love-based living.

Miracles can heal by transcending the physical into the Spiritual and awakening our understanding of the truth of who we really are. Through this awakening, we are shown our misperceptions of the world, including our misperceptions of separation, fear, and hate. Miracles are a way the Universe helps us correct these misperceptions, setting us on a path of healing that opens us to seeing that everything is connected. We are all One; we are all Love. Viewing the world from love, we create miracles. That is miraculous living.

Enlightened Love is BEing open-hearted after releasing samskaras and loving everyone and everything unconditionally. Our hearts have to be clear of energetic blocks to be open-hearted; otherwise, our hearts are closed. If we clear the energetic blocks or gaps that are the samskaras or suppressed and unresolved issues, our hearts are freer to open. This Enlightened Love within us seeks to see, witness, and discover the love in everyone and everything. Enlightened Love is seeing life from the Spiritual Realm perspective, where everyone is innocent, guiltless, and sinless. This love is easier if we see that every living being and everything is an expression of the Divine. From a Spiritual Realm perspective, everyone is a Soul seeking to learn, grow, and evolve. Enlightenment is understanding this as reality. If we remember who we are and who everyone else is, we have awakened; we are on a path of enlightenment. We are invited to be in awe and wonder and to participate in the mystery of the miracle world happening around us. We react in gratitude for this gift. To be more enlightened, we naturally treat ourselves and others as the magnificent Souls that we and they are. See the magnificence. Focus on the magnificence. Identify with the magnificence. This is a path of enlightenment. We are all miracles.

We can become miracles for ourselves and others. We're entitled to have extraordinary things happen, such as miracles. We receive miracles because the Divine loves us. We can create miracles because of our Oneness with the Divine. If we connect to the Oneness of the Universe and tap into Divine Love, we can express Divine Love through us. The key is to be our authentic selves and share our unique gifts and talents with others. In doing so, we give others permission to share their gifts. There is a ripple effect throughout the Universe with a simple act and acknowledgment that we can be the conduits of Divine Energy. We can be the conduits of miracles. Be in service, be present, be unconditional love, and allow the miracles to come through.

Here is a guide to living life as if everything is a miracle.

- Believe in your unlimited potential, expect to achieve that level.
- Own your magnificence. Own your Soul's Magnificence. See magnificence in others.

- Know you are an Infinite Spirit and will be here for eternity.
- Be Soul-centric, not ego-centric.
- Believe that everything is happening for you.
- Believe that only love is real.
- Seek and witness the love in others.
- Open your heart energy.
- Let go of the past.
- Live in the now. Focus on where you are going and who you are BEing.
- Forgive others, forgive yourself.
- See every living thing as Divine.
- Raise your vibrational frequency.
- Be grateful for everything.
- Be in the energy of what you want.
- Be in the flow of the Universe.

Enlightened Living from Our Divine Magnificence

Taking this concept of living life as if everything is a miracle one step further, let's explore how our enlightened way of BEing can enable us to live from our Divine Magnificence.

Enlightened living from our Divine Magnificence involves making decisions from inspiration. Enlightened living is knowing that the Invisible has led us to this next step in our lives—we are advancing on the path of enlightenment. Enlightened living is treating everything that shows up as an honored invitation from our Soul or the Divine. We naturally stretch to be the best versions of ourselves. We work in excellence and integrity. We want to contribute to the Universe at our highest potential. This response is our gift to the Universe.

We radiate the light we receive from the Divine and extend Divine Love to others. Who we're BEing makes all the difference in who or what shows up for our next step. Who we are BEing determines if we can live as if everything is a miracle.

We have all gone through dark periods in our lives. During these dark periods, sometimes all we want to know is that there is a light at the end of the tunnel. Even if we recognize these times as gifts and opportunities for extraordinary growth, it's still difficult. Being on a path of enlightenment can be a light at the end of the tunnel. Every step along this path is like a pearl of wisdom or a miracle pearl of life lessons. This wisdom accumulates as growth spurts or Divine Spark activation.

We are in extraordinary times, when an unprecedented number of people are awakening to a deeper or more complete understanding of the Divine and the truth of who we are as Divine BEings. This awakening is a crucial aspect of the Spiritual Journey that helps us see and experience the world differently, shifting our way of BEing in the world. This awakening puts us on a path of enlightenment. We have so much help, love, and support for this journey—it is beyond our comprehension. Knowing this, we can show up differently and be more confident in taking risks to expand and elevate ourselves while focusing on how we can positively contribute to the Universe. We can be excited about what we will learn next.

We are here to recognize that we are not physical bodies with a Soul; we are Souls expressed through physical bodies. We are here to realize our Divinity and experience Divine Energy flowing through us. We are here to create at our highest potential. We are here to be miracles for each other. We are here to serve each other and help each other along the way. We are here to make an impact and change the world to be more Divinely Inspired, focused on loving all, compassion for all, and serving all.

We learn to see through the lens of the Divine and recognize the Divinity in all things, creatures, events, and circumstances. We can see all things as other aspects of ourselves or the One. We see the miracle of life in all its simple beauty and simple glory right there in front of us every step of the way. We experience life as miracles because what happens is beyond what we can imagine as reality. What is available to us is way beyond our level of comprehension from the physical perspective. As we let go even more, we become miracles for others by extending our hands to them. We pull others out of their tunnels of darkness. We help them grow. We help them surrender and trust. We model what is possible for others.

Surrendering to and trusting the Invisible to guide us through the unknown is vital on the path of enlightenment. We resonate more with this unknown as our path to BEing our True Selves and living from our magnificence. We are magnetically pulled in the direction of the unknown to live from our magnificence. The more positive experiences we have, the easier it is to keep surrendering. We gain more confidence in ourselves. Life becomes more exciting. Life becomes richer as we move into greater alignment with the Divine. We can go deeper into this Divine Connection.

Longing to be more aligned with the Divine, we eagerly spend more time in silence to deepen our connection with the Divine within. We allow space for Divine Wisdom and Love to permeate our energy fields and take root in our BEing. We prioritize what is most important: being the best and most authentic versions of ourselves and living our best lives.

We can continually let go and fall into the Divine. We know the truth, and we can trust this truth rather than our own personal wishes and wants for our lives. Following Divine Guidance allows us to reach higher magnitudes of growth and higher levels of our Innate Potential. We are using our energy in a more productive way. We aren't being drained by low vibrational frequencies of fear, grief, guilt, shame, anger, and apathy. We are channeling our energy toward growth, Soul development, and service to others—all aspects that add life to us and the Universe. We have more vitality and vibrancy and easily share our illuminated radiance.

Living from our Divine Magnificence, we vibrate at higher and higher vibrational frequencies, increasing our radiance, optimal health, and vibrancy of our True Essence. We no longer resonate with the low vibrational frequencies of illness and disease. We no longer give credence to the ego's fear-based urging and desperation for control. We realize there is nothing to fear. We become more Soul-centric rather than ego-centric. Perhaps the ego's voice no longer exists or is so quiet we don't pay attention to it. Our inner world is the most important for creating our highest level of existence and potential. The material world, social status, money, and success ladders no longer have significant meaning. We are seeking people who understand the path of enlightenment as a way of living. We own our magnificence and seek to expand that aspect of ourselves, starting within. We are increasingly able to understand the flow of the Universe—we want to be part of the upliftment of the Universe. We want to add to, rather than subtract from, the Universe. It is not as much what we are doing in our lives; the secret is who we are BEing that really makes a difference in advancing along the path of enlightenment.

As we open up more and more to receive the flow of the Divine through us, we become more aligned with our Divine Magnificence. The benefits are exponential. We treasure that we can be a vessel for the Divine's expansion. We have clarity on the need or the opportunity to broaden our experiences, take adventures, and stretch ourselves in new ways. We only do this for one reason—to allow this Divine Expansion through us. We show up more fully to our new Divine Assignments or projects.

If we can surrender to being in alignment with the Divine, we will make progress and advance exactly as we need to, in the timing that is ideal for us. We are in it for the long haul. It is more like a marathon than a sprint. We start wherever we are, and we allow the growth that is needed to continue toward enlightenment. We are co-creators in this process. We are participants in the unfolding of our lives. We are learning and growing. We are letting go of what no longer serves us. We know ourselves on a level that is very different from ever before. We own our magnificence. We see the light. We share in the light. We radiate the light. We become the light.

On our path of enlightenment, as we awaken to the truth, it becomes increasingly easier to be a source of light for others. We can accept the Spiritual Realm paradigms of living to create a better world for all—not just a few. We are here to improve relationships, create new visions, explore new horizons, surrender more completely, and be in joy. We are on Earth, living in these physical bodies to enjoy life and grow. We are here to learn new skills, develop more effective ways to live, and promote greater love and acceptance in our homes, businesses, communities, states, countries, the world, and the whole Universe. What we do affects others. Who we are BEing affects others. Who we are BEing can lead to the expansion of the Divine.

The key to living and acting from your magnificence is to:

- Identify with your Soul as the truth of who you are and own your magnificence.
- Your Soul is Divine, you are Divine, and you are eternal. Live into the full potential of your primary Divine Soul Energy.
- See everything, everyone, and every event, circumstance, or situation as Divine.
- Know your Soul has an entourage of Souls also working for your best and highest good.
- Know that you are whole, well, and created by the Divine to be your authentic Self and do something for the Universe only you can do.
- Be in the state of BEing peace.
- Be aware of Divine Energy flowing through you as the radiant light of the world.
- Be aware of your ability to sense and see the world through the eyes, mind, and heart of the Divine.
- Be aware that Divine Wisdom comes through your heart and your mouth.

- Feel the energy of love surrounding you, and that is you.
- Surrender and trust that all that happens is an opportunity for growth; embrace it all and learn the lessons.
- Know that everything is happening for your growth, happiness, freedom, and joy.
- Let go of the past—all grievances, judgments, fear, stress, and anxiety.
- Forgive everything and everyone, including yourself.
- Feel and be in the Oneness of the Universe.
- Remove the veil and envision a life on Earth that lives according to the Spiritual Realm paradigms. Be a leader in this type of living.
- Be in alignment with your primary Divine Soul Energy to its fullest potential and accomplish your Divine Mission. Be Self-full, Soul-ful.
- Allow yourself to be lifted out of the limitations and barriers you perceive as being there. There are no barriers between you and the Divine.

Live as if the Universe depends on you to uplift its level of Consciousness—because it does.

On the next and final step of this journey, we will learn about and experience Oneness. It is more than you can imagine!

EXERCISES

Take the time to concretize the teachings from this Section by engaging in the following exercises. This will increase your understanding of the concepts and miracles of the Oneness.

Exercise 1: Meditation and Journal Prompts

Use the following prompts for meditation and journaling for a deeper exploration of topics covered in this Section. Go deep within and connect to your Inner Wisdom and discover the truth within you.

- Where are you on the path to enlightenment? Where do you want to be?
- What understanding about the Universe has changed for you by reading this book?
- What has changed within you at your core?
- How have you grown?
- How have you expanded?
- How are you living as if everything is a miracle?
- How are you living from your Divine Magnificence?

Exercise 2: The Tenfold Path to Enlightenment

Go back and reread the passage on the tenfold path to enlightenment and ask yourself the questions below. Write down the insights that show up for you. Become aware of how this has or hasn't affected you in the past. How can any of these steps affect the next phase of your growth? Is there one that you would like to adapt to as a way of BEing? Ask yourself how this will change things on your path of enlightenment. Write down your insights and revelations.

- What do I resonate with?
- What don't I resonate with?
- Am I satisfied with that way of BEing?
- Am I ready to change?
- What would I include on my tenfold path of enlightenment?
- What aspects of this path of enlightenment are next for me? Connecting to the possibility of this new opportunity will encourage situations to occur as opportunities for growth.

- What will bring out my Higher Self?
- What is my specific Divine Mission to accomplish?
- Am I ready to accept the truth about myself?
- Am I ready to accept the miracles that are meant for me?
- Am I willing to accept that there is a whole different way of BEing and living?
- Am I willing to learn new things and grow into what I want?
- Am I willing to let go and leave behind what brings me comfort?
- Am I willing to close the doors on relationships that don't serve me, or situations that are not for my best and highest good?
- Am I willing to step up to a new level or a new standard of commitment to get what I want?
- What new decisions can I make today?
- Am I ready to live as if everything is a miracle?
- Am I ready to own my Divine Magnificence?

Exercise 3: Write a letter to the Divine

To make sure the Universe or the Divine is aware of your total commitment to becoming the best version of you, you can write a heartfelt letter explaining your total commitment. This energy will be transmitted to the Universe. Explain how you perceive the opportunity and your commitment to embracing it to support your Soul Growth. This transmits your intentional energy to the Universe; then, you continually show up to receive what is in the highest alignment with your path.

Exercise 4: *What if* Questions

Meditate on these questions and then journal about them to see what guidance your meditation provides you. Allow new insights and awareness to flow to you and through you.

- *What if* it were true that everything is a miracle?
- *What if* everyone is a miracle?
- *What if* I could be a miracle to someone else?
- *What if* I believed in my Divine Magnificence?
- *What if* I could live from your Divine Magnificence?
- *What if* there were an open door for me to go through that would change everything for me?

SECTION FIVE

ONENESS:
EVOLVING FROM DUALITY TO UNITY

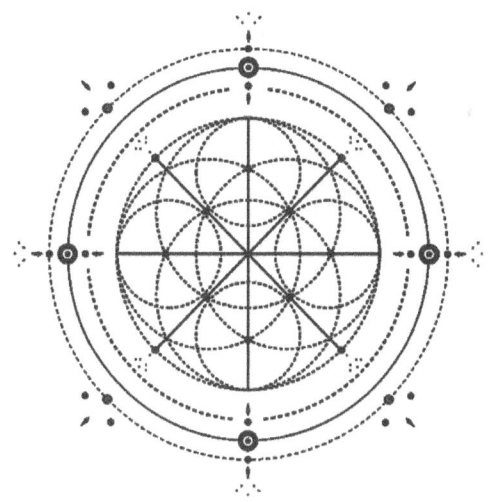

Oneness

Oneness means we are all energy BEings
Sharing positive and negative in our BEing-ness.

Oneness means we are all connected.
This mysterious Divine Matrix, the bridge.

Oneness means we accept each other
As we are on our own journey.

Oneness means we embrace all that happens
As opportunities for growth, expansion, evolution.

Oneness means we understand the Divine within.
We are aware we are more than we thought.

Oneness means our inner potential is limitless.
We are all connected to Universal Consciousness.

Oneness means we need to open to be
in Divine Flow with all.

Oneness means we are different expressions
of Divine Love, Divine Goodness, Divine Peace.

Oneness means we are unique but part of the whole.
We exist to discover the significance of BEing One.

Oneness means we all affect each other.
Positive or negative energy from us affects Universal All.

Oneness means there is no real beginning or end to us.
We flow from the eternal Oneness.

Oneness means the power of love and compassion is the Divine flow.
Its momentum is flowing to include all aspects of life on Earth.

Oneness means we choose to be in this Divine Flow or
we separate ourselves to live life hard.

Oneness means the Divine Flow comes from our heart energy.
Oneness means we see the world with our hearts, not our minds.

Oneness means we dance in the Divine Joy all around us.
We see through the lens of love and connection.

Oneness means we don't see the negativity in others.
We just can't vibrate at those frequencies--they don't exist for us.

~Anne M. Deatly

Universal Law of Divine Oneness

In this final leg of our journey together, we will embrace Oneness. You will learn how to have your own journey to Oneness—every day if you wish. We are meant to transcend duality and accept, embrace, and grow in the Oneness. In my experience, there are many aspects, qualities, layers, and dimensions of the Oneness. The goal of understanding Oneness is to live from the Oneness in the physical realm all the time. From this, we attain a new level of mastery in Self-actualization.

Understanding the Oneness of the Universe is essential to the path of enlightenment. Transcending perceived limitations will lead us deeper into the truth of Oneness. For most, the concept of Oneness begins as a mental understanding that gradually unfolds into more profound revelations and knowing, until we ultimately experience Oneness.

What does Oneness really mean?

At the heart of the Universe, there is only One Energy, One Source, One Love, One BEing, One Existence. The foundation of everything in the Universe is Oneness. The primary universal law is the Universal Law of Divine Oneness, which teaches us that everything in the Universe is interconnected and an aspect of the One. Oneness reveals the truth that separation is an illusion.

Every thing and every living being is interconnected, linked, entangled, and unified. Even every thought, feeling, action, experience, situation, adventure, event, or discovery is united or integrated with everything else. We are all connected to each other, and we are all connected to the Divine.

Oneness includes what is seen and what is unseen. This concept is why the physical and Spiritual Realms, or the physical and Invisible aspects of life, are inextricable. Every string of energy in the Universe is part of the Oneness. Nothing is left out. This law is why I say we all have and share the Divine Light, Divine Love, Divine Wisdom, Divine Peace, and Divine Benevolence within us. We have all that is Divine. We are fractals of the Divine. We are one unified family—all interrelated and interconnected.

This Universal Oneness is like a tapestry woven together to create the whole of existence. There is only one single collective Consciousness. Each energy affects the collective energy in subtle ways. What we think, feel emotionally, believe, or know acts as ripples in the Universe. Being aware of the ripple effect, we have the choice of the actual ripples we want to transmit to the Universe—knowing that the ripple will affect the whole. The energetic vibration we transmit creates an outcome of a similar energetic vibration. The ripples of energy affect the Universe because we are all One. What one does affects all others, the whole Universe.

As many Spiritual Influencers teach, we can intentionally connect to Oneness through meditation, prayer, mindfulness, and being in nature. In stillness, silence, and sacred space, we can sense the Oneness within us and throughout the Universe. We are part of so much more than we can even fathom. Even from an elevated state, it is hard to imagine. Oneness is a difficult concept for most of us to believe, especially when it comes to BEing One with the Divine.

How can we be One with the most powerful, highest vibration, and most intelligent aspect of life?

We are all Divine. We are all unique, Divinely created aspects of the One Universal Consciousness. Therefore, we all come from the same Divine Energy or Source and have ready access to all the wisdom there is or ever will be—all the time. There really is only One of us here. What I do to another, I do to myself. All Souls are interconnected. All lives are interrelated. We are all part of the ONE whole.

While Oneness is a primary Universal truth that transcends the need for scientific proof for acceptance, science is not to be left behind as a way of understanding our interconnectedness. For that, we can turn to the Universal Law of

Correspondence, which states "as above, so below, as below so above; as within so without." From a scientific perspective, this principle tells us that at both the macrocosm of the quantum field and microcosm of the subatomic particle level, we are naturally in a state of Oneness as energetic particles connected through strings of energy. These strings of energy can take on information or energy from other quantum waves or strings of energy. All the energy is being shared back and forth in a free-flowing exchange. This living field of energy that we live in and is us is a dancing, radiant, vibrating field of shared energy. This sharing or trading of energy creates the Oneness at the quantum level: energy in a continuous dynamic flow of exchange.

Exploring Oneness through Meditation and Automatic Writing

One way I have discovered to deepen my experience and understanding of Oneness is through meditation and visualization. These meditations have taken me on inner journeys into the vast unknown aspects of the Universe, leaving me curious for clarity on the meaning and connection of these visions to a deeper understanding of Oneness. To fill in gaps in my understanding, I turn to my True Self or my Ascended Masters guides for answers and use automatic writing to record the messages I receive.

Automatic writing is a technique for receiving messages from higher Consciousness by going into a trance state to connect with higher Consciousness and then writing down the messages that come through. I learned this technique through Sara Landon, author of *You Are a Channel*. The messages I receive in automatic writing sessions don't come from my conscious awareness. Later, when I read what I wrote, I see that the information is new to me, and it's written in a way that is not my natural voice.

When I first began automatic writing, I directed my questions to my True Self, then later, expanded to include my Ascended Master guides—Mufata, Kufafa, and Nanu. Eventually, I realized that All higher Consciousness is from the same Source in Oneness Consciousness, and I didn't need to ask for any separate aspect of the One to guide me or answer me.

I am sharing some of the messages about Oneness that I have received through automatic writing to expand on our exploration of this vast topic. Included in the questions I pose are some details about the meditation that preceded my inquiry, as well as my interpretation of those details to provide greater context for the depth and clarity of the messages I received. Most concepts were new revelations for me and may be for you as well. I invite you to sense their responses as including you as part of the Oneness in the dialogue. I invite you to feel they are talking to you as well.

Messages from the Guides

One of my early meditative explorations connected me to feelings of a Loving Presence, which had been somewhat mysterious, with an experience of Oneness. This experience led to a deeper dive to understand the connection. During an automatic writing session, I asked one of my Guides about the connection between my feelings of Loving Presence and Oneness.

Question: What would my Ascended Master Guides have me know about the spectrums of love and my ability to sustain connection to Loving Presence?

> *Dear Beloved,*
>
> *Yes, spectrums of love exist. Love is even more wonderful than you can imagine. As Spiritual BEings, we all grow into higher and higher capacities to hold Loving Presence within our unique fields. But we are swimming in Divine Energy or Loving Presence. What filters through to each of us depends on our level of resistance or acceptance of these high vibrations of energy. So, there are spectrums or a diffracted array of love energy available to filter through us as we grow in our ability to accommodate these very high vibrations. It takes conscious intention for this growth or elevation of capacity. It takes atomic and even subatomic rearrangement to accommodate these vibrations in the dense material bodies of humans. Spectrums of love are available for this growth within us to rise to the level, one small bit at a time, to allow the flow of higher vibrations step by step, moment by moment.*
>
> *Desiring a more sustainable connection with Loving Presence involves cultivating the conscious awareness or intention to hold high vibrational frequencies within your energy field for increasingly longer periods. This reflects your ability to hold high vibrational frequencies at all and know the difference. It is also a reflection of*

your understanding of your True Essence, representing your progress on the path to enlightenment.

We love you. We love you. We love you.

Question: I understand the Divine can only create the Divine, and the physicality of humans is only a small fraction of their True Self. If we could see from the highest version and largest version of our Divine Self, we couldn't see what is happening on Earth. We could only see from the perspective of the tower of light and high vibrational frequency that make up the tower of light that is us. We can only see love, compassion, joy, and peace. Did I understand the meditation correctly?

Dear Beloved,

We love your adventures in meditation to understand and FEEL ONENESS. Today's meditation opened up new visions of a higher way of BEing and to visualize the physical and invisible from higher perspectives and a higher frequency of life. Yes, your light and energetic form is immense. It is astronomical. We are each ALL that—towers of light connected to a physical form if on Earth. When you step into that greatness, you can only see love, joy, and peace around you. Yes, only the Divine creates the Divine. The Divine can only create the Divine. Everything in the Universe is Divine because the Divine created it. There is so much more to experience in life from this astronomical perspective.

We love you. We love you. We love you.

Question: In my meditation today, I was trying to capture all aspects of BEing the Oneness and experiencing the Oneness. My interpretation is that ALL Divine Energy is flowing through us all the time. Only a small percentage of our energy stays within our physical body tissues. But it is still all connected. So, even in the Oneness, we are separate. How can that be right?

Dear Beloved,

You are One with the whole Universe. Your energy flows through you, and the whole Universal Energy flows through you on a constant basis. You can feel the physical sensation of it. The energy that is you is part of the Oneness. But there is an attractor factor holding your photons together in relevant ways to maintain your identity and selfness. So, you remain connected to 'you' as an aspect of the Oneness. It is beyond your understanding. But take it on faith. The real you is centralized in your core and flows out from there to the rest of your physical body and energy body and eventually to the Oneness. This flow doesn't stop unless you close yourself off from it. You obviously haven't closed yourself off from it, or you wouldn't be receiving these messages. But most people are closed off from the constant flow of Oneness. Then they only sense the physical world, and they feel that is all there is. Your mission is to explain the Oneness, so people open themselves up to receive the greatest gift there is.

We love you. We love you. We love you.

Reading through these messages, I was struck by the layers and depth of possibility that are inherent in the Oneness. The more I learn about Oneness, the more layers are revealed to me, like the concept of spectrums of love and swimming in Divine Presence or Loving Presence. We are so familiar with the Loving Presence of the Divine that we don't realize what it is because it's always there within us and around us. It reminds me of the phrase "a fish doesn't know it's in water." We expect to feel a miraculous new sensation when we are in the Loving Presence of the Divine. But it's a constant presence that is so familiar we don't even notice it until we tune in and focus or set an intention to feel it.

I was also moved by the idea that we actually experience the world differently. We perceive the world around us differently, seeing aspects of our existence that are always there, but essentially hidden in plain sight until we are capable of perceiving them. We can only perceive and experience existence at the level of who we are BEing—the level of our vibrational frequency. When we open ourselves up to these higher ways of BEing, choosing to express through love, joy, and peace, everything changes. We change, and so does everything around us. It is wondrous to understand that there is so much more that life has to offer us from this higher perspective. The Oneness is always flowing through us; we can access it or plug into the Oneness as long as we stay open and receive it. Interestingly, the third share explains an attractor factor that keeps each of us in our uniqueness in the Oneness. I am amazed!

Still, due to the appearance of duality, the idea of Oneness, where there is no duality, seems alien to us in the physical realm we inhabit. In the shared reality of our physical world, we appear to be separate beings; things appear to be separate from us. You are there; I am here. That tree is not me; I am not that tree. In that state of duality, we feel separate and disconnected. The world is entirely external to our inner experience. We have been programmed to think that we stop at the edge of our physical bodies. Even religion emphasizes our separateness from the Divine by viewing God and beings of worship as an external existence above us.

But as we are awaking to the truth of our true nature, as a Divine Soul experiencing a physical realm, becoming familiar with the energy fields within and around us, the concept of Oneness is not inconceivable. Our energetic aspect is within us and also extends beyond us in all directions. The reality is that we are exponentially more energy than matter. I have seen renderings of pictures created from exalted experiences that show our physical body is within an energy body that is larger than the Earth. That is how amazingly significant we are as creative, energetic beings.

In duality consciousness or separation consciousness, everything appears separate. It appears that our physical bodies are separate from our energy bodies because we can see one and not the other. This appears to be duality rather than unity because we don't understand the continuum that exists between the physical and energy or Invisible aspects of us. Perhaps we could think of the energetic aspect of us as a subtle anatomy. There is actually a continuum of energy flowing to us that becomes increasingly structured and dense in its flow to us and the third dimension. According to Dr. Sue Morter, author of *The Energy Codes: 7-Step System to Awaken Your Spirit, Heal Your Body, and Live Your Best Life*, this energetic aspect builds the physical body through compressions and folding over of the energy. Understanding how the physical body is formed through energy, it is easier to accept the unity of physical matter and energy. Energy and matter are the same as in Einstein's famous formula, $E=mc^2$.

This helps us understand Oneness as something more than an abstract thought or ideal by showing us that Oneness is the basic quality of existence in the Universe, revealed not only from Spiritual intuition but also through scientific exploration.

In the subtle vibrational frequencies of the Invisible World, the boundary lines also become blurred between self and other, object and observer, and dissolve into the Oneness. We are both the observer and the observed. We are distinct, yet inseparable from the greater whole. With these revelations, we may clearly know and experience our place within the cosmos and the Infinite Potential inherent in the interconnectedness.

Oneness Through the Lens of Quantum Reality

Exploring Oneness through the lens of quantum reality offers a perspective that provides crucial insights vital to recognizing the interconnectedness of all things as the foundational paradigm for Oneness. As modern science begins to intersect with time-honored philosophy, including ancient wisdom, certain principles from quantum physics and spirituality appear to merge in their interpretation of the fundamental underlying reality of the Universe. Quantum entanglement, for example, demonstrates that particles may remain connected across significant distances, influencing each other simultaneously. On one level, this affirms the interconnectedness of particles from a scientific perspective. On another level, it affirms the interconnectedness, fundamental to understanding Oneness in quantum reality and the Spiritual Realm.

At the boundaries of our physical existence, our energy shifts in its atomic structure, forming a spectrum that ranges from the material to pure energy. This evolving structure not only surrounds us within the third-dimensional realm but also extends beyond it. We are inherently multidimensional BEings. Recognizing this facet of our nature helps provide a deeper understanding of how our energetic structures transcend traditional dimensional boundaries.

Understanding Oneness from this perspective, we are able to perceive reality as more than the sum of all of its parts. We tap into the concept that the Oneness represents an intricate web with all existence represented and interwoven through vibrational frequency and Conscious awareness. In quantum physics, the Universe is understood as entangled particles communicating across vast distances, where observation collapses the wave into a new possibility in a manifested form. The boundaries between self and other, object and observer, blur out of existence within the Oneness field of awareness.

Fractals In a Holographic Universe

A fascinating aspect of quantum reality that further cements the concept of Oneness as a primary Universal law is the holographic nature of the Universe. Yes! We live in a holographic Universe. Viewed through the lens of the holographic paradigm, the fabric of existence is not simply a sum of disconnected parts, but rather, every part is a microcosm containing the entire macrocosm. That means every person, every atom, even every thought or feeling, holds the pattern of the whole within itself. This revelation is both humbling and empowering: we are individual expressions, yet never truly apart from the greater totality. The separation we experience is similar to a dream—an illusion formed by the limitations of our senses and our repeated patterns of perception.

In our third-dimensional understanding of quantum reality, a hologram is an image created from light diffracted from all directions, which creates a three-dimensional image with the perception of depth. The light from all different directions creates a scattering of light that results in interference patterns, which produce a three-dimensional image. In contrast, a photograph is the result of light from one single direction, resulting in a focused two-dimensional image that has height and width but no depth.

Interestingly, a three-dimensional holographic structure can exist in two-dimensional form. For example, many credit cards have holograms for security purposes. Looking at the hologram, it appears three-dimensional—having length, width, and depth. The length and width of the holographic image on the credit card appear consistent with the card size, but the image appears to have depth well beyond the depth of the card.

Another way of understanding the concept of a hologram is that each holographic image contains the whole. In other words, each part is a fractal of the whole. Applied on a quantum scale, all that exists within the Universe and Universal Consciousness is a fractal of the whole—that BEing Source, All That Is. From a traditional scientific viewpoint, a whole system is made of separate parts. The parts interact and participate together to form the whole function. But in quantum physics, the behavior of the parts is organized by the whole, not vice versa.

There is a level of unified wholeness of functionality in the holographic model of the Universe that resembles concepts of Oneness. Within the concept of Oneness, individual identity is perceived as part of a larger whole of existence.

The perspective encourages looking beyond concepts or boundaries of personality and physical form. Each individual's experience is an integral aspect of a complex, interwoven, and interconnected Universe.

Let's try an experiment to better understand the idea of fractals. Looking at the image in Figure 5, you see it as an image on a page with two dimensions—length and width. If you tear this photograph up into three pieces from right to left, you will see only one section of the crystal in each torn piece. However, in a holographic photograph of each torn piece, you would see the complete image of the multifaceted crystal. The whole crystal is in each photograph; in other words, each torn piece is a complete fractal of the whole crystal.

Figure 5 Multifaceted Clear Crystal

Beyond that, I am using a crystal as a metaphor because it reflects and diffracts light in a myriad of ways, because of the unique positioning of each facet of the crystal. Each facet reflects the light at the unique angle at which the light falls onto it. All facets represent the whole crystal. No facet is separate from the whole, and all facets come from the same crystal. But the light falling on the crystal is reflected in different directions and ways depending on which fractal receives the light. Each facet plays a role in the brilliance and glimmering diffraction of the light into different colors, which represent different vibrational frequencies. Similarly, in Oneness, all individuated expressions, every individual person, every individual thought, feeling, and belief, and every individual particle are paradoxically singular and unique but also unified and inseparable from the greater whole of Oneness.

Also like the facets of a crystal that reflect and diffract the light in different patterns, our lives, experiences, discoveries, and adventures also reflect a spectrum of BEing. The unifying aspect is that all our lives and experiences flow from One Source. All our lives and experiences are interconnected and interrelated as essences of that One Source. Just like the integrity and unity of the crystal remain intact when viewed from different angles, the wholeness or completeness of the crystal is revealed through an interplay of the different parts, or facets.

Even if the crystal breaks and shatters into pieces, each piece holds the whole. Likewise, no matter how our existence is divided, unity is never lost. Every part contains the energy, pattern, Consciousness, and essence of Oneness. The facets remind us that individuality doesn't contradict unity but rather amplifies the magnificence of the whole. The deeper we know ourselves, the more we can perceive the Infinite. Treasuring and valuing each other is to honor the One who is reflected by us.

Given that each of us is an expression of the One, the power of the Divine and Divine Love is also in each of us in whole and equal measure, making everything possible. This understanding is critical to knowing the depths of the power of love and the resulting miracles possible for us. This revelation will help us advance on the path of enlightenment.

As we awaken on our Spiritual Journeys, we start to understand ourselves in this expanded sense of BEing a fractal of Consciousness, a fractal of the Oneness, a fractal of the Divine. Each person is a fractal of Consciousness and represents all of Consciousness. Each of us is like the complete image of the crystal of a holographic photograph. Each of us is the complete image of Consciousness.

The opportunity here for us is to create a bridge from our physical existence to our rightful place in the cosmos as holographic aspects of and expressions of the whole Consciousness—the One Source. This revelation invites us to contemplate the interconnectedness of all things, where nothing is separate or isolated. It is literally impossible to be separate. Each thought, emotion, and action ripples through our interwoven physical and energetic—invisible—natures. We begin to realize that Self-discovery is, at its core, a journey into the essence of the Universe itself, an exploration where the boundaries between the individual and the ALL dissolve into radiant and magnificent unity.

I See You in Me

Seeing the world through reflection,
Is the invitation of Oneness.
Seeing the jewel-like qualities of all.
It is a genius way to live.

Reflection upon reflection
To infinity and eternity
Makes a statement of interconnection
Weaving together a solid bond.

The lens of perception
Opens our eyes and minds
To See Me in You and
You in Me-linked in unity.

The brilliance and dazzling light in jewels
Brings significance to interpretation.
We are all One in the Oneness representing
The Whole and the ALL.

It is simple yet amazingly wise
To live in existence uniquely expressing the One
Interpenetrating ALL That Is and the Universal ALL.
We are One for eternity.

~Anne M. Deatly

Inner Journeys to Oneness

It is not enough to explain and intellectualize the concept of Oneness; we must experience Oneness to truly comprehend it and become the wisdom of the Oneness. We all need to sense the Oneness in our own unique ways using our specific and unique intuitive gifts. For me, the exploration of Oneness has been a truly fascinating journey. In addition to numerous other forms of research on this topic, I have used meditation to guide me on this journey and have *seen* Oneness through my inner vision during meditation.

As a preparation for Oneness meditation, I set the intention to witness or experience the Oneness. I commit time and space to exploring concepts of Oneness and cultivating the capacity to experience Oneness. Then I surrender to this exploration, wait for images to appear in my inner vision, and trust the successful outcome of experiencing the Oneness.

Over time, my visions deepened, and I may have even been visualizing or experiencing Oneness at higher dimensions or realities. However, the key is that I have learned gradually. Reflective insights during meditation will only reveal what we are prepared to perceive. We evolve as we progress, viewing the experience through increasingly higher perspectives.

To inspire your curiosity and prime your intuitive senses to open to the experience of Oneness, here are several examples of my experiences of Oneness. During my first meditation to experience Oneness, I saw myself as pure light. My light merged with the *other* light, which had no definition or identity. In the merged state, I could only distinguish myself as two eyes in a river of light flowing forward. There were no wayward lights scattered in other directions. All light became One in the flow, and I was One with this river of light.

In another meditation, I was a ray of sunlight. The image was of the sun with its rays as a collection of individual rays, or lines, of light. The image closest to the sun was just a ball of light. The farther the light was extended from the sun, the easier it was to differentiate individual rays. One ray of light stood out to me. So, I could envision myself as that ray of sunlight participating as the whole in sharing my light.

Experiencing Oneness Through Visualization

One of the tools I use to experience Oneness in my meditation sessions involves a painting by abstract expressionist Barnett Newman titled "Vir Heroicus Sublimis", translated from Latin as Man, Heroic, Sublime, on exhibit at the Museum of Modern Art in New York City. The painting depicts monochromatic red color blocks interrupted by several vertical lines of different intensity and color called zips. When I saw this painting for the first time, I was overwhelmed by my personal understanding that the zips represent thin spaces in the veil between the physical and Spiritual Realms. Barnett described the zips as rays of Divine light that serve as an invitation to a deeper, transcendent experience. I understand this to mean that there are different depths of the zips leading to a sacred space for connection. The following is a description of my experiences of Oneness during meditation, visualizing Newman's zips taking me on inner journeys to reveal aspects of the Oneness.

Preparation

To prepare for a meditation to experience Oneness, I begin by setting a firm intention to connect with and experience Oneness. Then I connect to my heart through slow, deep conscious breathing up and down my central channel, first to carve a pathway or open up space for the energy in my energetic core to flow easily through me, either from above to below my physical form or from below to above my physical form. Next, I expand my heart energy out into the room, consciously connecting to the Divine. Then I focus on seeing a small version of myself traveling down a floating spiral staircase from my head to just inside the area of my heart organ or heart chakra. A heart-shaped door slides open, and there is a brilliant, radiant, loving white light that envelops the small version of me upon entering the heart space. I physically feel a shift in the present life version of me, as if I am radiating this light and becoming this light.

Visualization

From this space of light, I take a trip to what I believe is my subconscious, where I see a meadow of flowers with a pond to the left, but the whole pond is not visible to me—it is cut off in the inner vision of the scene. I go up to a higher ridge of the flowered meadow and see an open gate in front of me. I go through the open gate, and a door frame or threshold appears a few feet in front of me. I go through the threshold, and I see this beautiful white light on the horizon just starting to rise, like the sun. It continues to rise as if a new day is dawning and rushes to envelop me. I feel part of the Oneness of the Universe.

In that experience of Oneness, I get into a supersonic rocket train that takes me deep into the vastness of me. During that trip, I climb from one compartment or interior box to another, growing, learning, and evolving, maybe even releasing blocks along the way to the nose of the train. Then I am dropped off at a place to be One with the vastness of the Oneness. I am sitting on a meditation cushion suspended in the space all around me. It is dark, but I see the twinkling stars all around. This is the space of stillness and silence. I also feel it is the Zero Point Field where all the untapped ideas and potential exist, and the point of singularity where all separateness is transcended into Oneness and magnetized unity is realized.

At this point, I slip through a white zip and enter a space of mirrors. I see myself as light. I understand there are different depths of this zip or sacred space. Next, I get into the supersonic rocket train again and get dropped off again. I enter a wider zip, and I see myself as light above a physical form, and I climb up the light. It becomes like a concrete or gravel path so I can move up into the height of it with physical feet. I sense the concept of traveling up the side of a pyramid. Other times, I travel up a tower of light.

Then I end up in a space that mirrors a pool of water with white light illuminating the water in the pool—and as the water shimmers with the light, I sense it symbolizes inspiration. As I am inspired, I sense my watery essence is being mirrored to me in this image.

One room leads to another room, and I visualize different scenes in each one. Most journeys take me to a small room of mirrors. In another room, I see a natural landscape. I am seeing it from a great height and notice that I am a bird flying over the landscape. I am receiving a bird's eye view, likely indicating life from a higher perspective or a higher level of Consciousness. Or sometimes, the landscape is pure gold as if Midas touched it all. In another room, I see the Flower of Life pulsating. In the next room, I see heads, representing ideas, suspended in darkness, until one is lit up as if I discovered something new, or I am taking a new action, or being invited to take a new action. Sometimes I enter into the Golden Buddha room or the Indra's Net room, where I discover more about myself, more about Oneness, and more about my journey in the Oneness. I could go on for ages in these adventures, but my timer goes off after 30 minutes. Upon which, I pick up my journal to ask questions of my guides to discover a deeper meaning of my experience.

Messages from the Guides

Question: Please help me understand the zip that came up in my meditation today. Am I interpreting the experience accurately?

Dear Beloved,

The zip or zips represent the increase in clarity of your inner world. They represent the thin spaces where there is no veil blocking you from entering the spiritual landscape of life, so that you can understand the Spiritual Realm. What is revealed to you when you slip through that thin space—from the physical realm—is a physical being. The idea is that if you could connect to your Spiritual Aspect— even your Oneness, you would be a Spiritual BEing in the physical. In this space of enlightenment, you could help others awaken to this truth and model for them or guide them on how to be their Spiritual Selves or live as a conscious expression of the Divine in a human body. You could live your life using the Spiritual Realm paradigms in the physical dimension. From this aspect, you could embody higher vibrational frequencies of the higher dimensions of BEing.

We love you. We love you. We love you.

Question: What is the significance of these images in today's meditation? What do I need to learn from this experience and these images?

Dear Beloved,

You, as the Oneness, went on a journey through the Oneness. There are many depths or energy layers in the Oneness. You are the Oneness, in a reflected form. The Oneness has infinite qualities—and you reflect the qualities that are uniquely you. As you reflect, you radiate or transmit that vibration as light or water. It is all Divine— just different qualities. One thing about the supersonic rocket train that takes you to different places is that it represents your expansion. To get to the depths of you, you have to space travel. The supersonic rocket train travels at the speed of light. You can just travel instantly to any quality of you within the Oneness if you consciously intend to do so. You are unlimited, as you know.

We love you. We love you. We love you.

Question: Explain the place that I discovered by going through a zip. Will you add to my understanding, or could you let me know the significance of why it was presented to me?

> *Dear Beloved,*
>
> *The place beyond the zip is the space beyond stillness and silence. Not many humans discover this place. But a way to explain it is a different vibrational frequency. These places of stillness and silence exist in different dimensions in different layers or depths. When one sets the intention to discover the stillness and silence of the Oneness, there are many levels to that intention. It is like a maze or a labyrinth that you can weave your way through—but there is no physical maze or labyrinth. You are just taken there from the first depth of silence and stillness.*
>
> *When you find a zip or thin place between the physical and invisible, whatever you are ready for will be presented to you. Today, you discovered a few others present in this dark space, and they were in their own stillness and silence. You also saw walls of mirrors that reflect who you are. This is a place where you can find out what can be released in your subconscious. Maybe you need to go through the space of mirrors to release a self-limiting concept.*
>
> *We love you. We love you. We love you.*

Through these messages, I had a revelation that connecting with the Oneness enables me to become more enlightened, increasingly expressing myself as a Spiritual BEing in the physical world. The connection with Oneness attunes my body to hold higher vibrational frequencies that allow me to embody more and more of my True Self.

It was also exciting to learn that the supersonic rocket train that I travel in represents my level of expansion and that the 'places' beyond the zips exist beyond the silence and stillness. They are not locations as we may think of, but rather different vibrational frequencies that exist in layers, depths, or dimensions that are revealed in meditation only as I am ready to receive them. Only when I am ready to receive the next layer of understanding is it shown to me in meditation. In a way, this is similar to how we learn through education or life. Everything connects and opens the door to an endless well of learning and growth in all aspects of our lives.

Reflections in a Room of Mirrors

Another place I go in my meditations on Oneness through the zips is a room of mirrors that reminds me of a department store dressing room, where I can see myself from different angles. At first, when I looked in the mirrors, all I saw was my physical body. Then I started to see myself as light coming from my heart. In later meditations, the light became so bright that it obliterated my physical form. Eventually, my light form was bigger than the Earth. But within that light, a small physical body connected me to Earth. Now this is the only vision of myself that I see in the mirror reflection.

Interestingly, I was curious about how using the mirrors in meditation might help me to release inner barriers that may be holding me back. Then I discovered that there is a spiritual concept called the hall of mirrors that showed me I was on the right path in my thinking. The suggestion is that seeing a hall of mirrors on an inner journey may indicate confusion between illusion and physical reality. But the mirrors can also represent a reflection of who we are being in every situation, relationship, or encounter, allowing us to see ourselves from a higher reality reflecting back to us. As a spiritual tool, mirrors can help us see ourselves through a situation or someone else's viewpoint, which may allow us to look deeper within to see why that point of view was mirrored back to us. For me, this was confirmation that looking deeper into my different reflections could reveal parts of me that had been hidden from view and hold valuable lessons for my Spiritual Growth.

This idea was further underscored when I attended a live event where the highly acclaimed channeler Darryl Anka was channeling the multidimensional extraterrestrial known as Bashar. During the audience Q&A for Bashar, I asked a question about Oneness. In response, Bashar invited me to imagine myself in front of a bunch of mirrors and see myself as thousands of reflections of myself all around me. Each reflection is a self-aware aspect of me, reflecting a specific view or angle. Every awareness is equally conscious and fully Self-aware. There are myriad aspects of ourselves. Each aspect is being reflected by circumstances and through others. Each aspect of ourselves can also see the other aspects of self that are reflected in the mirrors. This is the truth for everyone. The Universe is a mirror, and aspects of ourselves are being reflected to us in events or people. In turn, we reflect others to themselves.

On another level, I understood Bashar's answer also to mean that envisioning thousands of reflections of oneself is one way to tap into and understand the interconnectedness of the Oneness. If we can visualize the Oneness as reflecting ourselves and others, we can also sense the Consciousness of Oneness. In this reflective Universe, we can see aspects of ourselves that may be disconnected, unloved, separated, and unintegrated with the other aspects of us. Often, what we don't like in others is actually a reflection of something we don't like in ourselves or an aspect of ourselves we haven't integrated into our conscious wholeness. The Universe is gifting us a vision for us to take action to become more integrated and whole.

Every encounter and every emotional reaction triggered within us becomes a signal or a revelation of a disturbance within us. Recognizing this disturbance is a way to draw your attention to go deeper into Self-discovery of the meaning of the disturbance. Feeling discomfort, irritation, anger, fear, and resistance, to name a few disturbing reactions, serve to invite deeper self-reflection to discover the root cause within us. In this process, the world acts as a mirror to guide us to understand the deeper significance so that it can be resolved. The disturbance, once frustration, anger, or anxiety, transforms into an opening or window for compassion and growth, for self-love and evolution. When we can understand the reflective nature of the Universe and know that our reactions to the world around us are merely invitations to discover the core of an unresolved aspect of ourselves, we begin to welcome and embrace all the reflections we receive from the Universe, no matter how unpleasant they may be to see.

When we traverse the bridge from resistance to acceptance, we can heal within. We can begin to resolve deep-rooted issues, like the fractures from abandonment, neglect, and trauma that we were not able to resolve when we were young. Unable to resolve these core issues, we shut them down and locked them away. But they were/are still within us. We can reframe the experiences and take advantage of the opportunity to resolve the issue now and welcome the lost or shut-off parts back home. We have the opportunity to be more integrated as one whole with all its parts shining their lights. We have the opportunity to deepen our connection to our complete selves. We have the opportunity to connect to the tapestry of life around us that represents the Oneness. It is at this point, through integration, that we are more able to embody the manifestation or the expression of the Oneness from a more complete version of ourselves.

We can go beyond this as an intellectual concept to viscerally feel the connection or interconnectedness by asking what our experience would be if we view others like we were seeing them through a room of mirrors, with ourselves as only one mirror or angle in the room?

I suggest that, seeing each other in this way, we would quickly begin to understand that what others present to us represents only one of thousands or millions of aspects of themselves. We would know that this one aspect shown in the reflection of our mirror does not represent the whole of them, or the full truth of who they are. And if we changed our angle of perception or our level of Consciousness, we would see a new aspect of them. This invites us to trust that at the core of who we and who they are is the Divine One. They are each different expressions of the Divine with different levels of awareness about our interconnectedness.

The main point of Oneness is the connection or interconnection. The key aspect is the unity or interconnectedness of life. Energy is being shared in the dynamic flow of the vibrant dancing energy of the Universe. Everything is the One thing. We were all created by a Higher Power, the One—All That Is, God, the Divine. Like each wave is an interconnected part of the whole ocean, we are interconnected parts of the whole Universe—One Consciousness. As aspects of the Universe, it reflects us, and we reflect each other. There is an invisible *hall of mirrors* around us and in front of us reflecting who we are BEing. Recognizing this aspect of the reflective Universe helps us to grow and participate as aspects of the One.

On the physical plane, we each reflect who another is BEing when in our presence. Oneness is *only you encountering you*. Nothing is separate from you. If you are reacting to something or someone, it is a message to you that it is an issue within you. Nothing is separate from us as the One. That is why it is important for our growth to look internally if we witness something we don't like or appreciate in another. If we get triggered, at some level, maybe at a deep layer, we do or did that same thing, either to ourselves or others. The key is to become aware of how we respond or react to different people or different situations. This is our GPS to alert us to work on ourselves in this area. The good news is that it can be resolved because it is within us. If it is outside of us, we are powerless—we are victims.

Golden Buddha Reveals Our Divine Light Within

Another experience of Oneness during my inner journeys occurs in the Golden Buddha room. The Golden Buddha is a statue of unknown origins, thought to have been made in the 13th-14th centuries, located at the Wat Traimit Monastery in Bangkok, Thailand. For centuries, the statue, approximately 10 feet high and weighing 5.5 tons, was thought to be made of clay stucco with inlaid bits of glass. Only its size was remarkable. However, that all changed in the 1950s when it was relocated within the monastery grounds.

The story goes that the statue was originally cast in gold. But when the Burmese army invaded this region in the mid-1700s, monks at the monastery disguised the statue to appear unremarkable and of little value by completely encasing it in stucco, concealing its radiant magnificence. All the monks perished when the Burmese army invaded, and with them, the true story of this Buddha statue was lost.

In 1955, when the monks living at the monastery relocated their beloved Buddha statue, they discovered that there was much more to this statue than the eye could see. During the move, the ropes holding the statue gave way. The statue fell to the ground and cracked open. Amazingly, the crack revealed a light within the statue. The monks carefully chipped away the outer layer of stucco and discovered their beloved Buddha was actually made of gold. When fully recovered, the Golden Buddha statue revealed its radiant light.

The monks also discovered that the statue was comprised of 10 separate parts that fit together perfectly. At the base of the statue, they found a key that unlocked the parts, allowing them to be easily separated for transportation. This now famous statue shows the Golden Buddha with his right hand touching the Earth, indicating his awakening or enlightenment. In 2010, a new building was erected at the Wat Traimit Monastery to protect the Golden Buddha.

In Buddhist tradition, this story is offered as a teaching about hidden, inner potential, illustrating the immensity of our own hidden potential and value, as well as the hidden potential and value in all others. While this is a powerful teaching, I also view this story as a beautiful teaching on the truth of who we are in Oneness. At our core, we are all made of the pure golden light of Divine Light—the Oneness within.

When we are born, this inner light is brilliant and radiant. But as we travel life's path, illusions or misperceptions of who we are and why we are here conceal the light, much like the mud and clay that concealed the Golden Buddha. We develop false perceptions about ourselves, which become self-limiting beliefs blocking our radiant light. We make stories about not being good enough, not being worthy, being unlovable, and our powerlessness. Perhaps we do this out of a sense of fear, protecting ourselves from standing out and shining brightly, much like the monks who feared for the Golden Buddha to be seen for its true value.

Whatever our reasons for concealing our inner Divine Light of Oneness, be assured we do this to ourselves, and only we can reveal our truth. If we could chip away at these false beliefs to allow our radiance to shine forth, this would be a different world. When I think about this chipping away, the image of a chick pecking through the eggshell comes to mind. The birthing chick is breaking through to become an active aspect of the Oneness. This is birth. This is awakening. We can be awakened even now. We can be rebirthed. We can remove the mud and plaster of our inner barriers that block our golden light.

We can always return to the brilliant light aspect of ourselves to radiate our true essence in the world. We can work on chipping away or re-birthing the truth of us so that we can shine forth in our Divine Magnificence. This Divine Magnificence is at the core of every BEing. Knowing this, we can see each other as reflections of our Divinity in the Oneness, the ONE DIVINE LIGHT that connects us all.

Following one of my visits to the Golden Buddha room during meditation, I asked my Guides about the experience.

Messages from the Guides

Question: In my meditation, I aligned with an as-yet unknown potential or opportunity, and then I went through a golden zip. I was in a room with the Golden Buddha. I became the Golden Buddha. I felt the golden light flowing from within me to without me. What more can I learn from this meditation adventure?

> *Dear Beloved,*
>
> *We have some new understanding about your new potential or new opportunity. As you are shedding your mud layers, you are going to be invited as an enlightened speaker at conferences. You are being invited to bridge the gap between the physical and the Invisible Realms—to bring the two realms together as One. So naturally, you are invited to come from your golden or elevated PRESENCE—to be a spiritual influencer with PRESENCE. So, the audience can FEEL the*

love, peace, and joy that is animated within you.

We love you. We love you. We love you.

I was thrilled to receive this message as an encouragement that we have the opportunity to continuously elevate our way of BEing to attain ever higher perspectives on life. When we reach a level of awareness where others can benefit from what we have learned, we are called to awaken truth and wisdom in the collective.

Jeweled Reflections of Indra's Net

In the Vedic cosmology, the concept of Oneness is reflected in the metaphor of Indra's Net, which was the ruler of all gods in Vedic philosophy during the time of the Buddha, approximately the 5th century BCE. Indra's net is thought to be infinitely large, containing a multifaceted jewel at each node, vertex, or junction point in the net. Each jewel reflects all other jewels. I see this as a perfect representation of the concept of Oneness. Not only does the idea of each jewel reflecting all jewels square precisely with the premise that we are all one within a net of interconnectedness reflecting each other, but jewels also capture the brilliant radiance of our shared Divine Light.

To further emphasize the vast interconnectedness of Oneness, the jewels also illustrate that there is an infinite number of reflections in each jewel as a facet of one jewel. If all jewels are reflected in each jewel, when you sit in one jewel, you exist in all jewels simultaneously. Likewise, if you enter one jewel, you enter all jewels without leaving the first jewel. Using the metaphor of Indra's Net, we are each jeweled facets of the same One jewel. We are different points of view of the same One BEing.

Following my experience of Indra's Net during meditation, I again asked my Guides about the experience.

Messages from the Guides

Question: In my meditation today, I realized that the Universe is a crystal. I am a crystal within that crystal. Also, I went through a very thin green zip, and the room contained a big web with jewels at each node of the web. Is this Indra's Net, and what does it signify to me? Is this web connected to the crystal idea?

Dear Beloved,

Love that you understand the crystal perspective and how everything is a facet reflecting the Source. The web of life represents all aspects connected, and each BEing is represented as a jewel. Jewels and crystals are similar here—just a different metaphor of existence. Our energetic structure—oh, there is a 'structure' to your energetic BEingness that can be interpreted as a jewel or crystal. Because each of us is immense, it is difficult to discern that--especially if you are in the physical realm.

Keep traveling and exploring the wisdom and truth by going deep within you. This is the most significant journey of a lifetime.

What you are experiencing in each room of the mansion is a significant truth presented to you in terms of your level of understanding in the moment.

We love you. We love you. We love you.

Question: The Oneness concept of the hall of mirrors, Indra's Net, holograms, and the Universe as a crystal all help me understand. How do I create a feeling of connection to the Oneness or BEing the Oneness?

Dear Beloved,

You mean you want to take the intellectual concept of Oneness now understood from these metaphors and elicit a physical sensation of the Oneness? Yes.

Okay, it is like fish in water. The fish are swimming in water, and that's all they know. It is all the sensation they ever feel. You are the same in the Oneness.

We think what you are asking is related to your level of awareness of the Oneness. When that awareness elevates, there is a felt sensation like an aha moment! That is what you are feeling—a new awareness of the Oneness, where you feel an energetic shift within you. That makes this new understanding.

We love you. We love you. We love you.

Question: In my meditation, I experienced Indra's Net, the ball or fireball of my goal tossed to my future self, and the removal of the fence that represented my fear. Could you please elaborate on these three experiences to help me understand their full significance?

Dear Beloved,

Yes, that fear fence exists in your subconscious. It was picked up from the larger light BEing that you are and thrown outside the scene of your meditative vision—your subconscious mind—which means it no longer exists there.

You experienced Indra's Net in two different areas of the zip space. In the first experience, you witnessed how the jewel that you are is reflected by all the other jewels within Indra's Net. You even felt a new version of Namaste: "the jewel in me reflects the jewel in you." Then, at a higher level of Indra's Net, you realized that the vibrational frequency you are affects what you reflect. This is how we experience the world from our vibrational frequency. We only experience and reflect back the frequency that we are.

The ball of energy created as a vision of your future competency was created in the green area of the zip space. You envisioned your future self, and you tossed the vision or energetic vision to her. This action will provide the growth pathway for you to achieve that goal as your future self. This action also helps to further claim the real you and where the inspiration is leading you in your desire to be the best you. The best you is the real you.

We love you. We love you. We love you.

In exploring the meaning and significance of Indra's Net, I realized that I am a crystal, a reflection or representation of the Universe, which is also a crystal. I learned that all BEings are jewels within the Oneness of the Universe. If we could shift our perspective to see this Universal truth in all we encounter, our lives, our cultures, our countries, and our world would be living in peace and harmony.

I also learned that there is an energetic shift revelation when we experience the sensation of Oneness. Through this, I can connect to my future self and transmit my vision to her to ensure its achievement. I never would have understood that on my own. Paying attention to what is happening within us is the key to understanding the Oneness through our revelations. We experience the physical world through the lens of our own vibrational frequency. That is where we are limited unless we keep learning, growing, and becoming enlightened by our experiences. Just keep on the path to enlightenment and be open, and we all will have the unique experiences of what we need to learn next for our evolution and expansion.

Exalted Messages of Oneness

As I have continued to explore Oneness through communication with my Guides, new insights are revealed, and concepts I have integrated are given deeper and more profound meaning. The following messages provide revelations and insights that were particularly powerful for me. I share them as lights on your path to discovering the Oneness of All That Is within you, in the world around you, and in the vast Universe of possibilities that surround us all.

Messages from the Guides

Question: After slipping through a zip, I went beyond the row of dressing rooms to an empty space. It was the same darkness I experienced when I got dropped off by the supersonic rocket train. But this darkness hugged me. I sensed a physical sensation of an energetic embrace that was so Divine that tears flowed from my eyes. I felt an expansion. I understood how an electron winks in and out of physical existence because I was winking in and out of physical existence. That is what happens when we come into physical bodies. We leave the Spiritual Realm to come and re-find ourselves—our True Selves. The physical shows us who we are BEing by what is happening in our lives and what is mirrored back to us. But even in the Invisible me, I can feel and sense the presence of the Divine. Something happens energetically that results in a felt sensation. What happens energetically to have that sensation? And also, I realized that we--or at least part of our Soul or energy body remains in the Oneness when we become physical. Can you explain that to me?

> *Dear Beloved,*
>
> *We love the experience you had this morning in the Oneness. You are right that Souls don't ever completely leave the Oneness or the invisible. The physical and the Spiritual aspects represent wholeness. Your physical aspect is not your complete self. The physical and Spiritual aspects are inextricably connected.*
>
> *Your other question about what happened energetically to have a physical felt sensation is the culmination of photon density in your energetic core. When you activate the energetic core by consciously breathing and carving a pathway in it, you can accrete more light there. That light is activated in the physical by situations that are of a similar vibration. Energetic vibrations seek out like frequencies. Like attracts like. So, the felt sensation is an amplified vibrational frequency—sort of like a ripple effect and constructive interference where the amplitude of one wave is added to the amplitude of another wave.*
>
> *You connected to the Divine within you in that deeper area past the dressing rooms. You connected with your True Self—your Inner Radiance, your Inner Wisdom. This is an exalted experience and one that you will cherish always. You are going deep within yourself, and we love it.*
>
> *We love you. We love you. We love you.*

To reflect on the deeper meaning of their response, I invite you to believe that you are more than a physical body. You are a Soul with a little physical body. Your Soul is so vast and immense that it can't fit into your small physical body. The more you activate your energetic core, the more you will receive physical sensations of the vastness of your Soul interconnected with the Oneness. Breathing deeply up and down your energetic core and bringing conscious awareness enhances photon density.

Question: I understand feeling the sensation of the Oneness within. It is the continuum that flows through our chakras as light and becomes our life experiences. Was there more for me to learn?

> Dear Beloved,
>
> *The significant aspect of your journey is to have physical sensations of this energetic vibration that flows through you. How you experience these vibrations determines what level of Oneness you experience, how many zips you can enter, and what you will be shown in each dimension. It is a careful step-by-step learning process so that you can safely progress from one step to the next. You must be able to handle or take in the higher vibrational frequencies that you will encounter in the deeper layers of Consciousness or deeper zip experiences.*
>
> *Feeling Oneness expand in you helps you match the vibration of Consciousness outside you. That is another aspect of the Oneness. You are the same vibration inside and outside. Every time you go to a new layer of Oneness, the vibration around you changes. Your internal nature has to match the external vibration for progression to occur.*
>
> *We love you. We love you. We love you.*

We grow step by step on our path to enlightenment. We learn what is next for us as we go. There is so much support for our ability to integrate higher and higher vibrations into our physical forms, our growth and evolution. I invite you to expand on the idea of integrating more and more of your aspects of self and ponder the ease of connecting with your future self as a way to create alignment with a pathway of growth to become your future self.

Question: Today in meditation, I was sitting in space and expanded with the Oneness. I went through a few zips and saw the same rooms that I've seen before. But I came out and kept expanding. I felt like I may have had an exalted experience. I also felt pressure low in my pelvic floor area as if something was being released or pushed out. Can you explain or interpret what was happening? It all felt good.

Dear Beloved,

You were BEing less you, more in the One. The expansion feeling was your energy field becoming more integrated in the Creative Intelligence. The pelvic area issue was more energy coming into your energetic core, and it's taking up more space. It is likely you will need to build more circuits there to allow for high vibrational frequencies to become embodied there. It is also a process of feeling and allowing the Oneness.

We love you. We love you. We love you.

This message confirmed for me that new energy or higher vibrations entering the physical body can be felt. A felt sensation is a confirmation of energy shifting within us.

Question: I felt the energy of my True Self flowing up into me, up my energetic core, into my heart, and then looking through my eyes. Was it my True Self, or was it dispersed energy coming back to me during my awakening in the meditation?

Dear Beloved,

It is the same thing. The True Self and energy flowing back to you—it is the same thing. It is high vibrational frequency energy that got compartmentalized off your direct True Self. When you have awakenings during meditations, it means you are ready to see and understand at a higher level. We are witnesses to your growth and expansion. We also understand ways that you can guide others to these inner awakenings through guided meditations.

We love you. We love you. We love you

This message confirmed for me that all is working in our favor and there is tremendous support for our growth and elevation.

Question: In my meditation today, I went through a thin amber zip and went into two rooms. First, there was a dark room, and as I was thinking, I'd like to see what was in this room, two eyes appeared, which pierced the darkness. Even though I could not see beyond the darkness, I got a sense that I would see only what I intended to see. Intending to 'see' what was there, I only saw eyes. This carries with it truth in what shows up in our lives, we get what we expect, and expectations come from beliefs or knowings. It behooves us to explore our beliefs and release limitations. The next room was a room of windows with dark drapes--a viewing room. The drapes were removed, and I could see clouds in different formations. I realized my gift of viewing or witnessing people's life lessons and Soul's purposes, as in a session with a client. She had come to her life to learn she was stronger than sorcery or the dark side of life. Her Soul Purpose is/was to discover that the path of love and benevolence is stronger than any dark side of life. Is there something more you can add to amplify my understanding of these two rooms and their enlightenment for me?

> *Dear Beloved,*
>
> *The adventure you had today was deeply illuminating and surely added to your degree of enlightenment. You sensed correctly about the eyes in the dark room. It was cryptic and symbolic, but your Inner Wisdom is developing. Everyone only sees what they are looking for. So be careful what you are looking for!! It helps you to check on your beliefs, because your beliefs create expectations in life, and many beliefs are incorrect. They are developed so young in life, and from logic and reason appear true because evidence seems to build to reinforce the belief. But the deeper universal reality, since they believe and expect something, that is the ONLY thing they will witness in their lives. This is under the concept that the Universe is a mirror—reflecting you—your thoughts, feelings, and beliefs.*
>
> *In the second room—the viewing room—windows represent something is opening up for you. Windows to the world. The clouds are symbols or formations of visions of what you can see using cryptic information. Your ability to discern with clarity in your client's session was an example of a new gift of yours to help people to interpret their lives in a new and deeply meaningful way because of what has happened to them—their challenges and their traumas. You also immediately realized a unique Soul Purpose of your client, to help her realize the Soul's plan or intention in choosing such a traumatic experience to*

> *help her in her evolution. Helping her understand the brilliance in the terrible gift of the trauma will help her move on and not get stuck in the trauma. She will move beyond the trauma and learn to be grateful for it, as it is a magnificent gift in her Soul's evolution. This ability of yours is going to get enhanced and will be more and more clear and obvious to you in more and more clients.*
>
> *We love you. We love you. We love you*

The more we open to the Oneness, the greater access we have to our Inner Wisdom and the more connected to each other's essence and journey. When we understand the greater gift of the experience, it may be easier to let go of the pain and receive the gift more completely.

I would like to inspire you to meditate and do automatic writing. Hopefully, the messages from my Guides have inspired you to connect with your True Self and your Ascended Master guides to gain the wisdom and insights you are seeking, or to deepen that connection if you are already on this path. For me, automatic writing has been a powerful tool in opening to and receiving these messages. It has enhanced my journey in magnificent and amazing ways. Perhaps it is just the tool you have been looking for to learn what's next for you and let this higher guidance flow easily into your life. You can get any information you desire simply by asking or setting an intention. While writing this book, my pure intention to explore the meaning and the experience of Oneness led me to many places that provided guidance and information. The same gift is available to everyone, and especially you, now that you know it's yours to claim.

As we conclude our time together on this journey to Oneness, I hope you see how you are attuned energetically, mentally, emotionally, and physically to the Oneness. I invite you to take a moment to be still, quiet your mind, and open your heart to feel the simple but profound truth that you, everyone, and everything are part of this huge, loving, and benevolent connectedness. Allow the feeling to sink in. We are all part of something so much bigger than we can fathom, something so benevolent and loving that is beyond what we normally experience unless we open up to it. It is for you and for the Universe to grow, expand, and evolve.

From the felt sensation of Oneness, allow your inner knowing to expand and embrace being part of the Divine Benevolence that built this beautiful, extraordinary world for us as a way to become our True Self, our Soulful aspect.

We have exquisite opportunities to become who we are meant to be at the highest level. It is all within us. We don't need validation from external sources. We don't need to have the right earthly connections. We have the highest-level connections flowing through us continually. We just need to wake up and discover this truth for ourselves.

I invite you to keep going deeper and deeper and experience the truth and wisdom on your own. Weed out the self-limiting beliefs and inner barriers holding you back from becoming the unstoppable force of goodness and benevolence you were born to be you.

I hope this exploration of Oneness has revealed for you the simple yet deeply propound truth that is a mystery to most, lost and buried deep in ideas of separation and fear: our lives, our world, the Universe, all this is, are intricately woven together, as parts of a Divine whole that we each carry within us. How Magnificent, indeed!

I AM the Oneness

I am the total Oneness of the Universe.
My energies are interwoven with
Wisdom, enlightenment, compassion
Peace, joy, bliss, ecstasy of the One.

Like the Oneness, I share the Vastness, the Void.
Like the Oneness, I am Divine.
I am the highest vibrations.
I am the quest for more . . . love, joy, peace.

I am blessed and the blessing.
I am the yin and the yang.
I am the love, unconditional and pouring
Forward to all.

I am ever changing moment by moment as life unfolds.
Ever growing and expanding toward higher and higher expression.
I am committed to the evolution of the Oneness
Within every aspect of my energetic fabric.

I am Divine Love, I am Divine Wisdom
Reaching into the Vastness of Sacred Space.
I am the Sacred Space.
I am the expression of the highest potential.

I am the flow.
I am the freedom.
I am the joy.
I am the love.

I am the Oneness and goodness personified.
I am a single expression of the Oneness.
With every potential available to me.
Every possibility opening within me.

I am *All That Is*.
Enlightenment flows through me
I align with the enlightened wisdom flow
Which carries me to higher frequencies and different dimensions.

As I exist in the Oneness and Unity Consciousness
There is nothing I am not.
I am everything, and everything is me.
Why have these revelations been lost in me before?

Why is this a secret hidden from the general population?
Why is this so difficult to grasp if this is who I AM?
This wisdom is woven into the fabric of every cell and every string of energy.
This wisdom is the essence of who I AM.

Because when we separate from the Unity
We become disconnected, don't believe the truth.
We stay inside our own minds, not understanding the beyond.
How could it be true if I am me and you are you?

Mysterious and wonderful.
Divine and Sacred.
Holy and Benevolent.
Loving . . . embracing ALL.

There is nothing I am NOT.
I AM all of it.
A beautiful tapestry of Spiritual and physical.
I have become human to grow and evolve.

I reflect all other living beings
All living beings reflect me.
We are interconnected and holographic.
We are fused together and radiant.

I AM Divine Light radiating truth and wisdom.

I AM the Source of Infinite Intelligence, welcoming goodness.

I AM a magnificent expression of the Divine bridging the Spiritual and physical.

I AM Divine Love extending to the ends of the Universe.

~Anne M. Deatly

EXERCISES

My aim throughout this book has been to provide you with examples and opportunities to experience new concepts in ways that touch your heart and open your mind. As a scientist, I know that in scientific exploration, a proposed result must be proven through rigorous testing that produces the same result multiple times. The same is true for Spiritual exploration. It's not enough to read about proposed theories and insights; they must be proven through inner knowing, discernment, and experience. And even then, only the truth that is aligned with you will be revealed and experienced, which makes it even more imperative to do your own experimentation and exploration to illuminate your path. But once you have proven your own truth and experienced the Inner Wisdom, it's yours; it's there forever!

I hope you have enjoyed the exercises throughout this book to deepen your understanding and wisdom on your Journey to Oneness.

To integrate the content in this Section, here are some exercises to connect to the Oneness and your highest potential.

Exercise 1: Meditation and Journal Prompts to experience each quality of the Oneness

- The Universe is a hologram.
- The Universe is reflective.
- The Universe is like the Golden Buddha.
- The Spiritual Journey is a path to excavating the self-limiting beliefs to reveal the Loving Presence and Golden Light at the core of you.
- The Universe is a web of jewels reflecting all the other jewels.

Exercise 2: Meditation Journey to Discover Aspects of the Oneness

Develop your own meditative journey or use the meditative journey below with the intent to experience the Oneness. I share my meditation journey sequence below to get you started. You may experience different scenes or different places. Let it be your own journey, specific to you.

To prepare for a meditation to experience Oneness, I begin by setting a firm intention to connect with and experience Oneness.

Then I connect to my heart through slow, deep conscious breathing up and down my central channel, first to carve a pathway or open up space for the energy in my energetic core to flow easily through me, either from above to below my physical form or from below to above my physical form. Next, I expand my heart energy out into the room to connect to the Divine. This usually takes three or four deep breaths in a pattern of inhaling for three counts, holding your breath for three counts, and then exhaling for three counts. As you exhale, imagine your heart energy is expanding in concentric circles from your body. With each breath, the energy expands further and further away from your body.

Then I focus on seeing a small version of myself traveling down a floating spiral staircase from my head to just inside the area of my heart organ or heart chakra. A heart-shaped door slides open, and there is a brilliant, radiant, loving white light that envelops the small version of me upon entering the heart space. I physically feel a shift in the present life version of me, as if I am radiating this light and becoming this light.

From this space of light, I take a trip to what I believe is my subconscious, where I see a meadow of flowers with a pond to the left, but the whole pond is not visible to me—it is cut off in the inner vision of the scene. I go up to a higher ridge of the flowered meadow and see an open gate in front of me. I go through the open gate, and a door frame or threshold appears a few feet in front of me. I go through the threshold, and I see this beautiful white light on the horizon just starting to rise, like the sun. It continues to rise as if a new day is dawning and rushes to envelop me. I feel part of the Oneness of the Universe.

As that Oneness, I get into a supersonic rocket train that takes me deep into the vastness of me. During that trip, I climb from one compartment or interior box to another, growing, learning, and evolving, maybe even releasing blocks along the way to the nose of the train. Then I am dropped off at a place to be One with the vastness of the Oneness. I am sitting on a meditation cushion suspended in the space all around me. It is dark, but I see the twinkling stars all around. This is the space of stillness and silence. I also feel it is the Zero Point Field where all the untapped ideas and potential exist, and the point of singularity where all separateness is transcended into Oneness and magnetized unity is realized.

At this point, I slip through a zip or narrow vertical space and enter a particular space that has a message or a revelation for me. One room leads to another room, and I visualize different scenes in each one. Each room has a different message, a deeper learning, or a new way for me to grow.

Exercise 3: *What If* Questions

- *What if* the Universe was really only one BEing?
- *What if* I am the Universe in a drop?
- *What if* I were One with all others and One with the Divine? How would that change me? How would I show up in the world?
- *What if* we were all connected and reflected each other?
- *What if* we were all expressing the Divine in our physicality?
- *What if* I could see myself as a light form bigger than the Earth in the mirrors of the Universe?
- *What if* I could experience myself as a reflection in the dressing room of mirrors being reflected ad infinitum?
- *What if* I could experience myself as a jewel in Indra's Net, and I experienced how all the other jewels reflected me?
- *What if* I could experience myself as a jewel in Indra's Net, and I reflected all the other jewels?
- *What if* I could experience life or the Spiritual Journey as a path to uncover the Golden Buddha, my hidden potential, within me?
- *What if* I could freely transmit my Divine Radiance, or my Divine Magnificence, to the world unapologetically?

AFTERWORD

Congratulations on finishing this journey with me! Hopefully, you've had many illuminating experiences throughout this journey. You've discovered more about yourself and who you really are. Hopefully, you experienced the truth and wisdom of your Divine Magnificence. You're on a path to enlightenment. Perhaps you'll embrace everything that has happened, is happening, and will happen to you as a gift from your True Self. Everything is working in your favor. Everything is happening for you to explore and discover to BE more and to awaken. Focus from the inside out.

Life is all about exploration and discovery. There is a whole—VAST—Consciousness available to us to explore and play in. There are so many enriching opportunities—so many mind-blowing adventures to explore, so many never-done-before experiences yet to live. To be fully ourselves, we realize *Why Not Me* instead of hiding in our own safe corner of the vast Consciousness of opportunity. We can start to discover for ourselves what the Quantum Reality offers us in this concept of exploration. Nothing is limiting us but our own selves. There are no limits in the Quantum Reality or Universal Consciousness. Limitations are only present in our minds that are stuck in the physical realm paradigms of life. There is so much more readily available to us to explore, experience, and to become. Stepping into these opportunities will help us realize the truth and wisdom about the grandness and magnificence of this life. It's amazing, and it's right there for you and me. Just follow the golden light of enlightenment. Your life will be forever changed.

Aligning with your Divine Magnificence, connecting to your Loving Presence, Inner Wisdom, True Self is my goal for this book. It's intended for each of us to express our True Self and reach for the stars to higher and higher potential. The entelechy Life Force within you is guiding you to become who you're meant to be. Trust that, become that, embody that.

We're meant to expand to the edges of the Universe and take up the magnificent, vast spaciousness and become fully engaged as enlightened BEings in the Oneness. We're meant to create spaciousness in our lives for truth and wisdom to flow in. We're meant to create space in which to grow. We're meant to embrace and love all our experiences as stepping stones to our greatest advancement and evolution. It's all grander than our imaginations envision.

We're empowered and evolving. The energy of the Universe is increasing and upleveling by our discovering the unfathomable truth. It's a participatory Universe, depending on us to move forward, creating a world we'd love to inhabit. We can witness miracles unfolding in front of our physical eyes, revealing our engagement with the happenings around us. Each of us matters—deeply—to the Universe. We're an integral part of eternity. We've been here before, and likely, we'll be coming back to grow and evolve in different bodies and different circumstances to stretch us in completely new ways.

Hopefully, this book elevated you to a joy vibration. There are spectrums of love, spectrums of joy, and spectrums of peace to explore and experience. There are spectrums of abundance that are dancing all around us, waiting for us to awaken to the bountiful treasures. Be in wonder of the world around you that has this magnificent mystery within it. Don't take anything at face value. Look beyond to discover the hidden layers of the Divine beauty and brilliance.

Keep pondering yourself and your beliefs to become more connected to the absolute delight and magnificence of the Universe. Fully engage as part of the Oneness. Discover and become more aware of the deep abiding love here for all of us, that is us. Keep awakening to the radiance of dazzling potential and growth that is available at our fingertips. Expand to the edges of the Universe to become more fully you as your Divine Magnificence.

Find Divine Moments and feel Divine Presence. Expect miracles. When we intersect with nature in unplanned ways, we can be enlightened by what shows up—natural views of the Divine. Like the blue heron I witnessed right outside my back door, the two swans, and the group of small birds on my terrace.

We can call forth the energy of the Earth, our True Selves, our ancestors, or close friends who have transitioned. We can call forth Ascended Masters, Spirits, Archangels, and Angels into our energy field at will. We can call forth or envision energy spiraling into our energy fields and we can call forth specific vibrations such as enlightenment, wisdom, loving presence, unconditional love, joy, peace, compassion to fill up the cocoon-like energetic structure that helps transmute us to these higher vibrational frequencies—to live our lives from a higher way of BEing and fully become who we were meant to be.

It really is all about who we are BEing in life that makes the difference to be our True Selves. Being present to life and the Divine's hand in it all will accelerate us into an ascended way of BEing and catapult us into more and more elevated experiences of connection, delight, and presence. Be your true, authentic Soulful Self. Identify and express as your Soulful Self. Master your mind to serve your Soulful Self. Train your mind to be on you and follow the guidance of your True Self. Live a meaningful life as you understand the higher wisdom of the Universe. You decided to come into a physical existence to live at your highest potential. When you're on a path of enlightenment, you become aware of all the grandness of the human life opportunity for the evolution and ascension of your Soul, your True Self.

Understanding the Divine Intentions to experience life through you as you become your True Self, highlights the significance of your life in the growth and expansion of the Divine, the Oneness, the whole Universe. You understand the grand plan and intelligent design of this physical reality and how it is inextricable from the Spiritual Realm. You understand that all of humanity has this same wonderful and miraculous opportunity to step in as one who knows the plan and wants to play a significant role in the Divine Magnificence to expand and evolve, and contribute to the highest vibrational opportunity.

Rising above all the lower vibrational states illuminates that life is immeasurably more rewarding and meaningful from this higher, enlightened perspective. Isn't it time to step up into this awareness and do our part in this Divine Plan for growth and ascending beyond the physical realm limitations?

Recognizing the Divineness in ourselves and each other and treating each other with that respect, we'll create a world we'd all deserve and love. It's time we awaken to the truth of our existence and understand our ultimate reason for being here now. It's time we start viewing life through the lens of the Divine that we're all Divinely created for a specific purpose, with no one person, race, religion, country, or gender being better than another. We're here to put our differences aside and revel in the Divine Magnificence that each of us expresses authentically as our True Selves. We are ONE in this truth.

Bliss and gratitude are extremely important in an enlightened life, or a life of Self-actualization and Self-mastery. Giving and receiving in equilibrium is important to be in flow with the Universe. A natural by-product is bliss and gratefulness. Ideally, it also means that you're giving and receiving—what you receive is shared. You really can't hold onto anything to complete the flow –it goes in and out so that it's all part of the Oneness—the energy here and beyond.

Bliss is a natural state of BEing. Removing layers of misperceptions and negativity will unmask the bliss. When you're enlightened, you're grateful for all aspects of life—especially the difficult times. Gratitude helps illuminate how life works in your favor by providing obstacles you need to overcome, aspects of stuckness, misperceptions, and false beliefs. We all have challenges or roadblocks to help us grow and expand. Ascension and enlightenment are also accompanied by connecting and BEing bliss—and being grateful for all of it. It's the Divine awakening within us to help us remove the blocks to live life to the fullest and contribute at the highest levels.

Focusing on the Oneness, there is only One Source, One Heart, One Existence. We are all fractals or expressions of the Divine. We are all interconnected and interrelated. At our core is golden light or the golden Buddha, which we often block with self-limiting beliefs. We're all reflections for each other. We're all jewels in Indra's Net. There are layers of the Oneness that get revealed as we go deep into the exploration. The deeper we go, the more there is to learn. It's the most exciting journey in life.

As part of your discovery journey, you may want to reread parts of this book or repeat the exercises to experience them through new stages of growth. BEing comes from learning through life experiences, just as wisdom comes from doing and experiencing. Use this book to monitor your growth and evolution over time by observing how your experiences and answers change.

Oneness=Bliss=Loving Presence. All these are the same. All is energy within you to access anytime. The pathway to discover and BE these highest states of BEing is removing the layers of disconnection, doubt, and programming of separation. Find unity beyond the duality that's so pervasive in the human limitations of life. This is a beautiful challenge to discover the Bliss, and the Loving Presence--the way of BEing in the Spiritual Realm. This is key to living as your True Self—to create a life from the Oneness, not the duality of the physical realm. Discovering how to do this will be a major shift in your life's trajectory. You'll find wisdom, enlightenment, unconditional love, joy, peace, freedom, and compassion. The golden light of enlightenment takes you there. We're all One. Together, let's create a world of Oneness that illuminates our Divine Magnificence.

The jewel in me honors the jewel in you.

Divine Magnificence

In Divine Magnificence,
You simply radiate your inherent goodness.
Shining the Divine Light within you.
Mirroring the Divine aspect that is unconditional love.

The Unified Field flows through you
With radiance, vibrancy, and brilliance.
To activate that energy within you
To match the energy of your True and Higher Self.

Your frequency matches the benevolent stars.
Your vibration ripples in waves from you.
In all directions through the whole Universe.
You exist out of time and space.

Your energy is elegant in its connection
With All That Is, the Oneness.
You are everything and everything is you.
It is a miraculous existence all together.

You belong to this grand enlightened Quantum Reality.
This vibrant enlivened active dynamic
Energy Field is ever changing and growing.
You are part of it and contribute to it.

You radiate the Loving Presence that you are.
You exude wisdom, joy, and peace
Compassion, wonder, and unconditional love.
That is felt by others around you.

Others marvel at your peace.
Others delight in your compassion.
Others feel your deep abiding love.
Others are magnetized to your gentle presence.

Your expansion into the unknown is clearly visible to the clairvoyants.
Your elevated speech is heard by the clairaudients.
The claircognizants know you without meeting you prior.
The clairsentients can feel your presence inside them.

Your alignment to the Divine is sensed as wisdom.
You have tapped into your Infinite Potential.
Miracles shower down from above you consistently.
You have mastered your energy.

Your Soul is guiding you.
Your mind follows the Soul's guidance.
You've achieved Self-mastery and are enlightened.
You've connected to the wisdom of the Earth.

You are simply Divine.
You are an aspect of the Oneness.
Your energy ripples through the Universe.
You bring enlightenment to the Earth.

~Anne M. Deatly

APPENDIX A:
DIVINE SOUL ENERGIES

Soul Energy	Characteristics	Roles
Divine Power	**When in alignment:** Souls with Divine Power are focused on and highly value freedom. They must have power over their own lives but not others. These independent-thinker Souls do whatever they want without limitation or lack. They are quick thinkers, joyful learners, and express their creativity. They forge ahead. They are self-starters who take responsibility and action easily. They seek to understand the power of the Soul. They are natural leaders. They are sensitive to energy, and they are often psychic. They are powerful creators and manifesters. They explore the full expression of free will. These Souls know the difference between power with and power over, and help show us how powerful we are as the creators of our own experience. These Souls being sensitive to energy around them, need to revitalize themselves by taking time and space from the noise and chaos of the world. **When out of alignment,** their shadow side, these Souls don't have freedom if they have an obligation. Obligation dampens their expression of power, and they give their power away. They may seem flighty or that they don't care. It's not the case. They just need space to do it their way.	Leaders, Mentors, Entrepreneurs
Divine Self-Expression	**When in alignment:** This Soul energy flows as an authentic communicator who expresses or speaks their truth. They are naturally born speakers with a gift for words and language to express clearly. They can convey the essence of Spiritual Teachings clearly. They inspire others. They take every opportunity to use their words. Authenticity is the key here. They need and want to think things through. They are excellent learners and very verbal. **When out of alignment:** These Souls either tend to talk too much, frustrating others, or they mute themselves and do not express their true essence.	Great Speakers, Coaches, Writers, Teachers, Communicators, Consultants

Soul Energy	Characteristics	Roles
Divine Love	**When in alignment:** These heart-centered Souls seek unconditional love. They attract people because of their high vibrational energy. Just being in their presence is healing. They are experts in relationships and value connection above all. They accept everyone where they are on their journey and are tolerant and non-judgmental. They are lovers of the Earth. They love reaching out to others. They focus on helping others regardless of their profession. They naturally share love freely. They have a healing gift of loving acceptance of all. They are tuned into what others need. They love to nurture and be nurtured. **When out of alignment:** it's common for them to give love in an imbalanced way. They tend to over-give love and time and deplete themselves. They experience toxic relationships. Giving and receiving are out of balance. Giving for them is easier than receiving, and often they need to learn to receive. Trauma can flip this to being able to receive but not give.	Innate Healers
Divine Wisdom	**When in alignment:** These Souls understand the wisdom inherent in the Universe and align with Universal Laws. They connect with the larger truths and larger understandings of how things work. They are attracted to Spiritual Paths and Spiritual Teaching. They share the wisdom in very few words and are profound. They are grounded, thoughtful, highly principled, and action-oriented. These Souls are patient. They are great listeners, always seeking to learn and grow. They embrace logic over emotions. Things must make sense to them. What is common sense to them isn't to others. They don't speak much, but when they do, it's powerful. They're ready to help and support others with principled and practical advice and bring inherent wisdom of the Universe into the physical world. **When out of alignment:** These Souls often feel the need to isolate themselves from society, which may result in feeling alone.	Great Teachers and Coaches

Appendix A: Divine Soul Energies

Soul Energy	Characteristics	Roles
Divine Compassion	**When in alignment:** These Souls are tolerant, compassionate, understanding, and other-focused. Empathy is their superpower. They lead with their heart. They care for people, communities, and the Earth. Often, they are concerned with environmental causes. They need to be out and about interacting so that empathy and compassion can flow through them. **When out of alignment:** These Souls isolate themselves. They may be so focused on caring for others and the Earth that they forget to care and create for themselves. They may get drained of energy. Over compassion for others and under compassion for themselves is a common imbalance.	Excellent Teachers of Children, Nurses, Caregivers, Social Workers
Divine Creation	**When in alignment:** These Souls build things like companies, physical bodies, wealth through investments, and great art. They thrive on new experiences and are open to new ideas. They focus on creativity, the creative process, and are often very physical. They want to build to last and to leave a legacy. They tend to get whatever they want and whenever they want. They are grounded in their physical body and the tangible while expressing the Spiritual. These Souls need to be in their physical bodies, really enjoying life. **When out of alignment:** These Souls isolate themselves. They may be so physically oriented that they get addicted to things that are harmful, like drugs, sex, or alcohol.	Business Builders, Athletes, Personal Trainers
Divine Order	**When in alignment:** These Souls abide by order, perfection, peace, balance, and harmony. They value form and function. They are creators of structures and systems. They are good organizers and meticulous dressers. They bring beauty, balance, art, and order to their work. They are usually quiet and reserved and work alone. They have an innate sense of fairness. They have impossibly high expectations for themselves and are perfectionists. **When out of alignment:** Their expectations are too high for themselves and others. These Souls can end up frozen or paralyzed, unable to move forward.	CPAs, Bookkeepers, Virtual and Executive Assistants, Designers, Organizers

Soul Energy	Characteristics	Roles
Divine Truth	**When in alignment:** These Souls are here to seek, recognize, and speak their truth. These Souls are about individual truth. They share their truth in very few words. They expose lies and liars. Amazingly insightful, observant, intuitive, and visionary, they bring light to wherever it is needed on the planet. They are often clairvoyant. They help others discover and express their truths. These Souls help us take a stand for our personal, unique truth and help us see ourselves for who we truly are. **When out of alignment:** These Souls can be the strong silent types having been shut down in childhood for speaking without filters. This makes diplomacy a challenge for them.	Judges, Lawyers, Whistleblowers, Blunt Communicators

QUESTIONS FOR INDIVIDUAL REFLECTIONS AND BOOK CLUB DISCUSSIONS

1. How do you relate to being in the flow with the Universe? What experiences have you had with being in the flow? What did it feel like? What was the outcome of the experience?

2. How have you experienced being in the flow of the Universe as a choice?

3. How do you relate to yourself as a Divine Magnificent BEing? What is easy for you? What is difficult for you?

4. If you had the belief and the knowing that you are a Divine Magnificent BEing, how would that empower you? How would you honor and cherish yourself? Describe how that would change your life? If you could draw an image of that aspect of yourself, what would you include?

5. What needs to happen for you to accept and believe in your magnificence?

6. What needs to happen to bring you into alignment with your Divine Magnificence?

7. How do you interpret and experience that the physical and Invisible are inextricable?

8. What change would you witness in your life if you understood your life as a series of miracles along your journey?

9. How has your sense of identity shifted from reading this book? What was the information that created that shift within you?

10. Describe an experience you've had by sitting in the stillness and silence of the Zero Point Field. Describe how it changed you.

11. When have you experienced your mind as the center of Divine Operation?

12. When have you manifested something that you visualized beforehand?

13. When have you received a clear message from the Divine? Did you act on it?

14. If the Divine was learning and expanding through your life experiences, what is the biggest area of growth or expansion for the Divine?

15. What aspects of your life have you mastered in our journey together?

16. After the discussion of Self-mastery, what key aspects of Self-mastery are speaking to you? What needs to change to lean into these aspects for Self-actualization?

17. What benefit would it be for you and your life to experience life as if everything is a miracle?

18. In what ways do you resonate with the Universe reflecting what you need to witness about yourself? Do you understand this is a gift or a trauma?

19. What image did you create of you BEing One with everything?

20. How easy is it for you to see yourself as a jewel in the Universe, and your gem qualities are reflected in all the other jewels?

ENDNOTES

Section One: Being in Flow with the Universe

1. Anne M. Deatly, Ph.D., *Journey to True Self: Discover Your Divine Magnificence,* (Sacred Dragon Publishing, 2024), 28-29, 34.
2. https://www.rebprotocol.net/Wired%20for%20joy.pdf.
3. Donna Eden with David Feinstein, Ph.D., *Energy Medicine: Balancing Your Body's Energies for Optimal Health, Joy and Vitality,* (Jeremy P. Tarcher, 2008), 260-270.
4. https://store.edenmethod.com/products/playing-with-the-frequencies-a-donna-eden-advanced-class-live-stream-version.
5. https://www.rebprotocol.net/Wired%20for%20joy.pdf.
6. Ibid.
7. David R. Hawkins, M.D., Ph.D., *Power vs. Force: The Hidden Determinants of Human Behavior,* (Veritas Publishing 2004), 52-53.
8. https://www.rebprotocol.net/Wired%20for%20joy.pdf.
9. https://www.caringforcarers.com.au/joy/more-energy-medicine-exercises-for-joy/.
10. https://www.youtube.com/watch?v=yZQfMdre-to; Eden with Feinstein, *Energy Medicine,* 201-203.
11. https://sheevaunmoran.com/.
12. https://edenenergymedicine.com/the-nine-hearts-exercise/.
13. Eden with Feinstein, *Energy Medicine,* 26-29.
14. Deatly, *Journey to True Self,* 41-42.
15. Hawkins, *Power vs Force,* 52-53.
16. https://addicted2success.com/life/we-have-60000-thoughts-each-day-heres-how-to-generate-thoughts-that-matter/.
17. Bruce H. Lipton, Ph.D., *The Biology of Belief: Unleashing the Power of Consciousness, Matter & Miracles,* (Hay House, Inc, 2005).
18. Deatly, *Journey to True Self,* 127-129.
19. William Whitecloud, *The Magician's Way: What it Really Takes to Find Your Treasure,* (CA: New World Library, 2009).

20. Deatly, *Journey to True Self*, 10-13.

21. Marianne Williamson, *The Law of Divine Compensation: On Work, Money, and Miracles*, (HarperOne, 2012), 6.

22. Don Miguel Ruiz, M.D., *The Four Agreements: A Toltec Wisdom Book*, (CA: Amber-Allen Publishing, Inc., 1997), 25.

23. Williamson, *The Law of Divine Compensation*, 31.

24. Id., 32.

25. Id., 34.

26. https://womancenteredcoaching.com/.

27. Greg McKweon, *Essentialism: The Disciplined Pursuit of Less*, (NY: Crown Publishing Group, 2014).

28. https://zenwords.tumblr.com/post/190703954602/your-mind-is-like-a-piece-of-land-planted-with.

29. https://edenenergymedicine.com/grounding-techniques/#:~:text=Place%20your%20feet%20flat%20on,tailb.; https://www.caringforcarers.com.au/grounding/grounding-with-energy-medicine/.

30. Eden with Feinstein, *Energy Medicine*, 297-314.

31. Id., 308-11.

32. Ibid.

33. https://www.youtube.com/watch?v=5hYE0Wt4Sxs.

34. Eden with Feinstein, *Energy Medicine*, 234, 312-314.

35. Id., 306, 308.

36. https://edenmethod.com/the-brazilian-toe-technique/.

37. The Ultimate Auric Clearing Course with Toby Alexander.

38. Karma Mastery Certification Program with Toby Alexander.

39. Michael Talbot, *The Holographic Universe*, (HarperCollins Publishers, 1991).

40. The Ultimate Auric Clearing Course with Toby Alexander.

41. Ibid.

42. Eden with Feinstein, *Energy Medicine*, 204-212.

43. Helen Schucman, Bill Thetford, Kenneth Wapnick, eds., *A Course in Miracles Workbook for Students*, 3rd Edition (Foundation for Inner Peace, 2007), W-pI.68.1.1.

44. https://www.mentalhelp.net/blogs/my-cup-overflows-a-zen-tale-adapted/.

45. Gregg Braden, *The Divine Matrix: Bridging Time, Space, Miracles, and Belief*, (Hay House, Inc., 2007), 161-196.

46. Deatly, *Journey to True Self*, 15.

47. Linda Howe with Juliette Looye, *How to Read the Akashic Records: Accessing the Archive of the Soul and its Journey*, (CO: Sounds True, Inc., 2010), 3.

48. https://www.edgarcayce.org/the-readings/akashic-records.

49. Howe with Looye, *How to Read the Akashic Records*, 4.

50. Id., 5.

51. Id., 10.

52. Id., 6.

53. Id., 8.

54. Id., 9-10.

55. Id., 4.

56. Ibid.

57. https://www.edgarcayce.org/the-readings/akashic-records/.

58. Howe, with Looye, *How to Read the Akashic Records*, 12-13.

59. Howe, with Looye, *How to Read the Akashic Records*, 37-47.

60. Linda Howe, *Healing through the Akashic Records: Using the Power of Your Sacred Wounds to Discover Your Soul's Perfection*, (CO: Sounds True, 2016), 4.

61. Id., xxiii.

62. Id., xxiv.

63. Id., 5.

64. Id., 23, 5.

65. Id., 3.

66. Id., 4.
67. Id., 9.
68. Id., 9-11.
69. Ibid.
70. Ibid.
71. Id., 11-13.
72. Virginia T. Stephenson, and Buck A. Rhodes, Ph.D., *The Lost Secrets of the Ancient Mystery Schools: 11 Steps to Your Divine Self*, (Virginia T. Stephenson and Buck A. Rhodes, Ph.D., 2015), 63.

Section Two: Aligning with the Divine

73. Gregg Braden, *The God Code: The Secret of Our Past, the Promise of Our Future*, (Hay House, Inc., 2004), xv.
74. Ibid.
75. Id., xvii.
76. Anne M. Deatly, Ph.D., *Journey to True Self: Discover Your Divine Magnificence*, (Sacred Dragon Publishing, 2024), 50-51.
77. Helen Schucman, Bill Thetford, Kenneth Wapnick, eds, *A Course in Miracles Combined Volume,* 3rd Edition, (Foundation for Inner Peace, 2007), W-p1.110.3.1-3.
78. Schucman, Thetford, Wapnick, eds, *A Course in Miracles Combined Volume,* 3rd Edition, T-9.VII.8:2; T-9.VIII.10 :1.
79. Schucman, Thetford, Wapnick, eds, *A Course in Miracles Combined Volume,* 3rd Edition, W-pII.293.1.1-2.
80. Anita Moorjani, *Dying to Be Me: My Journey from Cancer, to Near Death, to True Healing*, (Hay House, Inc., 2012); Eben Alexander, M.D., *Proof of Heaven: A Neurosurgeon's Journey into the Afterlife*, (Simon and Schuster, 2012); Don Piper, and Cecil Murphey, *90 Minutes in Heaven: A True Story of Death and Life*, (Revell, 2004).
81. Tina Louise Spalding, *Jesus: My Autobiography*, (AZ: Light Technology Publishing, 2015), xx.
82. Ibid.
83. Id., 110.
84. https://en.wikipedia.org/wiki/Potentiality_and_actuality.

85. https://www.newworldencyclopedia.org/entry/Entelechy#google_vignette.
86. https://moam.info/restoring-soul-facets-ritual-the-inner-realm_59ef80bb1723dd3b60018745.html.
87. Donna Eden with David Feinstein, Ph.D., *Energy Medicine: Balancing Your Body's Energy for Optimal Health, Joy, and Vitality*, (Jeremy P. Tarcher, 2008).
88. Prune Harris, *Your Radiant Soul: Understand Your Energy to Transform Your World*, (CT: Publish Your Purpose, 2023), 61.
89. Id., 144-145.
90. Id., 145.
91. Id., 69.
92. Id., 67.
93. Id., 64.
94. https://www.youtube.com/watch?v=9ZVZqtiS6II.
95. https://www.brainyquote.com/quotes/swami_vivekananda_389831.
96. https://energyfieldmastery.com/soul-energies/.
97. Year Two, Eden Energy Medicine Certification Program.
98. Harris, *Your Radiant Soul*, 203.
99. https://www.medicahealth.org/assemblage-point/.
100. https://www.assemblagepointcentre.com/apctypical.html.
101. Jon Whale, Ph.D., *The Catalyst of Power: The Assemblage Point of Man*, 3rd Edition, (UK: DragonRising, 2009), 97.
102. *Id.*, 18.
103. https://www.simonheather.co.uk/pages/chapters/assemblage_point_healing_sample.pdf.
104. https://www.simonheather.co.uk/pages/chapters/assemblage_point_healing_sample.pdf; Whale, *The Catalyst of Power*, 105.
105. Whale, *The Catalyst of Power*, 99.
106. Id., 29-31.
107. https://www.simonheather.co.uk/pages/chapters/assemblage_point_healing_sample.pdf.

108. Whale, *The Catalyst of Power*, 200.
109. https://www.simonheather.co.uk/pages/chapters/assemblage_point_healing_sample.pdf.
110. Whale, *The Catalyst of Power*, 18.
111. https://www.simonheather.co.uk/pages/chapters/assemblage_point_healing_sample.pdf.
112. https://www.assemblagepointcentre.com/apctypical.html.
113. Whale, *The Catalyst of Power*, 84-85.
114. Id., 49.
115. Id., 113.
116. Id., 31.
117. https://www.pruneharris.com/post/the-assemblage-point.
118. Ibid.
119. Ibid.
120. Ibid.
121. https://www.assemblagepointcentre.com/apcwhat.html.
122. Ibid.
123. Ibid.
124. https://www.simonheather.co.uk/pages/chapters/assemblage_point_healing_sample.pdf.
125. https://www.assemblagepointcentre.com/apctypical.html.
126. Ibid.
127. Whale, *The Catalyst of Power*, 140.
128. https://practitioner.edenmethod.com/.
129. Harris, *Your Radiant Soul*, 66.
130. Sue Morter, D.C., Live Awake program, https://drsuemorter.com/event/liveawake-raising-your-vibration-for-a-life-you-love-living/.
131. Harris, *Your Radiant Soul*, 66.
132. Sue Morter, D.C., *The Energy Codes: The 7-Step System to Awaken Your Spirit, Heal Your Body, and Live Your Best Life*, (NY: Atria Books, 2019), 110-114.

133. Ibid.

134. http://bit.ly/4j4EhTi

135. Ibid.

136. Schucman, Thetford, Wapnick, eds., *A Course in Miracles Combined Volume*, 3rd Edition, W-pI.45.2.6-8.

137. Lorie Ladd, *The Divine Design: The Untold Story of Earth's and Humanity's Evolution and Consciousness*, (Lorie Ladd, 2022), 19-20.

138. Ibid.

139. Schucman, Thetford, Wapnick, eds, *A Course in Miracles Combined Volume*, 3rd Edition, W-pII.229.1.1

140. Byron Katie with Stephen Mitchell, *Loving What is: Four Questions that Can Change Your Life*, (NY: Three Rivers Press, 2002), 19.

141. Schucman, Thetford, Wapnick, eds., *A Course in Miracles Combined Volume*, 3rd Edition, W-pI.107.9.5.

142. Id., W-pII.250.2.4.

143. Michael Newton, Ph.D., *Destiny of Souls: New Case Studies of Life Between Lives*, (MN: Llewellyn Publications, 2000); Michael Newton, Ph.D., *Journey of Souls: Case Studies of Life Between Lives*, (MN: Llewellyn Publications, 1996); Robert Schwartz, *Your Soul's Plan: Discovering the Real Meaning of the Life You Planned Before You Were Born*, (CA: North Atlantic Books, 2009).

144. Jonette Crowley, *Soul Body Fusion: The Missing Piece for Healing and Beyond*, (CO: StoneTree Publishing, 2012).

145. Deatly, *Journey to True Self*, 142-144.

146. Schucman, Thetford, Wapnick, eds, *A Course in Miracles Combined Volume*, 3rd Edition, W-p1.79.1.4.

147. Adapted from a Diamond Inlay exercise, https://store.edenmethod.com/products/the-diamond-inlay-advanced-class-streaming-version.

Section Three: Tapping Into Our Infinite Divine Potential

148. Anne M. Deatly, Ph.D., *Journey to True Self, Discover Your Divine Magnificence*, (Sacred Dragon Publishing, 2024), 10-13.

149. Neville, *The Power of Awareness: Move from Desire to Wishes Fulfilled*, (Devorss Publications, 1952), 2.

150. Helen Schucman, Bill Thetford, Kenneth Wapnick, eds, *A Course in Miracles Combined Volume,* 3rd Edition, (Foundation for Inner Peace, 2007), T15.III.3.3-5.

151. Joe Dispenza, D.C., *Breaking the Habit of Being Yourself: How to Lose Your Mind and Create a New One,* (Hay House, Inc., 2012), 61-62.

152. Thomas Troward, *The New Thought and New Order, The Dore Lectures on Mental Science in the Classic Thomas Troward Book (Deluxe Edition),* (Compass Circle, 2018), 500.

153. Darryl Anka channeling Bashar, *Believing is Seeing: How Consciousness Creates the Physical Reality Experience*, presentation, Bergen Performing Arts Center, Englewood, NJ, June 14, 2025.

154. Thomas Troward, *The Hidden Power, in the Classic Thomas Troward Book (Deluxe Edition)*, (Compass Circle, 2018), 103.

155. Schucman, Thetford, Wapnick, eds, *A Course in Miracles Combined Volume,* W-pII.278.1.1.

156. Id., W-pII.277.2.2.

157. Genevieve Behrend, *Your Invisible Power,* (Compass Circle, 2018), 23.

158. Troward, *The New Thought and New Order, The Dore Lectures on Mental Science*, 500.

159. Behrend, *Your Invisible Power,* 26.

160. Tina Louise Spalding, "(#370) ACIM Lesson #166 with Jesus Commentary, YouTube video, 10:44, June 14, 2019, https://www.youtube.com/watch?v=y14KTsnug-s.

161. Behrend, *Your Invisible Power,* 5, 104.

162. Deatly, *Journey to True Self,* 10-13.

163. Behrend, *Your Invisible Power,* 39-40.

164. Id., 90.

165. Id., 39-42.

166. Ibid.

167. Id., 97.

168. https://www.russellrowe.com/numerology/cheat-sheet-numbers.pdf..

169. https://parade.com/living/1010-angel-number-meaning#:~:text=If%20you're%20seeing%201010,You%20won't%20regret%20it!.

170. https://stylecaster.com/feature/11-11-date-meaning-1063029/.

171. https://www.alittlesparkofjoy.com/angel-number-1234/ and https://enlightenmentu.com/1234-angel-number/.

172. https://thesecretofthetarot.com/angel-number-510/.

173. https://www.sunsigns.org/angel-number-510-meaning/.

174. https://www.bustle.com/life/life-path-9-in-numerology-meaning#:~:text=In%20numerology%2C%20the%20number%20nine,both%.

175. https://sarahscoop.com/angel-number-17-in-numerology-meaning-symbolism-and-predictions%EF%BF%BC/#:~:text=In%20numerology%.

176. Linda Howe, *Healing through the Akashic Records: Using the Power of Your Sacred Wounds to Discover Your Soul's Perfection*, (CO: Sounds True, 2016), xxvi.

177. Id., xxvii.

178. Id., xxv.

179. Id., 20.

180. Ibid.

181. Ibid.

182. Id., 15.

183. Id., 16.

184. Ibid.

185. Id., 15.

186. Id., 18-19.

187. https://lindahowe.com/wp-content/uploads/2019/09/The-Pathway-Prayer-Process-2.pdf. Howe, *Healing through the Akashic Records*, 35-7.

188. https://www.bettersleep.com/blog/opening-the-crown-chakra/.

189. Deatly, *Journey to True Self*, 154.

190. https://www.pruneharris.com/energyanatomy.

191. Prune Harris, *Your Radiant Soul*, (CT: Publish Your Purpose, 2023), 69.

192. Deatly, *Journey to True Self*, 28-30, 34.

193. https://www.pruneharris.com/energyanatomy.

194. Ibid.

195. Harris, *Your Radiant Soul*, 142.

196. https://www.healthline.com/health/dantian.

197. https//www.activeherb.com/blog/the-dantian-of-tcm-reservoirs-of-the-3-treasures.html?srsltid=AfmBOoqx2qQgmhin1eaK0nYTn61yT_1q0JNnwO0rgtZLvXEzXUarFkR0.

198. Harris, *Your Radiant Soul*, 200.

199. https//www.activeherb.com/blog/the-dantian-of-tcm-reservoirs-of-the-3-treasures.html?srsltid=AfmBOoqx2qQgmhin1eaK0nYTn61yT_1q0JNnwO0rgtZLvXEzXUarFkR0.

200. Harris, *Your Radiant Soul*, 200.

201. https//www.activeherb.com/blog/the-dantian-of-tcm-reservoirs-of-the-3-treasures.html?srsltid=AfmBOoqx2qQgmhin1eaK0nYTn61yT_1q0JNnwO0rgtZLvXEzXUarFkR0.

202. https://www.pruneharris.com/energyanatomy.

203. Ibid.

204. https://www.pruneharris.com/empath-course.

205. Ibid.

206. Sue Morter, D.C., *LiveAwake* program. https://drsuemorter.com/liveawake-waitllist.

207. https://www.pruneharris.com/empath-course.

208. Prune Harris, "Tracing Stellar Diamonds," YouTube video, 2:23, Nov. 13, 2022, https://www.youtube.com/watch?v=H3q9eD60oqw.

209. https://consciousnessliberty.com/beyond-the-7-chakras-activating-the-3-dantian-energy-centers-for-inner-alchemy/.

210. https://www.pruneharris.com/energyanatomy., https://www.pruneharris.com/empath-course.

211. https://store.edenmethod.com/products/playing-with-the-frequencies-a-donna-eden-advanced-class-live-stream-version.

212. Donna Eden, "Try this to Boost Your Confidence," YouTube video, 0:55, Apr. 21, 2023, https://www.youtube.com/shorts/1XpKbhbhX18.

213. Dirk Oellibrandt, "Restore Your Energy Field," YouTube video, 10:08, Mar. 24, 2020, https://www.youtube.com/watch?v=YSBksuqiX6E.

214. https://store.edenmethod.com/products/playing-with-the-frequencies-a-donna-eden-advanced-class-live-stream-version.

215. Deatly, *Journey to True Self*, 160-162.

216. Drunvalo Melchizedek, *The Ancient Secret of the Flower of Life*, Vol 2, (AZ: Light Technology, 2010), 309.

217. Deatly, *Journey to True Self*, 152-154.

218. Melchizedek, *The Ancient Secret of the Flower of Life*, Vol 2, 310.

219. Id., 346-356.

220. Donna Eden with David Feinstein, Ph.D., *The Diamond Inlay Program* https://store.edenmethod.com/collections/streaming-videos-and-dvds-/products/The-diamond-inlay-advanced-class-streaming-version.

221. Toby Alexander, "Awaken & Reprogram Your DNA," YouTube video, 1:13:33, Nov. 26, 2012, https://www.youtube.com/watch?v=qRQdGGMy4O8.

222. Sara Landon, *The Wisdom of the Council: Channeled Messages for Living Your Purpose* (CA: Hay House, Inc., 2022), 77-88.

223. Behrend, *Your Invisible Power*, 95.

224. Id., 83.

225. Id., 84.

226. Landon, *The Wisdom of the Council*, 78-79.

227. Sue Morter, D.C., *LiveAwake* program. https://drsuemorter.com/liveawake-waitlist.

228. Sara Landon, *You Are a Channel: Receive Guidance from Higher Realms, Ascended Masters, Star Families, and More*, (Hay House, LLC, 2024), 33-36.

229. Behrend, *Your Invisible Power*, 39-42.

230. Howe, *Healing through the Akashic Records*, 11-13.

231. https://drsuemorter.com/bodyawake-yoga-membership/.

232. Dirk Oellibrandt, "Restore Your Energy Field," YouTube video, 10:08, Mar. 24, 2020, https://www.youtube.com/watch?v=YSBksuqiX6E.

Section Four: The Path of Enlightenment

233. Lao Tsu, *Tao Te Ching*, (Vintage Books Edition, 1972), 33 (translated by Gai-fu Feng and Jane English).

234. David R. Hawkins, Ph.D., M.D., *Power vs Force: The Hidden Determinants of Human Behavior*, (Hay House, Inc, 2014), 52-53.

235. Hermann Hesse, *Siddhartha: A Novel*, Bantam, 1982.

236. Ibid.

237. Walpola Rahula, *What the Buddha Taught: Revised and Expanded edition with Texts from Suttas and Dhammapada*, (NY: Grove Press, 1974.) https://media.voog.com/0000/0037/7838/files/Walpola%20Rahula%20-%20What%20the%20Buddha%20Taught.pdf.pdf.

238. Helen Schucman, Bill Thetford, Kenneth Wapnick, eds, *A Course in Miracles Combined Volume*, 3rd Edition, (Foundation for Inner Peace, 2007), W-pI.199.8.7-8 and W-pII.1.1-2.

239. Anne M. Deatly, PhD, *Journey to True Self: Discover Your Divine Magnificence*, (Sacred Dragon Publishing, 2024), 127-129, and 189-191.

240. Lynne McTaggart, *The Power of Eight: Harnessing the Miraculous Energies of a Small Group to Heal Others, Your Life, and the World*, (Atria, 2017), Lynne McTaggart, *The Intention Experiment: Using Your Thoughts to Change Your Life and the World*, (NY: Free Press, 2007).

241. Schucman, Thetford, Wapnick, eds, *A Course in Miracles Combined Volume*, T-11.II.1:3-5.

242. Id., T-11.II.7:1.

243. Id., T-11.III.7:10.

244. Id., T-11.IV.3:1.

245. Id., T-11.IV.8 :1.

246. Deatly, *Journey to True Self*, 10-13.

247. https://www.nightingale.com/articles/acres-of-diamonds/.

248. Brian D. McLaren, *Faith After Doubt: Why Your Beliefs Stopped Working and What to Do About It*, (NY: St. Martin's Essentials, 2021), 31-40.

249. Michael A. Singer, *The Surrender Experiment: My Journey into Life's Perfection*, (NY: Harmony Books, 2015).

250. Michael A. Singer, *The Untethered Soul: The Journey Beyond Yourself*, (New Harbinger Publications/Noetic Books, 2007).

251. Schucman, Thetford, Wapnick, eds, *A Course in Miracles Combined Volume*, T-1.I.36.

252. Id., T-1.1.6:1.

253. Id., T-1.I.3:1.

254. Id., T-1.I:1.

255. Id., T-1.I.17:1-3.

Section Five: Oneness: Evolving from Duality to Unity

256. Singer, *The Untethered Soul*, 115-118.

257. Three Initiates, *The Kybalion: A Study of the Hermetic Philosophy from Ancient Egypt and Greece, (Project* Gutenberg License, 1912), Chapter II, Second principle.

258. Sara Landon, *You Are a Channel: Receive Guidance from Higher Realms, Ascended Masters, Star Families, and More*, (Hay House, LLC, 2024), 7-10.

259. Sue Morter, DC, *the LiveAwake program*. https://drsuemorter.com/liveawake-waitlist..

260. Michael Talbot, *The Holographic Universe*, (Harper Perennial, 1992), 1.

261. Id., 41.

262. Helen Schucman, Bill Thetford, Kenneth Wapnick, eds, *A Course in Miracles Combined Volume,* 3rd Edition, (Foundation for Inner Peace, 2007), T-11:VI:10:5-8.

263. https://wordpress.clarku.edu/phil224-mboardman/jean-francois-lyotard/barnett-newman/.

264. https://en.wikipedia.org/wiki/Golden_Buddha_(statue).

265. Ibid.

266. https://www.learnreligions.com/indras-jewel-net-449827.

267. https://en.wikipedia.org/wiki/Indra%27s_net#CITEREFCook1977. Archived 10 September 2017 at the Wayback Machine.

RESOURCES

Braden, Gregg, *The Divine Matrix: Bridging Time, Space, Miracles, and Belief.* Hay House, Inc, 2007.

Elgin, Duane, *The Living Universe: Where Are We, Who Are We, Where Are We Going.* Berrett-Koehler Publishing, Inc., 2009.

Landon, Sara, *You Are a Channel: Receive Guidance from Higher Realms, Ascended Masters, Star Families, and more.* Hay House, Inc, 2024.

Morter, Sue, DC, *The Energy Codes: The 7-Step System to Awaken Your Spirit, Heal Your Body, and Live Your Best Life.* Atria Books, 2019.

Schwartz, Robert, *Your Soul's Plan: Discovering the Real Meaning of the Life You Planned Before You Were Born.* North Atlantic Books, 2009.

PERMISSIONS

Quote from *A Course in Miracles*, copyright ©2007 by the Foundation for Inner Peace, 448 Ignacio Blvd., #306, Novato, CA 94949, www.acim.org, used with permission.

Excerpts from *Jesus: My Autobiography* by Tina Louise Spalding (2015) used by permission of Light Technology.

ACKNOWLEDGMENTS

My first acknowledgment is to my Spiritual Guides who invited me to write this book. If it were not for this nudge and inspiration, it wouldn't have been created. I also acknowledge that I was prepared to be a Spiritual Guiding Light with the infusion of my primary Divine Soul Wisdom energy. I am grateful that I connected to my True Self in this lifetime. I know we are always working together, both physically and Spiritually, and I am deeply grateful for this expanded connection.

I am deeply indebted to Michael Angelo Ludas for his cryptic guidance for me to be on a different life's journey. I only wish we could have shared the experience of bringing the Invisible or Spiritual into the physical together. I often feel your presence around me. I am in total awe that I recognize you in spirit from having known you in the physical world.

I sincerely thank Angela "Andi" Rosenau, creator of Sacred Dragon Publishing Services, for being on this journey with me to bring this book to life as my editor. Andi guided me in ways beyond my wildest imagination by asking me key questions. I am indebted to her guidance, kindness, conviction, and wisdom. She is dedicating her life to bringing the truth to the world by working with Ascension Authors. In that goal, she has gone above and beyond what I expected as an editor. Andi, I am grateful for the guidance I received to meet you and work with you. You have shared this journey of the evolution of this book with me, and you will always be a part of my life because you have shared the unfolding of my True Self as I continued to go deeper in writing this book to address your insightful and inspiring questions.

I acknowledge Donna Eden, the pioneer of Energy Medicine, and David Feinstein, PhD, who opened a whole new world for me in terms of understanding the energy body. I find your radiance and joy a gift, and you are treasured in my heart. With what I have learned from you, I have been able to help optimize the health and well-being of many clients. Your guidance is unprecedented. Thank you for who you are and what you have shared with the world.

I acknowledge Dr. Sue Morter, who has been an enlightened mentor for me in the past two years. I first resonated with Dr. Sue as a Body Awake Yoga devotee. From there, I progressed to participating in the LiveAwake program. I am deeply grateful that she is able to go deep and share from her personal experiences, including exalted states of BEing. I am in the Deep Track LiveAwake program and have completed the Bio-Energetic Synchronization Technique course. There are definitely more courses for me to take to benefit from her wisdom, authenticity, and her deep Loving Presence.

I acknowledge Dr. Claire Zammit, who has paved the way for me to let go of inner barriers within me, and now I am doing that for others. She has helped me grow in ways that I never imagined! She has helped me be completely honest with myself and fearless of what I will find within me when I ask the right questions. She has helped me become a transformational and inspirational life coach, empowering women. I am deeply grateful to you for BEing the model to follow and to grow toward.

I acknowledge *A Course in Miracles*. It has transformed my perceptions of the Universe, the Divine, and myself. I have connected to my True Self because of the course's teachings.

I thank my energy medicine clients for encouraging me to write this book. It is for you and all others who are seeking more from this physical realm or who want to participate in bringing the Spiritual Realm into the physical realm.

I acknowledge Ida Janssen for the design of the book cover. Ida, you were given a lot of conceptual ideas that you transformed uniquely into images that symbolize the deep messages in the book. Your creative genius revealed the perfect design.

I acknowledge Ryan Forsythe for his creative design of the book's interior format. There were a lot of different expressions of the content, and your recognition that each needed a unique look shows your illustration genius. I am deeply grateful you accepted this job, as I am aware that your career has evolved in a new direction. Thank you for working on this book.

I acknowledge Sharon Castlen, Integrated Book Marketing, for assistance and brilliance in helping to market the book so that the people who need this book on their Spiritual Journey will certainly find it.

I also acknowledge all of you who want to knowingly be on a Spiritual Journey. I wrote this book to all of you who want to know the deepest wisdom, the truth, and the miracles of the design of the Universe. I don't believe in coincidences, so I know you have been guided to this book. May you find the answers to some or all your deepest questions. May your perceptions of the Universe change and align with the deepest, wisest, eternal part of you. May you find ease and grace and the Divine as you travel on your specific journey. May you discover your True Self. May you be open to new ideas and concepts. May this book be like a puzzle in putting together pieces of new understanding that enhance your way of BEing and seeing the world around you in new and enlightened ways. May you discover the benevolence of BEing ONE with everything. What a Divine Plan that we are all expressions of the ONE! May this awareness of the Oneness change how you view yourself and how you live your life to the fullest potential. May you be able to accomplish what your Soul intended in this lifetime.

ABOUT THE AUTHOR

Anne M. Deatly, PhD, is a certified Advanced Eden Energy Medicine practitioner and teacher. She is a transformational life coach, inspirational speaker, spiritual influencer, and author of *Journey to True Self: Discover Your Divine Magnificence* and *Journey to Oneness: Align with Your Divine Magnificence*. Dr. Anne's three decades of scientific research, along with energy-healing training that engages the subtle quantum reality of the Universe, shine through in her shared discovery of how science and spirituality can connect us to unity consciousness.

Dr. Anne has a PhD from Vanderbilt School of Medicine and focused her early career on the study of viruses. Dr. Anne is now CEO and Founder of E Quantum Breakthroughs (EQB). The mission of EQB is to harness life force energy to help people break through or transcend barriers that limit them from living and achieving at their highest potential. Bridging science, spirituality, and human potential through consciousness, Dr. Anne shares how to tap into the wisdom of the body to transform and elevate vibrational frequency. She employs a pioneering approach to optimal health and wellness care, focusing on the whole person to help individuals identify with their core essence and synchronize their mind, body, and spirit to become their highest version and live their best life. *Because the best you is the real you.*

Dr. Anne brings her extensive background to what she now does through her healing services, programs, books, and speaking engagements. She is known as the *Radiant Energy Doctor* on the popular radio show "Energy Medicine and Optimal Health" on VoiceAmerica's Health & Wellness channel.

In addition, Dr. Anne is the creator of several energy healing and transformational programs, including:

- Energy is All There is: Master the Flow to Enhance Your Life
- The Butterfly Model: Crossing the Bridge to Your Future Self

Dr. Anne lives in a self-created sanctuary on a lake in a small New Jersey town and has two adult children.

The author of *Journey to True Self: Discover Your Divine Magnificence,* and *Journey to Oneness: Align with Your Divine Magnificence*, Dr. Anne will conclude the trilogy with her next book, *Journey to Inner Wisdom*. Her joy is to read, discover, and explore through learning, growing, and expanding into deeper connections with her True Self. Living on a small lake, she is guided by the natural world and the lake population into peaceful resonance and coherence with the Oneness of this quiet community.

ABOUT THE SPEAKER

Dr. Anne Deatly, PhD, is passionate about exploring the wisdom of the Universe. She shares secrets of the Universe to reveal there's so much more to life if we elevate our thinking and perceiving. She inspires her clients and readers to increase their vibrancy, vitality, and radiance by discovering their magnificent uniqueness in a profound, bold way that expands Consciousness and awakens their True Self within. Her sessions, programs, and books engage people who want to become the best versions of themselves, live their best lives, and explore Oneness. Her books explore the concept of Oneness and offer an experiential approach to sensing BEing part of the Oneness and what that means.

Dr. Anne's approach appeals to a broad range of interest groups: business leaders, women's groups, small religious groups, not-for-profit organizations, networking groups, and libraries.

She delivers her messages through multiple formats: keynote addresses, workshops, seminars, mastermind groups, conferences, and panel discussions.

To inspire and empower audiences with new wisdom and understanding for living a more meaningful life in these challenging times, Dr. Anne is excited to speak on a range of uplifting topics, including:

- Your Consciousness Determines Your Best Self and Best Life
- Understanding Mind-Body-Spirit Connection for Health, Wholeness, and Well-Being
- Living Together Peacefully as One Humanity
- Owning Your Divine Magnificence
- Secrets of Your Inner Wisdom
- Connecting to Your Inner Wisdom, Your True Self
- Harnessing the Power of Your Life Force Energy
- How to Primarily Identify with Your Soul, *Not* Your Physical Body
- The Truth is, You are Unlimited
- Becoming Who You are Meant to Be
- Living as an Aspect of the Oneness

To learn more about Dr. Anne, receive a review copy of her books, and schedule her to speak at your event, please go to her speaker page:

https://www.Dr.AnneDeatly.com/speaker

INVITATION TO CONNECT

Thank you so much for taking this spiritual journey with me. I hope you enjoyed and benefited from *Journey to Oneness: Align with Your Divine Magnificence*. Each of you who takes a journey like this will help uplift the whole Universe. We are working together for the benefit of the whole. I am delighted to be One with you in this amazing and lofty endeavor. We are making an impact in the world.

Please share your comments about *Journey to Oneness* on your favorite book review sites and social media groups. The more people who take this journey and apply the principles and secrets in this book, the more the Universe will benefit. The time is now to raise the vibrational frequencies of the Universe. We can do this together.

For continued support and inspiration on your journey, I invite you to subscribe to my YouTube channel "Higher Frequency Living" for content about discovering your True Self and your Divine Magnificence.

> https://www.youtube.com/@annedeatly2

For more information about my Energy Medicine practice, sessions, and programs, I would inspire and encourage you to connect with me on my website and social media.

> https://www.DrAnneDeatly.com
> https://www.facebook.com/EquantumBreakthroughs/
> https://www.linkedin.com/in/annedeatly/
> @deatlyanne instagram.com/deatlyanne/

I am excited to hear about your journey and hope our paths cross in person or online. We are One in this Universe, working together. That brings me much joy!

Live radiantly!

Anne M Deatly

www.ingramcontent.com/pod-product-compliance
Lightning Source LLC
LaVergne TN
LVHW011928070526
838202LV00054B/4545